Introducing Linguistic Morphology

LAURIE BAUER

EDINBURGH UNIVERSITY PRESS

© Laurie Bauer 1988

First published in 1988.
This paperback edition published,
with corrections, in 1992.

Reprinted 1994, 1995, 1999, 2001, 2002

Edinburgh University Press
22 George Square, Edinburgh

Set in Times Roman and
printed in Great Britain by
J. W. Arrowsmith Ltd,
Bristol

British Library Cataloguing
    in Publication Data
Bauer, Laurie
Introducing linguistic morphology
1. Language. Morphology
I. Title
415

ISBN 0 85224 582 3 Pbk

Introducing Linguistic Morphology

Preface

The aim of this book is to provide an introduction to linguistic morphology. The study of morphology has been influenced by all major groups of linguists: by the philologists of the nineteenth century, by the structuralists in the twentieth century, by the transformational grammarians in the second half of the twentieth century, and by linguists with other theoretical orientations as well. Part of the function of this book is thus to provide a coherent approach to the study of morphology, without gross distortion of the ideas that have come down to us from so many different sources.

In this book, Part One provides an introduction to the fundamental notions involved in the study of morphology. This Part provides a background in the morphological notions of the philologists and structuralists. Part Two provides an elaboration of this, going into considerably greater detail in a few areas of major importance, and specifically raising questions which are glossed over in Part One. Part Three provides an introduction to some of the major issues in morphology today, in the transformational or post-transformational era. In a course in General Linguistics, it is assumed that each Part will be studied as part of the course work for a different year. But in some Universities there may be a specialised course in Morphology, which will consider all three Parts, or sections of them. It is hoped that students who have worked their way through this book will have sufficient background to understand the current controversies in morphological theory, and to be able to approach the original articles and books in which the developments are taking place at the moment.

To support the theoretical exposition of this book students should ideally, especially in the early stages, carry out exercises in morphological analysis, using data from a variety of languages, to see how the theoretical constructs apply in practice. Such exercises are not provided in this book, although a series of study questions is given in Appendix B, including a list of English words for analysis. Individual teachers may choose problems from the many available in specialised workbooks, or invent their own.

In Appendix C there is a glossary of the technical terms of morphology, with definitions and, where appropriate, examples.

Technical terms from other areas of Linguistics such as 'phoneme' or 'direct object' are not listed, only those relevant to the study of morphology. Thus this appendix may be used as a quick reference source for the specialist terms in this book or as a means of revision. For technical terms from Linguistics that are not listed in the glossary, consult Crystal (1980) (or a later edition).

A brief note is also needed on my mode of glossing languages other than English. Morphs are separated out in the data by the symbol '·'. This symbol is also used in the English glosses to show which part of the English gloss corresponds to each morph in the original. Where a single morph in the original is glossed by more than one English word, the English glosses are hyphenated. Where necessary, a translation is also given between inverted commas. A simple example from French will illustrate this:

arriv·ons
arrive·1st-person-plural
'we are arriving'

In general I have tried to avoid abbreviations in the glosses, but *1st, 2nd* and *3rd* are consistently used, and *sing, pl* are occasionally used for 'singular' and 'plural'. Other abbreviations are explained in the text or should be clear from the context.

Transcriptions of data from other languages are dependent on the system used by my sources; in many cases an orthographic form is given rather than a transcription. Where possible, phonetic symbols of the International Phonetic Association have been used. Transcriptions of English employ the system used by Gimson in the *English Pronouncing Dictionary* (Jones, 1977).

I should like to thank all those who have provided me with help, advice and suggestions during the writing of this book. In particular, the following people have commented on parts of various drafts, and their aid has been invaluable: Winifred Bauer, Andrew Carstairs, Janet Holmes, Kate Kearns. They are not to blame if I have not always followed all of their advice, and they do not, needless to say, necessarily agree with what I have written.

Contents

Contents

Contents

ix

Part One: Fundamentals

1. Introduction

How many words are there in this book? Can we always tell precisely what a word is? Do *motet*, *motion* and *motive* have anything to do with each other? What ways do we have of making new words in English? Are the same ways of forming new words found in all languages? Is it just coincidence that although you can have a word like *people* which means much the same as 'a lot of *persons*', and a word *peoples* which means, more or less, 'a lot of lots of *persons*', you cannot have a word *personss* meaning the same thing? Is it just coincidence that the ablative plural of the Latin word *re:x* 'king', *re:gibus*, meaning 'by/from/with the kings' is so much longer than the nominative singular *re:x*? (I use the phonetic length mark rather than the traditional macron to show long vowels in Latin.) All of these questions relate to **morphology**, the study of words and their structure.

It is a well-established observation that words occur in different forms. It is quite clear to anyone who has studied almost any of the Indo-European languages. Students of these languages learn **paradigms** like those below as models so that they can control the form-changes that are required. As illustrations, consider a verb paradigm from Latin and a noun paradigm from Icelandic. (The word 'paradigm' means 'pattern' or 'example'.)

(1) amo: 'I love'
     ama:s   'you (singular) love'
     amat   'he/she/it loves'
     ama:mus   'we love'
     ama:tis   'you (plural) love'
     amant   'they love'

(2) *Singular*
     nominative hestur 'horse'
     accusative hest
     dative   hesti
     genitive   hests

     Plural
     nominative hestar

3

accusative	hesta
dative	hestum
genitive	hesta

In the nineteenth century, the term 'morphology' was given to the study of this change in the forms of words. The term is taken from the biological sciences, and refers to the study of shapes. In linguistics this means the study of the shapes of words; not the phonological shape (which can be assumed to be fairly arbitrary) but rather the systematic changes in shape related to changes in meaning, such as those illustrated in the paradigms above, or such as that relating the pairs of words below:

(3)	desert	deserter
	design	designer
	fight	fighter
	kill	killer
	paint	painter
	twist	twister

By extension, the term 'morphology' is used not only for the study of the shapes of words, but also for the collection of units which are used in changing the forms of words. In this sense, we might say that Latin has a more complex morphology than English. Again by extension, 'morphology' is also used for the sequence of rules which are postulated by the linguist to account for the changes in the shapes of words. In this sense we might contrast the morphology of language L with the syntax of language L (where the syntax is the sequence of rules postulated by the linguist to account for the ways in which words are strung together). In this sense we might also say that something is part of the job of 'the morphology of language L' or, more generally, of 'morphology', implying that this is true for all languages. We shall see later how all these senses fit together; such extensions of meaning are common within linguistics, and do not usually cause problems of interpretation.

Many traditional 'grammars' (in the sense 'grammar books') deal largely with such morphology as can be laid out in paradigms like those presented above, and have little to say about syntax. This has led to the situation where many lay people today still believe that languages like Chinese or English do not have much grammar, because they do not have extensive morphological paradigms. That is, for many people the term 'grammar' is equated with morphology. For most linguists today, however, 'grammar' includes both morphology and syntax, and most of the linguistic study of 'grammar' in this sense has, since the middle of this century, not been of

4

morphology, but of syntax. This is understandable. Syntax, especially from 1957 onwards, was a relatively new field of study, while morphology was considered well-researched and well-understood. It did not seem at that time as if there was a great deal that was new to say about morphology. Morphological descriptions of hundreds of languages were available, but all the languages differed in what appeared to be essentially random ways. There did not seem to be any cross-linguistic generalisations to be made in morphology. Syntax, in the middle of this century, was a far richer ground for linguistic discoveries. It was the excitement of the progress being made in the study of syntax which gave Linguistics such a boost in the 1960's. It was also progress in the study of syntax which eventually led to the realisation that there were still questions to be answered in morphology. As a result, there has in recent years been a resurgence of interest in morphology.

The theoretical background to this new interest in morphology comes from three distinct sources. Firstly, there is the philological study of grammar in the last century and the early years of this century. Secondly, there is the study of diverse languages under the influence of one or another of the structuralist schools of Linguistics. In particular the work of the American structuralists, especially Bloomfield and his followers, is important here. Finally, there is the influence of transformational grammar and the school of thought that emerged from the work of Chomsky. It is not always easy to separate out these three strands in current morphological theory, and sometimes one dominates, sometimes another. Nonetheless, all three influences can be strongly felt. This book provides an introduction to the study of morphology covering the input from these various sources, and attempting some kind of synthesis in the light of the most recent research. It discusses both the general background to all morphological study, and also some of the detail of recent theories of morphology.

REFERENCES AND FURTHER READING

At the end of each chapter there is a section of references and further reading. The book can be read without these sections, although in some later chapters there are discussions of a few matters of import which are tangential to the main text. The references in these sections (and in the text of the chapters in Part Three) are given in terms of the surname of the author and the date of publication, and full details can be found in the list of references at the back of the book. It is sensible to get into the habit of reading some of the works referred to. No textbook gives an unbiased presentation of the facts, and this one is certainly no exception. Only by reading other works can you make some attempt to counteract the inbuilt bias of the text. In other cases it is probably just as well to assure yourself that I have not given an unfair account of other people's research. Sources of data can be consulted either for extra data for analysis, or to see many of the extra complications which I have ignored for the sake of the example.

The data from Latin in this chapter, and in many other places in the book, is taken from Kennedy (1962). The data from Icelandic is from Einarsson (1945). Where references are not provided for language data, it is frequently because I am familiar with the language concerned. Much of the complex English data is gleaned from dictionaries and other reference books, only some of which are listed in the list of references at the end of the book.

2. The Basic Units

2.1 A close look at words
How many words are there in (1)?

(1)   The cook was a good cook as cooks go, and as cooks go,
       she went.

It probably didn't take you very long to come up with the answer
'15'. Now think about how you arrived at that answer. What you
did, in effect, was to count the items which appeared between spaces
on the page. We could say that a word is a unit which, in print, is
bounded by spaces on both sides. We will call this an **orthographic
word,** because it is linked to the spelling (orthography). In practice
we may not always feel certain just where words begin and end in
the written language, but strict application of the definition above
will provide us with consistent answers. Consider the next example:

(2)   I've been in hot water so often I feel like a tea-bag.

There are two places in (2) where we might raise questions about
how many words are involved. *I've*, we know, has two parts, and
could have been written as *I have*. But an apostrophe is not a space,
and so by applying the definition we formulated earlier, we can
say that *I've* is one orthographic word. Similarly with *tea-bag* in
(2). A hyphen is not a space, and we are thus able to say that
tea-bag is a single orthographic word, even though it is made up
of two parts. Just what those parts are is a question to which we
will return.
   Now let us turn to a different question with respect to (1). How
many different words does (1) contain? This question is more
difficult to answer, because the answer you give will depend on
whether you think *cook* and *cooks*, *go* and *went* are 'the same word'
or not. They are clearly different orthographic words: they have
different **forms** or shapes. So we might say that there are 11 different
word-forms (or orthographic words) in (1): *the, cook, was, a, good,
as, cooks, go, and, she, went.* On the other hand, there is another
sense in which *cook* and *cooks* are forms 'of the same word'. Let
us use the term **lexeme** for this sense, and say that *cook* and *cooks*
are different **word-forms** which belong to, or **realise**, the same **lexeme.**

7

Similarly, *go* and *went* are different word-forms which realise a single lexeme. There are two fewer different lexemes in (1) than there are word-forms, so there are 9 different lexemes in (1). The name by which we choose to refer to the lexeme is arbitrary, and depends on the classification required in the general theory within which we are working. We could call the lexeme realised by *cook* and *cooks* '762' or '85/a/17-U5' or 'Samantha', but to make things easier, we'll agree to call it COOK, using capital letters when we write it. We can now say, more succinctly than was possible before, that *cooks* is one of the word-forms which can realise the lexeme COOK. Similarly, we can say that *went* is one of the word-forms that can realise GO. The lexemes in (1) are THE, COOK, BE, A, GOOD, AS, GO, AND, SHE.

We can look at the same facts and the same terminology from a different angle. Suppose you were reading a book, and you suddenly came across the following sentence, which you didn't understand.

(3)   The posset was disembogued from the rehoboams.

Suppose you didn't understand the fourth word in (3). You might want to consult your dictionary to find out what it means. But you would not look up *disembogued* with a final *d* in your dictionary, because your knowledge of English is sufficient to tell you that *disembogued* is just a form of the lexeme DISEMBOGUE. Similarly you wouldn't look up *rehoboams*, but REHOBOAM, which is the name of the lexeme. Lexemes are dictionary words (not necessarily in the sense that they will be given a separate entry and act as a headword in the particular dictionary you happen to have on your shelf, but in the sense that you might expect their separate identity to be acknowledged in a large dictionary). A lexeme comprises all the word-forms which can realise that lexeme. Thus the lexeme REHOBOAM is sometimes realised by the word-form *rehoboam*, and sometimes by the word-form *rehoboams*.

The units which actually occur, which have a shape (whether that is an orthographic shape or a sound shape) are word-forms. Word-forms realise (represent, belong to) lexemes. Lexemes, correspondingly, do not actually occur but are abstract dictionary words: abstract in that each lexeme may comprise a number of possible forms. The lexeme is, in a sense, what all the word-forms associated with it have in common.

For the time being, we shall assume that the word-forms of the spoken language are identical with the word-forms of the written language (that is, with orthographic words). This is actually an extremely awkward point, and it will be taken up again in greater detail in Chapter 4.

2. The Basic Units

We are now in a position to distinguish between the lexemes and the word-forms in a sentence like (1), but this will not always be sufficient for all purposes. Consider the next four sentences.

(4) (a) Lee walked home.
     (b) Lee went home.
(5) (a) Lee has walked home.
     (b) Lee has gone home.

The word-form *walked* occurs in both (4a) and in (5a), and in both cases it realises the lexeme WALK. Yet *walked* in these two sentences is not precisely the same element, as we can see when we compare with (4b) and (5b), which contain equivalent forms of the lexeme GO. In (4a) *walked* realises WALK + past tense, while in (5a) it realises WALK + past participle. We might want to say that *walked* in (4a) and (5a) are different words, even though they are the same word-form and realise the same lexeme. We will say that they are different **grammatical words.** Grammatical words are usually discussed in terms of their descriptions rather than their forms, so that we are likely to talk about descriptions such as 'the past participle of WALK' as grammatical words.

We now have three different kinds of 'words': word-forms (including orthographic words), lexemes and grammatical words. The word 'word' might seem to be rather a liability under these circumstances. However, it turns out that the amount of specificity in the three other terms is not always needed, and it is useful to have a superordinate term for word-form, lexeme and grammatical word. This allows us to avoid, when appropriate, the precision implicit in these other terms. In this book, **word** will be used with this less specific meaning.

In the printed text, word-forms are already separated out for us. But even if they were not, we would still be able to discover the beginnings and ends of words fairly simply. Indeed, Ancient Greek was frequently written without gaps between the words, and this corresponds to the way in which we talk. There are no gaps between the words in normal conversation. If there were, schoolboy jokes such as asking someone to say 'I chased the bug around the tree', or 'I'll have his blood, he knows I will' would not work, and neither would elaborate jokes like the following French couplet:

(6) Gal, amant de la reine, alla, tour magnanime,
     Galamment de l'arène à la Tour Magne, à Nîmes.

     'Gal, the queen's lover, went (which was generous of him)
     gallantly from the arena to the Magne Tower at Nimes.'

9

2. The Basic Units

The two lines in this couplet are (or can be) absolutely homophonous, even though they mean different things because the word-breaks come in different places. So there are no gaps between words in speech, and what we hear could be represented by running all the words together in print, as in

(7) Menbecomeoldbuttheyneverbecomegood.

Even here it is a relatively straightforward task for a speaker of English to sort out where the word-forms begin and end. We do this because we can recognise patterns and carry out substitutions. Firstly, we recognise certain strings of letters (or strings of sounds in the spoken language) which we know are found in other sentences with a meaning which would also make sense here. So we can recognise the sequence *men* in (7) because it also comes up in sentences like

(8) Menareconservativeafterdinner.

(9) Menlosetheirtempersindefendingtheirtaste.

(10) Afterfortymenhavemarriedtheirhabits.

In a similar way we could isolate each of the word-forms in (7). Notice that we might try to isolate the first two letters of (7), and we would find *me* in other places, but then we would be unable to find a word beginning *nb*. So firstly we can recognise recurrent sequences. But even if we found a sequence which we did not recognise, we could substitute other things which we know are word-forms in the place of these strings. So for *men* in (7) we could substitute *people, lecturers, sopranos* etc., in place of *become* we could have *get, are, turn*, etc, but we could not replace the *m* in *men* or *menb* in (7) with a word-form like *weeds* and still end up with a sentence. So substitution allows us to determine word-forms.

2.2 Elements smaller than the word

Now consider the following sentence:

(11) He was born stupid, and greatly increased his birthright.

We could isolate all the word-forms in this sentence in the ways outlined above, but we can also look within the word-forms and isolate recurrent forms within the word-form. For instance, if we consider the word-form *birthright*, we can divide that into two parts: for the first part, *birth* we could substitute within the word-form things like *copy* and *water*, for the second part, *right*, we could substitute things like *day*, *place* and *rate*. In a similar way, we could divide the word-form *greatly* up into two parts. For the first part,

10

great, we could substitute other forms like *vast* and *incredible*, and within the word-form (though not within this particular sentence) we could substitute items like *-ness*, *-er*, *-est* for *-ly*. Again in a similar way, we can divide *increased* in (11) into two portions: *increase* and *-d*. For the first we could substitute items like *enlarge*, *minimise*, for the second, items like *-s* and *-ing*. In other words, the same techniques that allow us to segment sentences into word-forms also allow us to segment word-forms. The units which we arrive at within the word-form we will call **morphs**. A word-form may contain only one morph (*stupid, and*) or it may contain several (*great·ly, increase·d, birth·right*). In this book, the decimal point will be used to separate morphs. A morph, then, is a unit which is a segment of a word-form. It has a constant form and realises or is related to a constant meaning.

Some morphs have the potential of being word-forms on their own. In

(12)   Every·one live·s by sell·ing some·thing.

this applies to the morphs *every, one, live, by, sell, some* and *thing*. Such morphs are called **potentially free morphs**. Notice that the potentiality is not actually exploited for all of these morphs in (12). Indeed, only *by* is actually free in (12), but the others listed are potentially free. Morphs which cannot be word-forms by themselves but which need to be attached to other morphs are termed **obligatorily bound morphs**. In (12) only the morphs *-s* and *-ing* are obligatorily bound. Notice that there are words in English (and far more in many other languages) which are made up entirely of obligatorily bound morphs. Examples from English include: *Euro·crat, octo·pus, phil·anthrop·y, phonet·ic, quadra·phon·ic, wis·dom*, and so on. In (12), it so happens that all of the potentially free morphs realise lexemes, and none of the obligatorily bound morphs do. This is typically the case in English, but not invariably the case, as the examples above show. In other languages, such as Latin, for example, it is typically the case that the morphs realising lexemes are also obligatorily bound.

In most cases in English (and, indeed, in all languages), and in all of the cases in (12) – though there are exceptions which will be dealt with below – the morph which realises the lexeme does not also realise anything else. Any morph which can realise a lexeme and which is not further analysable (except in terms of phonemes) is termed a **root**. Obligatorily bound morphs which do not realise lexemes and which are attached to roots to produce word-forms are called **affixes**. In a word like *dealings*, *deal* is the root, and *-ing* and *-s* are affixes. In *something* in sentence (12) there are two roots.

Note that this implies that *some* and *thing* in *something* realise the lexemes SOME and THING, respectively, even though SOMETHING is also a lexeme in its own right. Affixes can be added directly to a root, as in *fool·ish* or they can be added to a root and some already attached affix, as is the case with *-ness* in *fool·ish·ness*. We can call anything we attach affixes to, whether it is just a root or something bigger than a root, a **base**. So in the formation of *dealings* the root is *deal*, but the base to which the *-s* is added is *dealing*. Note that in this case the final *-s* was not added to a root.

If an affix is attached before a base it is called a **prefix**, if it is attached after a base it is called a **suffix**, and if it is attached in the middle of a base it is called an **infix**. In the word *prepacked* there is a root *pack*, a prefix *pre-*, and a suffix *-ed*. All of the affixes that have been illustrated in (11) and (12) have been suffixes, which are more common in English than prefixes are. There are no infixes in English: the closest we have is the use of expletives in the middle of words like *absobloominglutely* and *kangabloodyroo*.

2.3 Inflection and derivation

Affixes can be of two kinds, inflectional or derivational. An **inflectional affix** is one which produces a new word-form of a lexeme from a base. A **derivational affix** is one which produces a new lexeme from a base. Take a word-form like *recreates*. This can be analysed into a prefix *re-*, a root *create*, and a suffix *-s*. The prefix makes a new lexeme RECREATE from the base *create*. But the suffix *-s* just provides another word-form of the lexeme RECREATE. The prefix *re-* is derivational, but the suffix *-s* is inflectional. In English (though not in every language) prefixes are always derivational. Suffixes in English, though, may be either derivational or inflectional. In the word-form *formalises* the root is *form* and there are three suffixes: *-al*, *-ise* and *-s*. *Formal* belongs to a different lexeme from *form*, so *-al* is a derivational suffix; *formalise* belongs to a different lexeme from *formal*, so *-ise* is a derivational suffix; but *formalises* belongs to the same lexeme as *formalise*, so *-s* is an inflectional affix.

There are a number of ways of telling whether a suffix is inflectional or derivational if you are not sure whether or not it produces a new lexeme.

(a) If an affix changes the part of speech of the base, it is derivational. Affixes which do not change the part of speech of the base are usually (though not invariably) inflectional. So *form* is a noun, *formal* is an adjective; *-al* has changed the part of speech; it is thus a derivational affix. *Formal* is an adjective, *formalise* is a verb; *-ise* has changed the part of speech; it is a derivational suffix. *Formalise* is a verb, *formalises* is still a verb; *-s* has not changed the part of speech; *-s* is likely to be an inflectional affix. Note, however, that while all prefixes in English are derivational, very few of them change the part of speech of the base.

(b) Inflectional affixes always have a regular meaning. Derivational affixes may have an irregular meaning. If we consider an inflectional affix like the plural -*s* in word-forms like *bicycles, dogs, shoes, tins, trees,* and so on, the difference in meaning between the base and the affixed form is always the same: 'more than one'. If, however, we consider the change in meaning caused by a derivational affix like -*age* in words like *bandage, cleavage, coinage, dotage, drainage, haulage, herbage, mileage, orphanage, peerage, shortage, spillage,* and so on, it is difficult to sort out any fixed change in meaning, or even a small set of meaning changes.

(c) As a general rule, if you can add an inflectional affix to one member of a class, you can add it to all members of the class, while with a derivational affix, it is not generally possible to add it to all members. That is, inflectional affixes are fully **productive,** while derivational affixes are not. For example, you can add -*s* to any non-modal verb in English to make the 'third person singular of the present indicative', but you cannot add -*ation* to any non-modal verb to make a noun: *nationalis·ation* is a perfectly good word, so it works some of the time, but none of **com(e)·ation,* **inflect·ation,* **produc(e)·ation* or **walk·ation* are words of English. We can summarise this criterion in the following way: affixes which show limited productivity with large numbers of gaps are derivational; affixes which are fully productive (can be used with all members of a class) may be either inflectional or derivational.

In fact, the distinction between inflectional and derivational affixes is more complex than this suggests, and the matter will be taken up again in Chapter 6. The criteria provided here, though, will cover most of the straightforward cases.

2.4 Allomorphs and morphemes

Sometimes two or more morphs which have the same meaning are in complementary distribution. That is, the two can never occur in precisely the same environment or context, and between them they exhaust the possible contexts in which the morpheme can appear. For example, there are two morphs in English which can be glossed as 'indefinite article': *a* and *an.* Some examples of their distribution can be seen below.

(13) (a) a man   (b) an oak
      a horse   an elephant
      a kettle   an uncle
      a university   an apple
      a green apple   an old man

2. The Basic Units

From the examples in (13) and from your knowledge of the rest of the language you can see that *a* occurs when the next word begins with a phonetic consonant, and that *an* occurs when the next word begins with a phonetic vowel. The word 'phonetic' is important, since *university* begins orthographically with a *u*, but phonetically with a consonant /j/. (In some rather conservative varieties of English this rule is not quite true, since it is possible to say *an hotel* and *an historical novel*. Not all such speakers pronounce these words without an /h/, which would make them conform to the general rule. We shall provisionally ignore these varieties.)

In this case the choice between the two morphs *a* and *an* is determined or conditioned by the following phonetic sound. We can say that their distribution is **phonetically conditioned.** In other cases the distribution of morphs may be determined by other factors. For example, there are various ways of marking plurality in English. The most common way is with an -*s* (variously pronounced), there is -*en* in *ox·en*, -*ren* in *child·ren*, -*im* in *seraph·im*, and a few other ways as well. The choice of these various ways does not depend on the phonetic environment, but on the lexeme involved. It is a peculiarity of the lexeme ox (as opposed to BOX, COX, FOX) that it takes a plural marker -*en*. No other word in English marks its plural in just this way. The plural marker -*en* is determined by the particular lexeme involved: it is **lexically conditioned.** Morphs can also be **grammatically conditioned.** In a language like German, adjectives change their form depending on the gender of the noun they modify. Thus in the nominative singular, we find the following pattern:

(14) ein gross·er Wagen   'a big car (masculine)'
       ein gross·er Fisch   'a big fish (masculine)'
       ein gross·es Haus   'a big house (neuter)'
       ein gross·es Tier   'a big animal (neuter)'
       eine gross·e Feder   'a big feather (feminine)'
       eine gross·e Schlange 'a big snake (feminine)'

The suffix on the adjective is not determined by the phonetic shape of the base or of the next word, nor is it determined by the particular lexeme following, but by the grammatical gender class that lexeme belongs to. The conditioning is thus neither phonetic nor lexical, but grammatical.

But if English *a* and *an*, or -*s*, -*en*, -*ren* and -*im*, or German -*er*, -*es*, and -*e* are clearly separate morphs because of their different shapes, they nevertheless have things in common. They have their meaning in common: 'indefinite article', 'plural' or 'nominative singular'. Between them, they divide up a single distribution: always before a singular countable noun, always on the end of a countable noun, or always on the end of an attributive adjective following an indefinite determiner. In the clearest cases, they even have a similarity in form. There is a sense, therefore in which *a* and *an* (and the other sets) are 'the same thing': We will say that these various sets of morphs realise the same **morpheme.**

As with lexemes, the name we use to refer to the morphemes is arbitrary. We could call the morpheme realised by *a* and *an* '9,673' or '99/o/7245-T2' or 'Zoe' – whatever made sense in our classification. But to simplify matters we will agree to call a morpheme either by a label describing its meaning (in this case 'indefinite article') or by one of its morphs, say 'a'. If we make the latter choice, we will usually use the morph that occurs most widely in the language. To show we are talking about a morpheme we will enclose this name in braces when we write it: {indefinite article} or {a}.

Notice that the morpheme, like the lexeme and the phoneme, is realised by something else. You cannot hear a morpheme or say a morpheme (just as you cannot say or hear a lexeme or a phoneme): you can only say or hear something which realises a morpheme (or a lexeme or a phoneme). You can hear or say a morph (or a word-form or a phone), but not what it realises. Morphemes (like lexemes and phonemes) are abstract units. The morpheme {a} is whatever all the morphs which can realise {a} have in common.

Morphs which realise a particular morpheme and which are conditioned (whether phonetically or lexically or grammatically) are called the **allomorphs** of that morpheme. (If we consider the written form of the language, it is also possible to talk about orthographically conditioned allomorphs of a morpheme, as in *come* and *com-*, the latter of which occurs in *coming*.) *A* and *an* are the two phonetically conditioned allomorphs of the morpheme {a}. Notice that every allomorph is a morph. The term allomorph is simply more informative than is morph on its own, because it says that the morph is one of several realisations of the same morpheme.

It should be noted that the terms 'morpheme' and 'allomorph' are frequently used by other linguists in rather different senses from the ones they have been given here. While the meanings used in this book are relatively common, they are not in universal use, and you will have to take care when you meet these terms in other works that you know precisely what is intended.

This abstractness of morphemes frequently causes problems of understanding for students who are new to morphology.

15

A parallel might be helpful. Consider the various symbols presented below:

(15)   R   r   *ı*

What do these symbols have in common? The answer, fairly simply, is that they are all kinds of 'R'. What is it about them that shows, then, that they are all kinds of 'R'? How can you tell that they are 'R's? The answer lies not in their particular shape, which varies depending on the kind of script they happen to occur in. The answer lies in their function; they all function as 'R', they all have the same value in the system, they all, for instance, can be used at the beginning of the word *rat*. But this is an abstract quality. The 'R-ness' of the symbols presented in (15) is something abstract. The 'R-ness' corresponds, in the analogy, to the morpheme. The different forms for these 'R's which have the same function in the system correspond to morphs. The symbol 'r' is just one of the morphs that can realise the morpheme, the abstract notion of what 'R' is.

2.5 Recapitulation
Armed with all this terminology, consider the word-form *was* in the sentence

(16)   While he was not dumber than an ox, he was not any smarter.

Was is a word-form which is probably not further analysable into morphs. This word-form realises, among other things, the lexeme BE, as we can see if we change the syntactic environment of (16), but not its meaning:

(17)   Being not dumber than an ox, but being no smarter, he was not a brilliant conversationalist.

(18)   I hope, at least, to be not dumber than an ox.

But there are also other morphemes realised by the word-form *was*. Firstly, *was* is singular, because if it had a plural subject it would be replaced by *were*:

(19)   While they were not dumber than oxen, they were not any smarter.

You cannot say in standard English

(20)   While they was not dumber than an ox, they was not any smarter.

Secondly, *was* also marks past tense. You cannot say

(21)   While he was not any dumber than an ox, he was not any smarter at the moment.

16

You have to say

(22)   While he is not any dumber than an ox, he is not any smarter
       at the moment.

In other verbs, pastness is shown by a separate morph (as, for example, in the difference between *compliment* and *compliment· ed*), but here this difference is included in the single word-form. So *was* is a single morph, but realises not only the lexeme BE (which contains a single morpheme {be}), but also the morphemes {singular} and {past tense}. A morph which realises more than one morpheme in this way is called a **portmanteau morph.**

To summarise, we can say that an actual speech event can be analysed into a series of word-forms, some of which will be made up of a single morph, others of which will be made up of more than one morph. The morphs realise (though not necessarily in a one-to-one manner) morphemes. Morphemes are abstract units of grammatical and semantic analysis. One or more morphemes may form a lexeme, an abstract vocabulary item. This is presented in tabular form (with a certain amount of simplification) in fig. 2.1.

LEXEMES	made up of one or more	MORPHEMES
realised by		realised by
WORD-FORMS	made up of one or more	MORPHS

Figure 2.1: Summary of basic terms

REFERENCES AND FURTHER READING

Most introductory linguistics textbooks cover the kind of material that has been covered in this chapter. It should be noted, however, that the terminology used here derives from a British tradition, which is, in this area, distinct from the American tradition. In particular, many American sources do not distinguish between 'morph' and 'morpheme' in the way that has been done here. For a discussion of the various ways in which the term 'morpheme' has been used in Linguistics, see Mugdan (1986). It is clear from that article just how careful you have to be when reading works which discuss morphemes.

Among the best books to consult for consolidation of the discussion here are Brown & Miller (1980), Lyons (1968) and Matthews (1974). Of these, I would particularly recommend Brown & Miller (1980) for beginners. Note that Matthews's use of the term 'word' is different from the one in this book.

2. The Basic Units

The discussion of abstractness in terms of letter-shapes is loosely based on Lass (1984).

Not all authorities agree that allomorphs can be lexically conditioned. Lyons (1968), for example, is in a tradition of excluding the use of the term 'allomorph' in such circumstances. It is true that it is far less clear that there is 'conditioning' involved in lexical conditioning, which is far more random than other kinds of conditioning. There are therefore advantages to this kind of restriction. But there are also advantages (albeit less obvious ones) to the wider usage of the term adopted in this book.

The sentences used as examples are, of course, not my own. Many of them can be found in Bentley & Esar (1951).

In Appendix A a feed-back exercise is provided to check and extend the student's knowledge of the terminology introduced in Chapter 2. This should be seen as an integral part of this chapter.

3. The Morphological Structure of Words

In this chapter, we shall consider the various processes by which words can be built. I shall illustrate these processes from a number of languages, some of which will be familiar to you, and others of which will not be familiar to you. It is the wide range of ways in which it is possible to build words which is the central focus of this chapter. In passing, attention will also be drawn to some of the difficulties that arise in morphological description, to show why linguists find morphology interesting. One reviewer said about morphology recently that 'we do not understand all that we know'. This is part of the interest and the challenge provided by morphology.

3.1 Word-building processes using affixes

By far the most common way of building new words in the languages of the world is by using affixes. The commonest type of affix by far is the suffix. There are several languages in the world which use suffixes to the exclusion of any other type of affix (Basque, Finnish and Quechua are examples), but only very few which use prefixes to the exclusion of other types of affix (Thai is an example), and none which use any other type of affix exclusively. Thus the obligatorily bound morph *par excellence* in the languages of the world is the suffix.

3.1.1 Suffixes. Suffixes are used for all purposes in morphology. They are used derivationally as in

(1)   *English*:   constitut·ion·al·ity
        Finnish: asu·nno·ttom·uus
                live·noun·without·abstract-noun
                'houselessness'
        Mam: txik·eenj
                cook·patient
                'something cooked'

and inflectionally as in

(2)   *Finnish*:   talo·i·ssa·an
                house·plural·in·3rd-person-possessive
                'in their houses'

19

Turkish: gel·é·miy·eceğ·im
come·be-able·negative·future·1st-person
'I will not be able to come'

Notice that all of the suffixes in (2) are inflectional, even though some of them are translated into English by separate lexemes. The meaning of an affix is not sufficient to tell you whether that affix is inflectional or derivational. This will be taken up again in Chapter 6. Neither is it the case that a given type of meaning is always realised in the same kind of way across languages. Even plurality may not always be an inflectional category. In Diyari, an aboriginal language of South Australia, plurality is marked optionally by a derivational suffix.

As is clear from the examples given above, suffixes can occur in sequences, although there is no expectation that they will. When both inflectional and derivational suffixes co-occur in the same word-form, the general rule (although it is by no means exception-less, see below section 6.5) is that the derivational suffixes precede the inflectional ones, so that the following cases are typical:

(3) *Diyari:* yiŋki·mali·yi
give·reciprocal (derivational)·present (inflectional)
'give one another'

Finnish: kirja·sto·sta·mme
book·collective (deriv)·out-of (infl)·our (infl)
'out of our library'

French: égal·is·a
equal·verb (deriv)·3rd-person-singular-past (infl)
'[he/she/it] equalised'

Portmanteau morphs are very common as suffixes in highly inflecting languages. This is illustrated by the case and number marking on the nouns in many Indo-European languages. The paradigm for the Latin noun ANNUS 'year' given below will provide an example.

(4)

	Singular	Plural
Nominative	ann·us	ann·i:
Vocative	ann·e	ann·i:
Accusative	ann·um	ann·o:s
Genitive	ann·i:	ann·o:rum
Dative	ann·o:	ann·i:s
Ablative	ann·o:	ann·i:s

3. The Morphological Structure of Words

In this paradigm it can be seen that there is neither a consistent realisation of singularity, nor one of plurality. Neither is there a single realisation of any one of the cases (and if the other genders were taken into consideration, this would be even more striking). Rather the final morph analysed in the word-forms in (4) has to be seen as a portmanteau morph, realising simultaneously the category of number and that of case. The alternative position, where a single morpheme is realised in more than one morph, can also be illustrated from Latin. Consider the realisation relations shown by the arrows in the Latin word-form *reːksisti* 'you (sg) ruled'.

(5) RULE   perfective   2nd   Singular

Each of the morphs analysed in (5) can be motivated by comparison with other forms of Latin, and the realisation relations can be justified since if any of the morphemes were changed, the morphs realising those morphemes would also change. Compare, for example, the form for 'I ruled':

(6) RULE   perfective   1st   Singular

3.1.2 Prefixes. Although they are rarer than suffixes, prefixes work in very much the same way. They can be derivational, as in

(7) *English*: dis·en·tangle
     Mam: aj·b'iitz
                 agent·song
                 'singer'
     Tagalog: pan·ulat
                 instrument·write
                 'pen'

or inflectional as in

(8) *Mam*:   t·kamb'
                 3rd-singular-possessive·prize
                 'his prize'
     Swahili: a·si·nga·li·jua
                 he·negative·concessive·past·know
                 'if he had not known'
     Tagalog: i·sulat
                 modal·write
                 'writing (participle)'

21

These examples show that, like suffixes, prefixes can occur in sequences. The norm is for derivational prefixes to occur to the right of inflectional prefixes within the same word-form, as is shown in the data from Achenese, a language of Sumatra, below:

(9)   (a)   jih ji·langŭ
             he 3rd-person-(younger) (infl)·swim
             'he swims (transitive, e.g. swims the river)'
      (b)   jih ji·mɨ·langŭ
             he 3rd-person-(younger) (infl)·intransi-
             tive (deriv)·swim
             'he swims (intransitive)'
      (c)   jih ji·pɨ·langŭ
             he 3rd-person-(younger) (infl)·causative (deriv)·swim
             'he makes [someone] swim'

Prefixes can, of course, co-occur in the same word with suffixes, and all possible combinations of derivational and inflectional are found in such cases.

(10)   *English*:   un·thank·ful
                     (deriv) (deriv)
       English: re·think·s
                     (deriv) (infl)
       Mam: ky·xoo·ʔkj
                     3rd-person-plural-ergative (infl)·
                     throw·processive (deriv)
                     'they went and threw'
       Turkana: ɛ̀·ràm·i
                     3rd-person (infl)·beat·aspect (infl)
                     'he is beating'

3.1.3 Circumfixes. In some cases a prefix and a suffix act together to surround a base. If neither of these affixes is used on its own, and the two seem to realise a single morpheme, they are sometimes classed together as a **circumfix**. This can be illustrated from German, where the past participle of weak verbs is made by adding a prefix *ge-* and simultaneously, a suffix *-t*. That is, the base is enclosed in affixes, neither of which can occur on its own in the forms in question. This is illustrated below.

(11)   film·en   'to film'   ge·film·t   'filmed'
       frag·en   'to ask'   ge·frag·t   'asked'
       lob·en   'to praise'   ge·lob·t   'praised'
       zeig·en   'to show'   ge·zeig·t   'shown'
       Ge·film etc do not occur.

Film·t etc do not occur in this meaning but only as 3rd person singular present tense forms.

If the circumfix *ge···t* is taken to be a single affix, it is a **discontinuous morph**. Discontinuous morphs are considerably rarer than continuous morphs.

3.1.4 Infixes. Since infixes create discontinuous bases, the rarity of discontinuous morphs also accounts for the relative rarity of infixation (the use of infixes) in the languages of the world. Consider the following examples, (12) from Chrau, a language of Vietnam, and (13) from Tagalog, a language of the Philippines.

(12) vŏh   'know'   v·an·ŏh   'wise'
      căh   'remember'   c·an·ăh   'left over'

(13) sulat   'write'
      s·um·ulat   'wrote'
      s·in·ulat   'was written'

In both these cases the infix is inserted after the initial consonant of the base. Note that in (12) the infix is used derivationally, while in (13) it is used inflectionally. Infixes can co-occur in the word-form with prefixes and suffixes. This is illustrated below from Tagalog. Verbs like *sulat* in Tagalog have three different passive themes. The first was illustrated above in (13), the second involves prefixation as well, and the third suffixation, as can be seen in (14a and b) respectively.

(14) (a) i·s·in·ulat   second passive theme (preterite)
      (b) s·in·ulat·an   third passive theme (preterite)

3.1.5 Interfixes. A rather special kind of infix can be found, for example, in many of the Germanic languages, where there is a linking element which appears between the two elements of a compound. This can be illustrated from German.

(15)		Element 1	Element 2	Compound	Gloss
	(a)	Auge	Arzt	Auge·n·arzt	'eye doctor'
		Schwester	Paar	Schwester·n·paar	'pair of sisters'
		Tag	Reise	Tag·e·reise	'day's journey'
		Uhr	Kasten	Uhr·en·kasten	'clock case'
	(b)	Bauer	Frau	Bauer·s·frau	'farmer's wife'
		Jahr	Zeit	Jahr·es·zeit	'season' (*lit.* year time)
		Tag	Licht	Tag·es·licht	'day light'
		Wirt	Haus	Wirt·s·haus	'inn' (*lit.* host house)
	(c)	Stern	Banner	Stern·en·banner	'stars and stripes'
		Strauss	Ei	Strauss·en·ei	'ostrich egg'

23

3. *The Morphological Structure of Words*

(d)	Arbeit	Anzug	Arbeit·s·anzug	'work clothes'
	Geburt	Jahr	Geburt·s·jahr	'year of birth'
	Liebe	Brief	Liebe·s·brief	'love letter'
	Verbindung	Tür	Verbindung·s·tür	'connecting door'

The linking element in the compound is an affix which only comes between two other forms. It is therefore sometimes termed an **interfix**. The -*o*- that occurs in neo-classical compounds such as *electrolyte* in English (see below, section 3.6) might also be seen as an interfix.

The German interfixes in (15) raise a small problem for morphological description. In (15a) the interfix has the same form as the appropriate morph of the morpheme {plural}. In (15b) the interfix has the same form as the appropriate morph of the morpheme {possessive}. In (15c) the interfix has the same form as the appropriate realisation of the dative plural. But in (15d), the interfix does not share the form of any morph which otherwise could be attached to the first element. Words like these suggest that these interfixes, whatever they are derived from etymologically, probably do not synchronically represent the morphemes {plural}, {possessive} or {dative}. That being the case, though, there does not seem to be any morpheme which these interfixes do realise. They seem to be morphs that do not realise morphemes, morphs which have no meaning attached to them. They are **empty morphs**. It is sometimes useful to have a label which can be used to refer to all kinds of morphs, whether or not they realise morphemes. The term 'morph' itself usually implies a realisation of a morpheme. The term **formative** can be used (rather untraditionally) to refer to morphs and empty morphs, or to be deliberately vague as to whether a particular recurrent form is a realisation of a morpheme or not.

3.1.6 Transfixes. Another special kind of infix involves not only discontinuous affixes but also discontinuous bases. These are affixes which occur throughout the base, and they are thus termed **transfixes**. Transfixes appear only in the Semitic languages. In these languages, roots are made up of a number of consonants, and can never occur in isolation. Transfixes are then added to these roots, sometimes also with prefixes or suffixes. The transfixes are made up of a number of vowels, and may also involve operations on consonants (for example, consonants may be doubled). The position of the transfix varies from transfix to transfix: some of them allow clusters of the consonants in the root, others do not. Each transfix occurs in a fixed position in the root. This very complex state of affairs is illustrated for the roots *ktb* 'write' and *drs* 'study' below, using data from Egyptian Arabic.

3. The Morphological Structure of Words

(16) 'katab   'he wrote'   'daras   'he studied'
     'jiktib   'he will write'   'jidris   'he will study'
     mak'tuub 'written'   mad'ruus 'studied'
     mak'taba 'bookshop'   mad'rasa 'school'
     ma'kaatib 'bookshops'   ma'daaris 'schools'
                           dars   'lesson'
     ki'taab   'book'
     'kaatib   'clerk'
                           mu'daris 'teacher'

Since they involve two sets of discontinuous morphs, transfixes are the most complex type of affix. Accordingly, they have received quite a lot of attention in recent times from linguists as test cases for various morphological theories. They raise very important problems for morphological description, but these need not concern us further here.

3.2 Reduplication

Reduplication, or using some part of the base (which may be the entire base) more than once in the word, is far more common across languages than the rarer types of affixation illustrated above. If the entire base is reduplicated, reduplication resembles compounding (see below, section 3.6). Reduplication can also form types of affix. That is, the part of the word which is repeated may be added to the end or the beginning of the base. All these types will be illustrated below. The examples in (17) are from Afrikaans, and show whole words being reduplicated. The examples in (18) are from Motu, a language of Papua New Guinea, and illustrate the use of reduplicated prefixes as well as whole word reduplication. In the Maori data in (19) the reduplicated part is used as a suffix.

(17) amper   'nearly'   amper·amper   'very nearly'
     dik   'thick'   dik·dik   'very thick'
     drie   'three'   drie·drie   'three at a time'

(18) tau   'man'   ta·tau   'men'
     mero   'boy'   me·mero   'boys'
                         meromero   'little boy'
                         memeromemero 'little boys'

(19) aahua   'appearance' aahua·hua   'resemble'
     hiikei   'step'   hiikei·kei   'hop'
     maakuu   'moisture'   maakuu·kuu   'rather moist'

Reduplication is frequently used iconically. By this, I mean that the form of the word in some way reflects its meaning. So reduplica-

25

tion is frequently used to indicate plurality, intensity and repetition, which are some of the meanings illustrated in examples (17) to (19). However, reduplication is also found in less iconic uses. For example, compare the data in (13) with that below:

(20)   sumulat   'to write'   su·sulat   'will write'
        bumasa   'to read'   ba·basa   'will read'
        ʔumaral   'to teach'   ʔa·ʔaral   'will teach'

In (20) it can be seen that the future tense in Tagalog is formed by reduplicating the first consonant and vowel of the base to form a prefix. The marking of futurity with reduplication is far less iconic than marking, say, plurality with reduplication. Note also that here reduplication has been used to mark inflection, while in most of the other cases illustrated here it has been used derivationally.

Reduplication, then, is in effect a special way of making affixes or a way of creating a special kind of compound. These affixes or compounds may, however, act differently from other affixes or compounds in the language concerned. This is, for example, clearly the case with the Afrikaans examples cited above, which are formally distinct from other compounds in that language. Reduplication is usually determined in phonological terms, so that a reduplication rule will state how much of the base is to be reduplicated in terms of consonants, vowels, syllables, and word-forms.

3.3 Word-building by modification of the base

Where affixes are not used for creating new words, the most common method is to make some kind of phonological change to the base. The change may be segmental or suprasegmental, and if segmental it may affect consonants or vowels and one or more segments. The terminology surrounding the various types of change is complex, and unfortunately not always illuminating, as will be seen below.

Consider first modifications to the segmental make-up of the base. In the examples below, a change from a voiceless fricative to a voiced fricative causes a change from noun to verb in English:

(21)   mouth   mouth
        sheath   sheathe
        strife   strive
        thief   thieve
        wreath   wreathe

There is no special name for this type of internal modification. It is found along with affixation in the following irregular English plurals:

26

(16)

(22) house   house·s
      mouth   mouth·s
      path   path·s
      self   selve·s
      shelf   shelve·s
      wharf   wharve·s
      wife   wive·s
      youth   youth·s

More common is modification to a vowel sound. Such modification has a different name depending on its historical source. Where it is the result of assimilation to a following vowel (even if that later vowel has subsequently disappeared) it is called **Umlaut**. Otherwise it is called **Ablaut**. Either can be referred to as **vowel mutation**. The following are examples of Umlaut from some of the Germanic languages:

(23) *Danish*
      gaas   'goose'   gæs   'geese'
      mand   'man'   mænd   'men'
      English
      mouse   mice
      foot   feet
      tooth   teeth
      louse   iice
      Icelandic
      stór   'big'   stærri 'bigger'
      mús   'mouse'   mýs   'mice'
      son·ur 'son'   syn·ir 'sons'
      full·ur 'full'   fyll·ri 'fuller'

Note that in some of the Icelandic examples, Umlaut co-occurs with a suffix, while in other examples there is no affix. Co-occurrence of modification of the base and affixation is, in fact, a very common phenomenon.

Examples of Ablaut from irregular past tenses in some of the Germanic languages are listed in (24):

(24) *Dutch*
      bijten 'bite'   beet   'bit'
      doen   'do'   dee   'did'
      dragen 'carry'   droeg   'carried'
      stelen 'steal'   stal   'stole'
      Frisian
      bliede 'bleed'   blette 'bled'
      drage   'carry'   droech 'carried'

27

gean	'go'	gong	'went'
glimme	'glimmer'	glom	'glimmered'
helpe	'help'	holp	'helped'
Icelandic			
ber	'I carry'	bar	'I carried'
gef	'I give'	gaf	'I gave'
kýs	'I choose'	kaus	'I chose'
tek	'I take'	tók	'I took'

That Ablaut is also found along with affixation can be illustrated from the past participle forms of the same verbs:

(25) *Dutch*

gebeten	'bitten'
gedaan	'done'
gedragen	'carried'
gestolen	'stolen'.

Frisian

blet	'bled'
droegen	'carried'
gongen	'gone'
glommen	'glimmered'
holpen	'helped'

Icelandic

bor·inn	'carried'
gef·inn	'given'
kos·inn	'chosen'
tek·inn	'taken'

Although these examples have all come from the Germanic languages, and the very names Umlaut and Ablaut are German loan words, vowel mutation is not restricted to these languages by any means, as can be seen from the examples below:

(26) *Dinka*

dom	'field'	dum	'fields'
kat	'frame'	kɛt	'frames'
met	'child'	miit	'children'

Welsh

singular	*plural*	*gloss*
bychan	bychain	'little'
byddar	byddair	'deaf'
garw	geirw	'rough'
caled	celyd	'hard'

Transfixes (see above, section 3.1.6) are viewed by some linguists as types of internal modification.

28

Turning now to internal modification in suprasegmental structure, consider the following data from Kanuri, a language of Nigeria. The example shows the differences between the 3rd person singular conjunctive ('s/he VERBS and ...') and optative ('s/he is to VERB') tenses in Kanuri:

(27) *conjunctive*   *optative*   *gloss*
      lezâ   lezá   'go'
      tussâ   tussá   'rest'
      kərazâ   kərazá   'study'
´ = high tone, ^ = falling tone

Such processes are relatively common in the tone languages of Africa. Since these morphs are suprasegmental in their realisation, they are sometimes treated as suprasegmental affixes, and called suprafixes or **superfixes**. It has been pointed out that such affixes are no more on top of the other morphs than they are underneath them, and that simulfix would probably be a better term, but this suggestion has not been generally adopted. Stress differences such as distinguish the following English pairs (at least in some varieties) are also superfixes in this sense, or cases of suprasegmental internal modification:

(28) 'discount (*n*)   dis'count (*v*)
      'import (*n*)   im'port (*v*)
      'insult (*n*)   in'sult (*v*)

Some authorities view cases of this kind as **replacive morphs**. They would claim that the replacement of one phonological sequence by another is a morph realising the appropriate morpheme in all the cases that have been discussed in this section. For example, they would say that the distinction between *mouse* and *mice* is marked by a replacive morph of the form '/aʊ/ → /aɪ/'. The replacive morph is everything between inverted commas in the last sentence. This analysis is controversial. The most usual understanding of morphs is that they are forms, while replacive morphs would be not so much forms as processes. This is clearly an extension of the term 'morph', although whether such an extension goes beyond what is justified, particularly within a generative framework, is less clear. Other analysts might see cases of infixation in these examples. The main argument against this position is that in most of these cases the form of the modification is lexically determined, and there is no constant form. There is also a typological argument, in that the languages which use modification most freely (for example, the Germanic languages) do not generally have any other infixes. It is partly for this reason, and partly in order to give some kind of

29

formal statement of internal modification that the term 'replacive morph' is used.

3.4 Relationships with no change of form

There are many instances to be found where, although there appears to be an inflectional or derivational relationship between two words, they have precisely the same form. Some examples are given below:

(29)   *English*

singular		*plural*	
deer		deer	
fish		fish	
sheep		sheep	

English

better (*adj*)	to betier	a better	
empty (*adj*)	to empty	an empty	
round (*adj*)	to round	a round	
clean (*adj*)	to clean		
	to farm	a farm	
nasty (*adj*)		a nasty	

French

devoir	'to have to'	le devoir	'duty'
pouvoir	'to be able to'	le pouvoir	'power'
savoir	'to know'	le savoir	'knowledge'

Yoruba

gígùn	'long'	'length'
dídùn	'sweet'	'sweetness'

The examples in (29) have to be distinguished in principle from the cases where there is no change of form, but equally no reason to hypothesise the existence of an extra morpheme. For instance, the English plural forms in (29) do not work in the same way as the Maori plural forms in (30):

(30)

korou	'channel'	korou	'channels'
kurii	'dog'	kurii	'dogs'
kuumara	'kumara'	kuumara	'kumaras'

In English it is normal for plurals to be overtly marked on nouns, while in Maori it is the exception for plural nouns to carry any morphological mark. Plurality in Maori is marked by determiners. Since morphemes have to do with both form and meaning, every morpheme must have both a form (or series of forms) and a constant meaning. If there is never any form, we cannot set up a morpheme. Thus we cannot postulate a morpheme {singular} for English nouns, because singularity is never marked by an affix on nouns.

3. The Morphological Structure of Words

Some linguists postulate a **zero morph** to account for the difference in function between homophonous forms such as those in (29). The argument runs as follows. In most instances where there is a change in the part of speech, there is an affix to mark that change. In *legal·ise*, for example, the fact that an adjective has been turned into a verb is marked by the suffix. In to *empty*, on the other hand, there is no overt affix. In order to treat both of these the same way, a zero morph is postulated on the end of *empty·∅*, marking its status as a verb.

Zero morphs, however, are controversial. They are most generally accepted in inflectional cases, where parallelism with other forms in a paradigm appears to demand an affix. Consider the following example from Russian, where the word for 'drinking glass' is a masculine noun, and the word for 'school' is a feminine noun.

(31)	'school'		'drinking glass'	
	Singular	*Plural*	*Singular*	*Plural*
Nominative	ʃkol·a	ʃkol·ɨ	stakan	stakan·ɨ
Accusative	ʃkol·u	ʃkol·ɨ	stakan	stakan·ɨ
Genitive	ʃkol·ɨ	ʃkol	stakan·a	stakan·ov

Here all cases and numbers are typically marked with a suffix (there are more cases than are illustrated here, and also a third gender), and the nominative and accusative singular of the masculine and the genitive plural of the feminine are the exceptions. The case of each individual noun can be worked out when its gender is known. A zero might thus be seen in such instances as a kind of place-holder. Note that if it were true that the nominative, say, was never marked in Russian, then we would not be able to talk in terms of zero morphs for that case.

In derivation, however, the case for a zero morph is less compelling. Consider the English data in (32) below:

(32) He walked *round* the car.
She was looking *round*.
They sat at the *round* table.
As soon as I *round* the corner, I want you to start running.
I always enjoy theatre in the *round*.

Let us assume that we can work out which *round* is the basic form of all of these (this is feasible, but not immediately obvious). That basic type of *round* presumably has no zero morph on the end of it. The others, though, would have a zero morph. So a zero is contrasting with nothing at all, a lack of even a zero. What is more,

31

all the other *round*s must have different zero morphs, so that different zeros contrast with each other. Even if this state of affairs is possible within a generative theory of morphology, it does not have much plausibility as an account of the way in which real speakers process language. For that reason, the term **conversion** will be used here for the derivational cases illustrated in (29), rather than **zero-derivation,** a term which is also current. A third term is **functional shift.** Some authorities differentiate between some or all of these terms, but for most they are synonymous.

3.5 Cases involving shortening bases
In rather rare cases the base may actually be longer than the form created from it. Consider the following data from spoken French:

(33)
masculine	feminine	gloss
mɔvɛ	mɔvɛz	'bad'
œʁø	œʁøz	'happy'
gʁɑ̃	gʁɑ̃d	'big'
lɔ̃	lɔ̃g	'long'
ʃo	ʃod	'hot'
vɛʁ	vɛʁt	'green'
fʁwa	fʁwad	'cold'
pəti	pətit	'little'
blɑ̃	blɑ̃ʃ	'white'
fʁɛ	fʁɛʃ	'fresh'
fo	fos	'false'

It is clear that the feminine form of these adjectives is the same as the masculine form, but with an extra consonant. However, there is no way to predict from the form of the masculine adjective which consonant will be added to make the feminine form. We can only make predictions if we start with the feminine form. Then it is quite simple: if we subtract the final consonant from the feminine form we have the masculine form. Some authorities term this final consonant a **subtractive morph,** a morph which is removed by a morphological process.

In cases where the element subtracted is (or looks like) a morph with an independent existence elsewhere in the language, and especially where the process is a derivational one, we talk of **backformation.** For instance, when P.G. Wodehouse writes

(34) I could see that, if not actually disgruntled, he was far from being gruntled.

he forms the word *gruntled* by the deletion of the prefix *dis-*. The lexeme GRUNTLE actually existed at the time that *disgruntled* first appeared in the English language, but now a sentence like (34) strikes us as funny because we do not expect to find a lexeme GRUNTLE; we are not familiar with it. *Gruntle* is thus a backformation for a modern speaker. In the line

(35)   Little spider, spiding sadly ....

the *-er* that has been deleted is not a real suffix; there is no familiar lexeme to SPIDE. It has, however, the same form as the familiar suffix in words such as *pointer, retriever* and *warbler,* and this is sufficient to allow it to be deleted in backformation.

There is one very important point about backformation: in retrospect, it is invisible. It is only noticeable when the backformed word (this is an example of backformation!) is unfamiliar. Unless the difference is pointed out by someone with an understanding of etymology, you could not tell that EDIT comes from EDITOR but that EXHIBITOR comes from EXHIBIT. This has led some linguists to deny that backformation has any synchronic status as a morphological process. But it must be remembered that backformation continues to be synchronically used to produce new lexemes, and thus must be included in any synchronic grammar.

Another type of shortening is **clipping.** Clipping is the process of shortening a word without changing its meaning or part of speech. As will be clear from the examples given below, clipping frequently does change the stylistic value of the word. As far as is known, there is no way to predict how much of a word will be clipped off in clipping, nor even which end of the word will be clipped off. Neither is it possible to say that any given syllable will definitely be retained in clipping. Some examples from English are given below:

(36)   binoc(ular)s
        deli(catessen)
        (de)tec(tive)
        (head-)shrink(er)
        op(tical) art
        sci(ence) fi(ction)

Since the parts that are deleted in clipping are not clearly morphs in any sense, it is not necessarily the case that clipping is a part of morphology, although it is a way of forming new lexemes.

3.6 Processes involving several lexemes
The formation of a new lexeme by adjoining two or more lexemes is called **compounding** or **composition.** It seems that no known language is without compounds, and in many languages compounds

33

are the main type of new lexeme. Some random examples are given below.

(37) Finnish

kirje·kuori
letter·cover
'envelope'
maa·talous·tuotanto
land·economy·production
'agricultural production'
huone·kalu·tehdas
room·article·factory
'furniture factory'
French
oiseau·mouche
bird·fly (n)
'humming bird'
ouvre·boîte
open·box
'tin opener'
année·lumière
year·light
'light year'
Kanuri
súro·zàu
stomach·pain
'stomach ache'
kɔm·cejí
man·he-killed
'murderer'
nóŋgù·ba
shame·no
'shameless'

Maori

puku·aroha
belly·love
'sympathetic'
whare·ruuna·nga
house draw-together·
nominalisation
'meeting house'
mate·wai
lack·water
'(be) thirsty'
Vietnamese
bàn·ghế
table·chair
'furniture'
hoa·xa
fire·vehicle
'train'
biên·chép
jot-down·copy
'transcribe'
Yoruba
í·gbà·lé
noun·sweep·ground
'broom'
ì·bọ·wọ̀
noun·insert·hand
'glove'
oní·ṣ·òwò
having·to-do·trade
'trader'

In the most typical cases, compounds do not contain internal inflections, but there are instances where internal inflections (or what appear to be internal inflections) are found:

(38) Danish

byg·ning·s·fejl
build·nominalisation·genitive·error
'astigmatism'
ny·t·aar
new·neuter·year
'new year'

34

Finnish
hallit·ukse·ssa·olo·aika
rule·nominal·in·be·time
'period in government'
kansa·n·taju·inen
people·genitive·grasp·adjective
'easily comprehensible'
Icelandic
barn·s·skó·r
child·genitive-singular·shoe·plural
'the shoes of a child'
barn·a-skól·i
child·genitive-plural·school·nominative-singular
'school for children'
Turkish
din·i·bütün
religion·possessive·whole
'devout'
el·i·açık
hand·possessive·open
'generous'

Most of the compounds that have been illustrated so far (though not all) are **endocentric** compounds, that is they denote a sub-class of the items denoted by one of their elements. A *sea-bird* is a kind of *bird*, in Finnish a *huone·kalu·tehdas* is a kind of *tehdas* 'factory', in French a *oiseau-mouche* is a kind of *oiseau* 'bird', and so on. Similarly, if you *type·write* you *write* in a certain way; if something is *grass-green* it is *green* in a certain way. In each of these cases the compound as a whole is a hyponym of its main or **head** element.

Exocentric compounds, in contrast, denote something which is not a sub-class of either of the elements in the compound, that is they are not hyponyms of either of their elements. An *egg-head*, for example, is neither an *egg* nor a *head*. In French, an *ouvre-boîte* is neither an *ouvre* nor a *boîte*. Names of people, animals and plants are often exocentric compounds, where the compound states some feature of the entity it names:

(39)   *Danish*
graa·ben
grey·leg
'stem canker'
lang·øre
long·ear
'long-eared bat'

English
high·brow
red·skin
yellow·tail
Turkana
ŋɪ·karì·mɔjɔŋ
plural·thin·old
'the Karimojong tribe'
lɔ·surù·lac
at·mosquito·louse
'type of tree used as medicine against vermin'

Exocentric compounds are sometimes called **bahuvrihi** compounds, 'bahuvrihi' being a Sanskrit exocentric compound meaning 'having much rice'.

Many languages also have compounds which denote an entity made up of the two elements mentioned in the compound together. These compounds are given the Sanskrit name of **dvandva** compounds, or are sometimes termed **copulative** compounds. Some examples are given below:

(40)   *French*
bleu-blanc-rouge
blue·white·red
'the French flag'
Tamil
appaa·v·amma
father·empty-morph·mother
'parents'
aŋŋan·tampi
elder-brother·younger-brother
'brothers' (e.g. 'do you have any brothers?')
Vietnamese
bàn·ghế
table·chair
'furniture'
sốt·rét
be-hot·be-cold
'malaria'

Compounds such as those that have been illustrated in this section are sometimes termed **root compounds** (or **primary compounds**). These are contrasted with **synthetic compounds** (or **verbal (nexus) compounds)** where the head element contains a verb as its base, and the modifying element contains an element which, in a sentence,

36

could function as an argument of that verb. For example, an English synthetic compound is *dish-washer*. The verb is *wash*, and the noun DISH could act as the direct object of that verb in a sentence like *We are washing the dishes*. When the compound created in this way is itself a verb, it is normal to speak in terms of **incorporation**. In the most typical cases of incorporation, the noun in the modifying element of the compound has the same semantic function as the direct object of the verb involved. The typical case is illustrated below from Maori:

(41)　Kei　　te　hoko a　　Tamahae i　　ngaa　　rare
　　　　at(pres) the buy　pers　Tamahae prep the(pl)　lolly
　　　　'Tamahae is buying the lollies'
　　　　Kei　　te　hoko rare　a　　　Tamahae
　　　　at(pres) the buy　lolly　pers　Tamahae
　　　　'Tamahae is lolly-buying'

In this example, a new verb *hoko rare* 'lolly-buy' has been created from the verb *hoko* and the noun *rare*. A similar pattern can be seen in the following example from Dasenech, a language spoken in Kenya and Ethiopia:

　　　　ʔaar a　　　　laalla
　　　　song verbfocus sing-imperfective-1st-singular
　　　　'I sing a song'
　　　　A　　　　ʔaar·laalla
　　　　verbfocus song·sing-imperfective-1st-singular
　　　　'I sing (a song)'

It is typical of incorporation (and indeed of compounding) that it is used most frequently to denote an activity that is seen in some way as general or characteristic, and only rarely for a single event. However, there is some variation among languages on this point, and in Maori, for instance, incorporation seems to be used to allow an indefinite direct object for the verb and without any of these other implications.

While, as was stated earlier, the most frequent type of incorporation involves the direct object of the verb, other patterns are also found. Firstly, sometimes a subject noun is incorporated, particularly with an intransitive verb. The first example is from Paiute:

(42)　pa:ɣinːa·xːqarɯ·puɣa
　　　　fog·begin-to-sit·remote-past
　　　　'It got foggy' (*lit.* fog began to sit)

37

The next example is from Takelma, a language of Oregon:

(43) moth·wo:kh
      son-in-law·arrived
      'he visited his wife's parents'

Nouns which are in other relationships to the verbs are also found. In (44) there are two examples from the Mexican language Nahuatl, in the first of which an instrument noun is incorporated, and the second of which an object of comparison is incorporated. In (45) there is an example from Paiute with an instrument incorporated; and in (46) there is an example from Dasenech with a locative incorporated.

(44) ni·k·tle·watsa in nakatl
      I·it·fire·roast the meat
      'I roast the meat'
      ʃo:tʃi·kwepo:ni in no·kwik
      flower·blossom it my·song
      'my song blossoms like a flower'

(45) wii·t:on:o·p:uɣa
      knife·stab·remote past
      'he stabbed with a knife'

(46) ʔanj tikkid' e·g'or·hiði
      goat one
      verbfocus-perfective-3rd-sing·tree·tie-perfective-3rd-sing
      'one goat he tied to the tree'

Compounds formed by reduplication were discussed in section 3.2 above.

In English and some other European languages there are also some words which are compounds in one sense, although of a rather unusual variety. The two lexemes involved in their make up are not English lexemes (or lexemes of the other European languages involved), but lexemes of the Classical languages, Greek and Latin. These are words such as

(47) biometry
      biology
      geology
      geometry

Their status and the rules governing their formation are not clear at the moment, and they are something of a linguistic oddity. For obvious reasons, these words are called **neo-classical compounds.**

3.7 Alphabet-based formations

Some ways of creating new lexemes (but not ways of creating new word-forms of lexemes) depend upon the existence of a writing system. They are thus not universal, since not all languages are written. Neither do they clearly belong under the heading of morphology, although they are included here for the sake of completeness. In particular, two types are relevant here, **blends** and **acronyms.**

Blends are also called **portmanteau words,** because, as Humpty Dumpty explained to Alice, they are 'like a portmanteau – there are two meanings packed up into one word'. In some cases two words are simply merged where they overlap, so that no information is lost, but repetition of letter combinations is avoided:

(48)   glass + asphalt → glasphalt
war + orgasm → wargasm
slang + language → slanguage
guess + estimate → guestimate
swell + elegant → swelegant

In many of these cases the overlap is phonetic as well as orthographic, but not in all, as can be seen from *glasphalt* in British Received Pronunciation. In most cases, however, there is no overlap, and the new word is created from parts of two other words, with no apparent principles guiding the way in which the two original words are mutilated. Some examples of this type are given below:

(49)   flimsy + miserable → mimsy
parachute + balloon → paraloon
hawk + dove → dawk

Here it is not possible to predict that the words would not be *fliserable* or *balachute* instead of what actually occurs. It is also extremely doubtful whether such words can be analysed into morphs, and thus whether they form a real part of morphology.

Acronyms are words coined from the initial letters of the words in a name, title or phrase. They are more than just abbreviations, because they are actually pronounced as new words. In many cases the acronym may actually precede the title which it purports to abbreviate, or at least, the title may be manipulated in order to give an acronym which is considered suitable for the group concerned. This is particularly the case with pressure groups which are in the public eye. Some examples are:

(50)   *AIDS* < Acquired Immunity Deficiency Syndrome
BASIC < Beginners' All-purpose Symbolic Instruction
Code

3. The Morphological Structure of Words

SALT < Strategic Arms Limitation Talks
WASP < White Anglo-Saxon Protestant

Acronyms tend to merge into blends when more than one letter is taken from each of the words of the title, as in the German *Ge(heime) Sta(ats) Po(lizei)*, 'secret state police' or Gestapo. Other even more complex forms of similar types are found. Consider the following examples from Indonesian, which illustrate both final and medial letters or letter combinations being used to form new lexemes:

(51)
danyon	← komandan bataliyon	'battalion commandant'
Ekubang	← Ekonomi, Keuangan,	'Economics, Finance
	dan Pembangunan	and Development'
hansip	← pertahanan sipil	'civil defence'
Irjen	← Inspektur Jendral	'Inspector General'
zipur	← zeni tempur	'combat troop'

It will be clear the blends share with compounds the fact that they involve two lexemes in the base. Clippings (see above section 3.5) may also, at least in some cases, be orthographically based.

3.8 Unique morphs

Unique morphs are morphs that only occur in one fixed expression in the language under discussion. Occasionally unique morphs can look like potentially free morphs, as English *kith* in *kith and kin* or (at least in the days before scouring powders) *vim* in *vim and vigour*. Even here, though, the morphs are bound to this particular collocation. More frequently there are unique morphs which look like obligatorily bound morphs. Examples are *-ter* in *laughter*, *-ert* in *inert*, *luke* in *lukewarm* and *cran* in *cranberry*. Because of this last example, such items are sometimes called **cranberry morphs.**

The status of unique morphs is determined by parallelism with other morphs which are not unique. The *-ter* in *laughter* is seen to be a suffix because of parallels with things like *arriv·al*, *marri·age*, *inject·ion* which also have a verb in first position, where the meanings are relatable, and where there are clearly repeated suffixes in parallel constructions. *Cran* is considered to be some kind of root because of parallels with *blackberry, blueberry, cloudberry, snow-berry, waxberry* and the like. We must demand parallels of a general type before we analyse a unique morph in order to avoid analysing a unique morph *h-* in *hear*.

The meaning associated with a unique morph is determined by subtracting the meanings associated with the known morphs in the construction from the meaning of the construction as a whole.

So the meaning associated with *cran* is precisely what makes cranberries a subset of all berries.

3.9 Suppletion

Although morphologists are continually seeking regularities in the patterns of language, there comes a time when they have to admit defeat, when word-forms of what appear to be the same lexeme are so different from each other that they cannot be derived by general rules at all. In such cases, we talk of **suppletion.** Consider, for example, regular verbs in French. The patterns in the present, future and imperfect can be illustrated with the regular verb DON-NER 'to give':

(52)   je donn·e   je donn·er·ai   je donn·ais

In this verb, the root *donn-* can be seen in all three forms. However, when we look at the verb ALLER 'to go', the pattern is completely different:

(53)   je vais   j'ir·ai   j'all·ais

Although some of the endings can still be recognised, the roots are so completely different that we talk of them as being **suppletive forms.** Historically this is explained by the fact that they are actually derived from different verbs. Suppletion is shown in English in the lexeme GOOD with the two forms *good* and *better*, and in the lexeme GO with the two forms *go* and *went*. In the examples cited, it is not controversial to claim that suppletion is involved. We shall see later, though, that the boundaries of suppletion are not clear, and that different people draw them in different places.

3.10 Conclusion

It can be seen that there are a large number of ways of building words in the languages of the world. Compounding is an extremely common method of forming new lexemes, otherwise affixation, and in particular, suffixation is clearly the most common way of building words. Other processes can, to a certain extent, be seen as deviations from this expected norm. In most languages which have morphological structure they are minority formations. They are the processes which cause problems of description. Some explanation of why this should be will be given in Chapter 12.

REFERENCES AND FURTHER READING

The quotation on p. 19 is from an anonymous review of Bauer (1983) published in the periodical *Choice*, for November, 1983.

3. The Morphological Structure of Words

Example (5) is taken from Matthews (1972: 132), and (6) is from the same work, p. 94. Many similar examples can be found in that book.

The terms interfix, circumfix and transfix, while not widespread in morphological discussions, can be found in, for example, Bergenholtz & Mugdan (1979). The term empty morph is from Hockett (1947). The use of the term formative here is my own, and others use the term in different ways, in particular within Chomskyan grammar. I would use 'formative' for what Aronoff (1976) rather unfortunately terms a 'morpheme' (unfortunately, because it is an idiosyncratic use of an already much abused term). The suggestion about simulfix is from Hockett (1954).

Although Lukas (1937) calls the forms in (27) 'tenses', 'moods' might be a better label.

For a discussion of how to determine which part of speech is basic in cases of conversion such as those in (32), see Marchand (1964).

Although it was stated on p. 33 that no known language is without compounds, there are some languages which have relatively few compounds, and in which compounding may not be productive. Dimmendaal (1983: 292) says that the Nilotic language Turkana is one such, but his suggestion that this is typical of verb-initial languages does not seem to hold up. The Polynesian languages show this.

Brandt (1984) points out that 'cranberry morph' is in fact a misnomer, since *cran* is etymologically speaking a regularly derived version of *crane* (the bird), and could thus simply be an allomorph of {crane}. There is plenty of comparative Germanic evidence to support this. He suggests a Danish replacement, *brombær* 'blackberry', where *bær* means 'berry' and *brom* has no independent existence. *Bilberry* might be a more coherent English example. Despite the etymological inaccuracy, the label 'cranberry morph' is widely recognised.

For more details on acronyms, backformation, clipping, blends, conversion and neo-classical compounding with specific reference to English, see the appropriate sections of Bauer (1983). For more detail on prefixation, suffixation, infixation, reduplication, replacive and subtractive morphs, see Chapter 7 of Matthews (1974).

Data from various languages has been gleaned from the following sources: Achenese from Lawler (1977), Afrikaans from Botha (1984a), Chrau from Thomas (1971), Dasenech from Sasse (1984), Dinka from Gleason (1955), Egyptian Arabic from Mitchell (1956, 1962), Finnish from Karlsson (1983), Frisian from Tiersma (1985), Icelandic from Einarsson (1949), Indonesian from Dardjowidjojo (1979), Kanuri from Lukas (1937), Mam from England (1983), Maori from W. Bauer (1981a, b, personal communication), Motu from Taylor (1970), Nahuatl from Sapir (1911), Paiute from Sapir (1911), Swahili from Ashton (1944), Tagalog from Blake (1925) and Gleason (1955), Takelma from Sapir (1911), Tamil from Asher (1982), Turkana from Dimmendaal (1983), Turkish from Lewis (1967), Welsh from Williams (1980), Vietnamese from Thompson (1965), Yoruba from Rowlands (1969).

Part Two: Elaboration

4. Defining the Word-Form

In Chapter 2 we defined word-forms in terms of orthographic words, and we noted that this was a matter which would have to receive further attention. As we saw in that chapter (p. 10), there are no gaps between the words in the spoken language as there are in the written language. Many of the languages of the world are still not written languages, and in the history of the world the majority of languages have not been written. We thus need to know how to define word-forms in languages where we do not have an orthography to help, or where the orthography is not helpful in this regard. We also need to know whether there is any reason for the division into orthographic words that happens to be used in English (or *mutatis mutandis*, any other written language), or whether that is merely convention. On the face of it, this seems fairly unlikely. Speakers of English have, on the whole, a fairly good intuition about what 'a word' is, although there are a few marginal cases where intuitions are unclear: cases such as *all right, nonetheless, insofar as*. This, it might be objected, could simply be the result of general literacy in the society. In response, it could be pointed out that even pre-literate children in our society have a reasonable notion of where the words begin and end, as is shown by questions of the type 'What does X mean?', where X represents some string that adults would happily term a word. There is also a certain amount of evidence (though perhaps not enough to make a categorical statement on the subject) that non-literate speakers of unwritten languages know where words begin and end in their languages. It thus seems that we are dealing with some fairly clear intuitions in this area. Of course, we need not necessarily expect that word-forms of the written language will overlap exactly with word-forms of the spoken language, but we should be surprised if there was no overlap at all.

There are two major sets of criteria which can help us to define a word-form for the spoken language. The first set is phonological, and defines what we might term a **phonological word**. However, the phonological criteria, such as they are, do not operate in all languages, and in some languages define strings which do not correspond to orthographic words or words defined by other criteria.

45

4. Defining the Word-Form

The best way of defining word-forms turns out to be by morphological and syntactic criteria, and a discussion of them will take up the main part of this chapter.

4.1 Phonological criteria

The phonological criteria that can be used to define the phonological word are a disparate group. They may not all function in the same language, and indeed may not define the same unit as a word in a single language. Nevertheless, there are a number of phenomena relating to the phonological word which recur across languages. These are dealt with here under three rather broad headings: stress, vowel harmony and phonological processes.

4.1.1 Stress. In many languages there is a tendency for each word-form to carry a single stress. This is to be understood in the following way. If a sentence is said in English as a statement, with falling intonation, there will usually be one neutral place where that fall will come: on the last potentially prominent word in the sentence. It will, however, be possible to move that intonational fall to virtually any other word in the sentence, usually then implying some kind of contrast. But whatever word the fall comes on in the sentence, there will only be one syllable in each word on which it can come. So in the sentence below, the intonational fall could, under appropriate circumstances, fall on any word, but only on the syllable preceded by a stress mark in those words

(1)   Antidisestablishment'arianism 'was sup'posedly 'the 'longest 'English 'lexeme.

In this sense there is only one stress for each lexeme in English. The same is not true in French, for example, where this criterion defines a phonological phrase.

Notice, however, that the description of English given above is not quite accurate. Other positions are possible for stress within the word-form when there is explicit contrast with another, partially similar word-form. Thus we can find utterances like

(2)   I didn't say aw'ful, I said or'chid.
       I said 'replay but I meant 'display.

where the stress apparently falls on 'the wrong syllable'. In cases like this, it is never possible to have two contrastive stresses in the same word-form. So both of these types help to define the word-form.

In some languages, stress regularly falls on a specific syllable in the word. In Czech, Finnish and Icelandic, for example, it regularly falls on the first syllable of a word, in Polish and Swahili on the

46

penultimate syllable of the word. In such languages stress serves a demarcative function, separating off the words from each other, and showing the position of the beginning or the end of the word. It also defines the word-form. Notice, however, that in a language like Icelandic, prepositions are not stressed, and will therefore, by this criterion, be designated as belonging to the end of the previous phonological word. Nevertheless, stress remains a useful way to help define word-forms.

4.1.2 Vowel harmony. In a language which has vowel harmony all the vowels in the word-form share some phonetic feature such as backness, closeness or unroundedness. Languages which have vowel harmony include Finnish, Hungarian, Turkish and Twi. Typically, this means that affixes have (at least) two distinct allomorphs, phonetically conditioned by the vowels in the base. Consider the following examples from Finnish:

(3)	otta·a	's/he takes'	pitä·ä	's/he likes'
	otta·vat	'they take'	pitä·vät	'they like'
	otta·vat·ko	'do they take'	pitä·vät·kö	'do they like'

It can be seen from these examples that the morpheme {3rd person plural} and the morpheme {interrogative} take different forms, depending on which root they are added to. If the root contains front vowels, then the affixes also contain front vowels, if the root contains back vowels, the affixes also contain back vowels. (Vowels marked orthographically with an Umlaut are front vowels.) In languages like this, the word-form can be defined in terms of the domain of the vowel harmony.

There are, however, some problems with this. First of all, in Finnish and Turkish (and every language that has vowel harmony?), compounds are defined as sequences of separate word-forms by this criterion, because vowel harmony only determines vowel quality in affixes. Secondly, some languages with vowel harmony allow a few exceptions to the harmony. In Turkish, for instance, there are a few foreign loan words which do not observe vowel harmony (although most do), and there are a few invariable suffixes which retain their form independent of the vowels in the base. Despite these few irregularities, in those languages which have it vowel harmony provides a good way of helping to define the phonological word.

4.1.3 Phonological processes. There are innumerable phonological processes in the languages of the world whose application is determined by the boundaries of units larger than the segment. Some can apply only at the end of a syllable, some only at the beginning of a morpheme, and so on. The application of some of these

47

processes is influenced by a unit which, for other reasons, we can identify as a word-form. These processes thus provide an extra way of determining where the boundaries of the word-form fall. It is, of course, not possible to give a complete list of such processes, but a couple of examples should suffice to make the point.

In German, the nominative and accusative singular forms of the lexemes RAT 'council' and RAD 'wheel' are homophonous: both *Rat* and *Rad* are pronounced /raːt/. The dative singular forms of these lexemes, however, are pronounced differently from each other. *Rat·e* and *Rad·e* are distinguished in pronunciation in that the former has a /t/ where the latter has a /d/, as shown by the spelling. It is, in fact, a general rule, that you never find any voiced obstruent in final position in the word-form in German. This is usually formulated as a phonological rule of obstruent devoicing which applies word-finally. Note that the devoicing does not occur morpheme finally (*Rade*), but only word-finally (*Rad*). Places where this rule of obstruent devoicing apply thus help to determine the final position in the word-form, and so help to determine the boundaries of the phonological word.

In Sengseng, a language of Papua New Guinea, geminate consonants occur within the word-form, but never across word-form boundaries. When like consonants occur at the end and beginning of adjacent words, they are separated with a schwa. Thus in (4b) below there is an inserted schwa marking the boundaries of the word-forms, although there is no inserted schwa between the identical /t/s in (4a), since these occur within a word-form. Again this allows a phonological definition of a word-form.

(4) (a) ɛt·tihon
         she·reflexive
         'herself'
     (b) ɛt mihin ə nis
         she head-3rd-person-singular-possessive hot
         'she has a headache'

4.2 Morphological and syntactic criteria
The Bloomfieldian definition of the word-form is 'a minimum free form'. This means that a word-form can stand as an utterance on its own, but also that it is the smallest unit which can do this: it is not made up entirely of smaller units which can also stand alone as utterances.

In fact, there are cases where elements smaller than the word-form can stand alone as utterances, but these are all in contexts such as the following:

48

(5)   A: Did you say 'incur' or 'recur'?
        B: In.

Examples of this type show language **mention** and not language **use**. The same is true of lists of affixes, such as can be found in Linguistics books. In language use it is not possible for prefixes and the like to occur as isolated utterances.

Even thirty-five years after this definition was proposed, it is still one of the best definitions of the word-form that are available; but there are some problems with it. The first is that by this definition compounds will always appear to be phrases and not word-forms. This is possibly not terribly serious. We have already seen that vowel harmony also treats compound words as sequences of two word-forms rather than as single word-forms. More seriously, it seems that words which can stand alone as utterances are precisely those words which can form a larger constituent by themselves: plural countable nouns, pronouns, intransitive verbs, etc. *Chair, must, consume* are not minimum free forms in language use, while *chairs, red* and *eat* are. This seems to imply that the definition actually delimits a subset of word-forms, and this only by accident. In particular, there are a number of items that we would normally consider to be word-forms (and that we would treat orthographically as word-forms) which will be completely excluded by this definition. These are words such as articles, conjunctions and prepositions, especially in their unstressed forms. You cannot simply walk up to someone and say 'The'. Nor will the form *the* be a suitable part of a dialogue, except in mention contexts like (5) and extraordinarily rare instances of contrast. By Bloomfield's definition, therefore, they will not be considered word-forms. Bloomfield himself was not very happy with this result, and tried to avoid it by saying that such words were paradigmatically commutable with units which were minimum free forms. So the word-form *the* could be isolated by parallelism with *that*, which can stand in isolation. There are various problems with this kind of approach, perhaps the most striking of which is that affixes could be claimed to be word-forms using the same kind of arguments, and this would be undesirable. Consider the following examples, for instance:

(6)   ex·president   metal(l)·oid
        former president   metal-like

It is perhaps better to conclude that forms like *the* are not word-forms according to Bloomfield's definition. There are then two possibilities. The first is that orthographic words do not coincide with word-forms in the spoken language, the second is that
49

4. Defining the Word-Form

Bloomfield's definition needs to be improved upon. Attempts to improve upon this definition, though, have not provided a better formulation of the definition, but discussed a number of criteria which units must meet in order to be considered word-forms. There are three major criteria which are discussed in this context:

(a) Positional mobility
(b) Uninterruptability
(c) Internal stability.

In fact, these three aspects of the word-form are interrelated.

Positional mobility means that the word-form as a whole can be moved relatively easily within the sentence. In some languages this mobility is greater than in others. In English, the mobility is mainly seen in sentences like the following:

(7)   This we must see.
       Plums I love.
       Shorts you'll never get me into.

where one particular part of the sentence comes under focus. In such cases (and also in cases like passivisation where, on some analyses, noun phrases swap positions) it is always at least a word-form which is moved, it is always a whole number of word-forms that are moved, and the word-form is always moved so that it does not interrupt other word-forms. In a language like Latin, word-forms show much greater positional mobility than they do in English. For example, under appropriate conditions, any of the following would be an acceptable sentence of Latin:

(8)   Bru:tus Caesarem occi:dit.
       Caesarem occi:dit Bru:tus.
       Occi:dit Caesarem Bru:tus.
       'Brutus killed Caesar'.

Not only is it the case that major constituents may occur in any order, but the elements of those constituents need not always occur together, as is illustrated by the following example from Classical Greek (Herodotos, I, 30, 3):

(9)   nun o:n   himeros epeiresthai moi   epe:lthe se
       now therefore a-desire to-ask   to-me has-come you
       ei tina   e:de: panto:n eides   olbio:taton
       if someone already of-all   you-have-seen most-fortunate
       'Now therefore a desire has come over me to ask you whether you have already seen someone who is most fortunate of all.'

Uninterruptability means that extraneous material cannot be introduced into the middle of the word-form. Consider the examples

50

below from Danish, which illustrate this point. In Danish there are two forms of the definite article, one preposed and one postposed. The postposed definite article forms a single word with the noun it is attached to, while the preposed one does not. (10a) is a piece of genuine literary Danish, and (10b - e) provide variant orderings of morphs to illustrate the point.

(10) (a) Lærer·en kunde se ud, som om han spiste smaa Børn ristede
         teacher·the could look as if he ate small children grilled
         'The teacher might look as though he ate small children grilled'.
      (b) de smaa Børn ristede
         the small children grilled
      (c) Børn·ene ristede
         children·the grilled
      (d) de smaa ristede Børn
         the small grilled children
      (e) *Børn ristede -ene
         children grilled the

This criterion is actually very difficult to formulate precisely. It is clear that there is a sense in which word-forms can be interrupted:

(11)   *Czech*:   zpívám   zpívávám
                   I sing   I am accustomed to sing
       English: sensationism   sensationalism
                   kings   kingdoms
       French: arrivions   arriverions
                   we were arriving we would arrive
       Latin: amat   ama:bat
                   s/he loves   s/he used to love

The point, according to Lyons, is that one can insert material between word-forms 'more or less freely', and that one cannot insert material into the middle of word-forms with the same degree of freedom. Matthews says that 'the point is that [the word-form] cannot be interrupted by rearranged material from elsewhere in a given sentence'. Even these general constraints appear to be broken by the exceptional case of the expletive insertion rule in English that gives rise to forms like *absobloodylutely* and so on.

Internal stability means that the ordering of items within the word-form is usually fixed and non-contrastive, as opposed to the ordering of word-forms within the sentence. Given a Latin word such as

(12)   reg·eːb·ant·ur   'they were being ruled'

it is not possible to rearrange the order of the morphs. *Reg·b·ur·eː·ant* is simply not possible in Latin. The word-forms in a sentence, however, are much more moveable (the criterion of positional mobility discussed above), so that all of the sentences in (8) are perfectly grammatical.

There are languages where the ordering of elements within the word-form does appear to be contrastive and meaningful. Some examples are given below.

(13)   *Japanese*:   nag·ur·ase·rare
                     hit·present·causative·passive
                     'is made to hit'
                     nag·ur·are·sase
                     hit·present·passive·causative
                     'causes to be hit'
       English: bibl·ic·ist   arm·chair
                     bibl·ist·ic   chair·arm
       Turkish: misafir·se·ler
                     guest·be-conditional·plural
                     'if they are guests'
                     misafir·ler·se
                     guest·plural·be-conditional
                     'if they are the guests'

It appears, however, that even here examples like this are rare. Languages such as Eskimo which appear to provide regular counter-examples, turn out not to provide genuine ones. In Labrador Inuttut, the following two examples, differing only in the order in which the morphemes are realised, have clearly different meanings (the allomorphy for the 3rd person singular is irrelevant here). What is more, the example is fairly typical.

(14)   pi·guma·jau·juk
       empty-base·want·passive·3rd-person-singular
       'He is wanted'
       pi·jau·guma·vuk
       empty-base·passive·want·3rd-person-singular
       'He wants it done to him'

However, in this case there are simply a number of positions in which the passive morph can occur, and it may occur in more than

4. Defining the Word-Form

one, as is shown by

(15) taku·jau·tit·tau·gasugi·jau·juk
see·passive·cause·passive·believe·passive·3rd-person-singular
'He was believed to have been made to be seen'

These three criteria of positional mobility, uninterruptability and internal stability could be classed together as defining the **internal cohesion** of the word-form. But to go no further than to consider these three criteria is to miss a very important point: namely that they, as well as several others, are criteria which are generally used to determine constituency in syntax. What we seem to be saying, therefore, is that word-forms are special kinds of constituents. In the classical languages, it appears that this special kind of constituent can be defined reasonably well in terms of the three criteria already discussed. In other languages, including probably English, they are not, it seems, sufficient. Under these circumstances it is worth considering other tests for constituency, and seeing whether they are also helpful in defining the word-form.

Most such tests, while they agree in isolating the word-form as some kind of constituent, do not isolate it uniquely: either they show that the word-form and units larger than the word-form are constituents, or they show that the word-form and units smaller than the word-form are constituents, or, most frequently, both. One test, however, does seem to be useful, namely that under appropriate discourse conditions a constituent may be omitted. For example, word-forms can be deleted in conversations like the following:

(16) A: Chris can't come.
B: But Jean can [*sc.* come].
A: Did you see the red file?
B: No, only the blue [*sc.* file].
A: Did you see her in January?
B: No, [*sc.* in] February.

It appears that affixes cannot be omitted under similar discourse conditions. The following are thus impossible conversations:

(17) A: I think it's disgraceful.
B: *And [*sc.* dis]gusting.
A: I think it's disgraceful.
B: *But hope[*sc.* ful].

There are two points to note about this criterion for English. The first is that it does allow us to isolate words like *the* as word-forms.

53

4. Defining the Word-Form

As far as I can make out, most people seem to find the following a perfectly possible conversation:

(18) A: We saw the engine.
      B: And [*sc.* the] guard's van.

Secondly, this test does marginally allow a base to be deleted when that base is a potentially free morph. The following conversation is perhaps a little odd, but perfectly comprehensible:

(19) A: Have you learnt to encode?
      B: And de-[*sc.* code].

This last criterion thus seems to allow us to define the word-form in English as the smallest unit which can be omitted when it would be identical with another element which occurred earlier in the discourse. This does not prove, of course, that this criterion will work for all languages. In fact, as far as I can see it will not work for French, in the sense that it will not isolate articles in that language. (We might conclude that articles are less word-like in French than in English.) Nevertheless, it does seem to indicate that word-forms are particular types of constituent, and this may explain why they are isolatable by pre-literate speakers.

An interesting question, but one that we shall not attempt to answer here, would be whether the way of defining a word-form for a given language correlates in any significant way with other syntactic facts about that language. It seems likely that a language in which positional mobility is a defining factor will be a language with a fairly free word order, and this is likely to be a language which is fairly highly inflected. In this context it would be very interesting to know just how the word-form can be defined in a language like Eskimo (see, for example, the word-form from Labrador Inuttut in (15) above) and to what extent the criteria that have been discussed in this chapter are useful there.

REFERENCES AND FURTHER READING
The source of the comment on speakers of unwritten languages on page 45 is Sapir (1921: 34).

Stress and intonation are very complex areas, and no attempt has been made here to be systematic in introducing the topics. Indeed, even the use of the term 'stress' is controversial. For an introduction to these areas, Brown (1977) is recommended.

Details of Finnish vowel harmony (which is presented here in a slightly simplified form) can be found in Karlsson (1983: 21). For details of Turkish vowel harmony, see Lewis (1967: 15-20). Suomi (1985) gives a clear discussion of the problems of isolating word-forms in Finnish despite demarcative stress and vowel harmony in that language.

4. Defining the Word-Form

The data on Sengseng is from Ann Chowning (personal communication).

The definition of a word-form as a minimal free form can be found in Bloomfield (1935: 178) (it is called there simply a 'word'). This definition is also discussed in Lyons (1968: 201-2), and the three criteria on page 50 are also discussed by Lyons. Lyons also makes the use/mention distinction, and discusses it again (rather briefly, but with references) in Lyons (1977: 6).

Some of the examples in (11) and the quotation on page 51 are taken from Matthews (1972: 98, fn). The quotation from Lyons on the same page is from Lyons (1968: 204).

On the rule of expletive insertion in English, see Bauer (1983: 89-91) and McMillan (1980).

The examples from Labrador Inuttut are from Smith (1982a).

For a discussion of constituency in syntax, see, for example, Chapter 2 of Radford (1981).

5. Productivity

In recent years, productivity has come to be seen as one of the key issues in the study of derivational morphology. It is also traditionally viewed as being one of the factors which separates inflection from derivation, as we shall see in Chapter 6. Yet despite its importance, it is still poorly understood, and the issues have not all been worked out. In this chapter I shall present a rather idiosyncratic view of productivity, though one which I believe is becoming more generally accepted in the linguistic community as a whole.

There are two important things to notice about productivity. The first is that productivity is not all or nothing, but a matter of more or less, and the second is that it is a synchronic notion. These two points are actually entwined, and frequently confused in discussions of productivity, but an attempt will be made here to keep them apart.

5.1 Productivity as a cline

Any process is said to be productive to the extent that it can be used in the production of new forms in the language. Let us illustrate this with some phonological processes, and then go on to some morphological examples.

In Middle English, there was a general tendency to shorten stressed vowels which were in the antepenultimate syllable of words. This applied particularly to words of foreign origin, but was to a lesser extent true of native vocabulary too. As a result of this process we today have a short vowel in each of the words listed in (1a) below, despite the long vowel in the related word in (1b).

(1)	(a) cavity	(b) cave
	cranberry	crane
	gratitude	grateful
	heroine	hero
	holiday	holy
	legacy	legal
	Michaelmas	Michael
	natural	nature
	situate	site
	solitude	sole
	specify	species
	tyranny	tyrant

5. *Productivity*

This rule was probably never fully productive. That is, it was probably never the case that this rule applied to all words of three or more syllables which were stressed on the antepenultimate syllable. Words such as *favourite* are probably genuine exceptions. Modern inventions and loan words, however, do not necessarily fit with this rule. Examples are

(2) 'autocite
kurcha'tovium
pene'tralium
'Tethian
'virion
Za'irean
Zhda'novian

In other cases, though, the rule is still adhered to by some or all speakers. In words like '*Piscean* and *para'cetamol* there is variation between a long and a short vowel in the stressed syllable, despite long vowels being the norm in the related *Pisces* and *acetic*, and in '*negritude* the short vowel is in general use. This shortening rule has thus gone, in the course of the last 500 years or so, from being extremely (though not necessarily entirely) productive, to being of limited productivity.

At the other end of the scale, we have a rule which is currently very productive. It is the rule determining the distribution of /n/ and /ŋ/ before a velar stop, i.e. before /k/ or /g/. The rule governing this process varies slightly from one variety of English to another, and is dependent to a certain extent on formality and so on, as well as on geographical variety. However, we can say that /ŋ/ is always found before a syllable-final /k/ or /g/, but may not be found before a word-boundary, a morpheme boundary, or a syllable-boundary. That is, in the following list, in any given style or variety, there is more likely to be /n/ at the top of the list, and bound to be /ŋ/ at the bottom of the list:

(3) John Gielgud
can go
in case
incredible
incoherent
syncopated
finger
blink

This rule is still productive, so that new words which fit the input conditions, that is which can be subject to the rule, are automatically

5. Productivity

included in the rule in the same way that existing words are included in that style or variety. This can be seen in words like the following:

(4)   Piscean guy
        in-crowd
        incapacitant
        oncogene
        rinky-dink
        funky

Here, therefore, we have a process which is extremely productive in current English.

Note, of course, that both these processes are productive in modern English: the shortening rule is used to produce some new forms, the rule determining the distribution of /ŋ/ is used in determining comparatively many forms. We can say that the second of these two rules is more productive than the first in current English, but we cannot give any real measurement of productivity. We cannot attach any numbers to the degree of productivity. Neither does just saying that something is 'productive' tell us a great deal, because we need to know how productive the process is before we can tell what that implies. This is extremely unsatisfactory, but the best we can do at the moment. Productivity has to remain a comparative notion. Theoretically we might be able to talk about complete or full or total productivity if we could guarantee that the process would apply without exception every time its input conditions were met. Unfortunately, we cannot even do that. Firstly, it is rare that we can state anything with that degree of certainty in Linguistics. Secondly, and less trivially, in morphology it is often extremely difficult to state the input conditions with the requisite degree of accuracy. We shall return to this point.

Turning now to morphology, consider the case of the suffix -*th* which creates abstract nouns. Here it is possible to give an exhaustive list of the lexemes of English which clearly contain this suffix, and also an exhaustive list of those lexemes which may, but there is doubt in the minds of many speakers. Lists are provided below as (5) and (6).

(5)	breadth	(6)	(after)math
	coolth		berth
	dearth		birth
	depth		breath
	girth		broth
	greenth		death
	growth		drouth

59

health	faith
highth	filth
length	girth
ruth	mirth
spilth	month
stealth	mowth
strength	sloth
tilth	troth
truth	worth
warmth	wrath
wealth	wreath
width	youth

Some of the words in both these lists may be unfamiliar, and not all of the words in (6) are etymologically derived with the -*th* suffix. This is, however, irrelevant for the present purpose, which is to show that the distribution of this suffix can be stated in terms of lexemes. It is not possible, except as a joke, to coin a word such as *newth* on the basis of *truth*, and speak of the newth of the growth in spring. *Greenth* is, in any case, extremely rare and old-fashioned, but on that basis you would not speak of the *blackth* of coal or of the night. This suffix is now non-productive.

At the other end of the scale, it seems that the suffix -*able* is extremely productive added to transitive verbs. It would not be possible in principle to make an exhaustive list of all cases of -*able* suffixed to a base which is a transitive verb, because every time a new transitive verb is formed, -*able* can also be added to it. You may not know what it means to *Koreanise* the US economy (because I have just this moment invented the word), but given that it exists, you know that it is possible to discuss the degree to which the US economy is *Koreanisable*. This is an extremely productive suffix.

As with the phonological cases, we cannot measure how productive a particular morphological process is, and this remains an unsatisfactory state of affairs. But we can say that one process is more productive than another or, in one limiting case, is not productive. Again, it would theoretically be possible to say that a process was fully productive, but that involves us in specifying the productive rule with great precision, and that we probably cannot do properly. In fact, it is not clear whether we could say that any morphological process is fully productive in this sense. We shall see later in this chapter why it is so difficult to tell. Even inflectional affixes, which are frequently assumed to be fully productive, usually show some exceptions (see below, section 6.4).

5. Productivity

5.2 Productivity as synchronic

It was stated above that the suffixation of -*th* to form abstract nouns in English is no longer productive. Yet clearly it was productive at some stage in the history of English, otherwise the relevant words in (5) and (6) could not have been formed. The process used to be productive, but no longer is. We cannot sensibly talk about the productivity of a morphological process without implicitly talking about the time at which this process is productive. When we say nothing about the time, the implication is that we are speaking of productivity in 1980's English. If we were discussing sixteenth-century English we would have to conclude that -*th* suffixation was productive, although there might be severe constraints on the bases with which it was productive, so that there were never very many words formed in -*th*. That is, we can speak of productivity in synchronic terms, or of changes in productivity in diachronic terms, but not of productivity as such in diachronic terms.

But this creates problems. The -*th* suffix in the words in (5), at least, can be clearly recognised, even in the 1980's. The linguist can analyse the words which contain this suffix, and thereby isolate the suffix. This suggests that we have to draw a clear distinction between morphs which are productive and those which are **analysable**. All productive morphs are also analysable, but not all analysable ones are necessarily productive. Furthermore, we need to be able to distinguish between the degree to which something is productive, and the degree to which it is analysable. Let us speak of the extent to which remains of a morphological process are analysable in the established words of a language as the extent to which that process is **generalised**. We can now say that the degree of generalisation of an affix in the vocabulary of a language is a reflection of the past productivity of that affix. The -*th* affix is not widely generalised: there are relatively few words in (5). But other affixes are widely generalised, even if they are not productive. One possible example is the suffix -*ment* that is found in words like *chastisement, government, shipment, treatment*. There are hundreds of established words of English that are formed with this suffix, as can be seen from a reverse dictionary of English, and yet there is some evidence that this suffix is no longer productive in English. If this is true, we can say that -*ment* is highly generalised, but no longer productive. The fact that it is so highly generalised shows that at some stage it was also highly productive. Generalised affixes are the result of productivity at some time, and the more widely generalised the affix, the more highly productive the affixation process has been.

With an affix that is still productive, it is usual, but not necessary, for the affix to be generalised as well. This is the case with -*er*

61

forming subject nominalisations such as *baker, camper, killer, proposer, singer, walker* and so on. These words, and hundreds of others established in English usage indicate the past productivity of the suffix. It is a highly generalised suffix. But more than that, it is still highly productive, so that nearly any verb can form a subject nominalisation in *-er*. Some more recent examples are *lander, inducer, converger, scrambler* and so on; and if you invent a new word like *Koreanise*, a person or instrument which does it becomes fairly automatically a *Koreaniser*.

Note that, in theory at least, it is possible to give some measurement of generalisation. This could be done, for example, by counting the number of occurrences of the process in some reasonably representative word-list or (more accurate, no doubt, but correspondingly more difficult), by counting the number of examples of the process in some large word-list as a percentage of the potential bases available for the process.

Notions such as counting word-lists, however, raise other questions about generalisation and productivity which we also have to consider.

5.3 Potential words and productivity in the individual
Until fairly recently, it has been usual for morphologists to discuss derivational morphology in terms of words which 'exist' and words which do not 'exist'. 'Existence' has usually been assumed to be defined by a listing in, for example, *The Oxford English Dictionary*. Such a procedure is dangerous for a number of reasons.

Firstly, words which are included in the *OED* are, in some senses, included pretty much at random. This is not true of a host of common words which the readers for the dictionary could not avoid finding, but with rarer words a listing in the dictionary depends to a certain extent on a suitable occurrence of the word having been found in the works the readers were considering, and not only found but recognised as a word worth noting. Without wishing to cast any slur upon the ability of the people who have read so assiduously for the *OED* over the years, I am sure that they would be the first to admit that they cannot cover everything, cannot note every attested word, cannot find suitable examples of every attested word. That this is in fact true, and that there are many words which have not made it into the *OED* (or by extension any other dictionary), is easily illustrated. You can probably find words yourself in any journalistic text which are not in the *OED*. For instance, none of the words in (7) is in the *OED*, and yet they have all been attested in writing, and repeated.

(7)   apartness
belongingness
cunningness
erraticness
givenness
maleness
scaredness
showeryness
wellroundedness

The second reason for treating the lists from any particular dictionary with care, is that some of the words which are included in dictionaries are included more or less by mistake. You might like to consider some of the words in (5), for example. *Greenth* is listed in the *OED*, yet it has never been a particularly frequently used word, and it appears to be listed mainly because it occurs in the works of George Eliot. It is therefore the case that some of the words entered in a dictionary like the *OED* are in extremely limited use (and have possibly never been widely used) while other words which are not listed are not listed for equally random reasons. To take a list such as that given in the *OED* as the gospel on what the words of English are is to do an injustice both to your data and to the editors and readers who are not, and would not claim to be, infallible.

Thirdly, and most importantly it seems to me, deciding on the basis of some list whether or not a word 'exists' is to cut derivational morphology off from both syntax and inflectional morphology, and to claim an entirely separate condition of relevance for this part of the grammar. If this is to be done, then it should be as a major conclusion of research carried out, not as a premise. But most morphologists today seem to feel that such a separation is in fact not justified. We shall return to this problem in Chapter 6.

The point can be made in relation to syntax in the following way. Syntacticians discuss sentences which are possible, but not necessarily occurrent. Only in rare cases do they limit themselves to actually attested sentences. Most syntacticians would find the following example to be a perfectly well-formed sentence, even though it has, I take it, never occurred in language use, and is unlikely to.

(8)   The Minister of Education announced that a sum of forty million dollars per year was being set aside to boost research in Linguistics, particularly Morphology, over the next ten-year period.

5. Productivity

If a sentence like (8) is a perfectly acceptable object of study in syntax, why should not possible but non-occurrent words be perfectly acceptable objects of study in morphology? We know that just as it is possible to create new sentences, it is possible to create new words. We thus know that not all the potential words of any language can be attested, just as we know that not all the potential sentences of any language can be attested. It is true that we appear to remember more words than sentences as complete units, but as words and sentences have different functions, this should be expected. In general, it seems to me, morphology and syntax are much closer to one another than would be realised by reading the range of literature that exists on each.

This is even more evident when it comes to the distinction between inflection and derivation. With only a few exceptions it is often assumed that all potential inflectional forms will be realised in a language, but that not all potential derivational forms will be realised. In languages with complex inflectional systems this may or may not be true. Who is to say whether the first person plural negative future inferential conditional reciprocal causative passive ('if as they say we were not about to cause to be VERBed to one another') of any hundred verbs of Turkish chosen at random is actually attested? The difference between inflection and derivation is not necessarily as great as one might conclude from a superficial reading of the literature, either.

One possible objection to the points I have raised here is that they confuse words which 'exist' in the society, and words which may or may not be found in the idiolects of particular individuals. Only the former type, it might be claimed, is of relevance to Linguistics. This is a serious point, and requires some consideration.

Let us assume that some speaker of English, familiar with the novels of George Eliot, produces the following utterance:

(9)   If I had been impressed with the greenth of the beech trees in the spring, I was even more impressed with their brownth that particular autumn.

The linguist/analyst might easily dismiss the coining of *brownth* as a case of analogical formation, of no general interest. Assume, however, that the same speaker, taken with this type of word, goes on to use words like *blackth, greyth, pinkth, indigoth* and even *cyanth*. Are all of these also to be dismissed as analogical formations rather than the result of a productive rule? The answer is not clear. I suspect that many would dismiss them in this way, although the use of *-th* then looks more like productivity than analogy (always assuming that the two can be distinguished). But these words would probably not (except in exceptional circumstances) pass into the general vocabulary of English. Even if we wanted to say that -*th* suffixation had become productive for this individual speaker, we would probably not wish to say that as a result of this it had become productive 'in English'. That is, we need to distinguish between productive for the individual, and productive within the speech community. Only if a particular morphological process is productive for a large enough number of members of the speech community will that process be said to be productive for the speech community. On the whole it is productivity within the speech community which is understood by the term 'productivity', and it is this type of productivity which gives rise to listings in dictionaries and the like. What we might call **individual productivity** will occasionally give rise to dictionary entries (as possibly with the example of *greenth*), will frequently give rise to *hapax legomena* (words with only a single attestation), and will even more frequently never come within the scrutiny of the professional linguist or grammarian.

The main problem with making a distinction between individual productivity and societal productivity is in drawing the line between the two. Clear cases at both ends can be recognised, but there is a middle ground where it may not be clear whether there is a case where individual productivity is the same for several individuals, or a marginal case of societal productivity. The dominating criteria distinguishing the two in our society are probably wide-spread use in the written and spoken media, and listing in dictionaries. In a pre-technological society it would probably be much harder to draw the distinction, and indeed in very small speech communities there may not be any distinction to be drawn.

Notice that even if we draw this distinction between what an individual does and what is generally accepted in the society as a whole, it does not affect the basic point that there are potential words as well as potential sentences which are not attested in the variety being described. The distinction between productivity *tout court* and individual productivity makes it possible to state definitively what words have been produced and accepted by the society (on the basis of the *OED* or some equivalent). Nevertheless, more words will have been produced and accepted by individuals, and there will be many words which might have been produced but were not, both in the society and by the individual. For instance, *princess·dom* must have been a possible formation at some stage in the history of English, if not still today, but it is not listed in the *OED*. For languages that do not have an equivalent lexicographical tradition, not even this pseudo-definitiveness is possible.

5.4 Blocking

One of the main reasons why very few morphological processes show total productivity is a phenomenon which is known as pre-emption or, more usually, by the rather unflattering title of **blocking**. Blocking refers to the non-existence of a derivative (in the societal sense discussed in section 5.3) because of the prior existence of some other lexeme. Some statements of this constraint formulate it so that only a previously existing derivative formed from the same root (possibly base) can block the production of a new derivative, but this is probably too restrictive. It should be noted that this formulation of what blocking is, refers only to derivational morphology. While there seems to be no *a priori* reason why blocking could not also be applied to inflectional morphology, in general use the term has been restricted to derivational morphology. In fact, in many instances blocking appears to be the derivational analogue of suppletion in inflectional systems. This is something of an over-simplification, and there are differences between inflectional and derivational morphology in this regard. Before any further discussion, however, we need an example of how blocking works.

The suffixation of -*er* to create subject nominalisations in English is, as we have already seen, extremely productive. Yet there are times when nominalisations in -*er* seem to be avoided. These are the occasions when there is already a word in existence which means just what the -*er* nominalisation would mean if it were used. So in (10) below, we tend not to use the word listed in (a), but rather to to use the corresponding word from (b). The existence of the (b) word blocks the productivity of the -*er* suffixation rule, and prevents the general use of the (a) word.

(10)   (a)   cycler   (b)   cyclist
           batter [in cricket]   batsman
           typer   typist
           studier   student
           raper   rapist
           stealer   thief
           deliverer   delivery boy (etc.)
           shop assister   shop assistant
           lift attender   lift attendant

There are a couple of important points to note about this blocking. First of all, blocking does not entirely prevent the coining of words like those in (10a) by individuals if, for example, they temporarily forget what the (b) word is, or that there is one. All that is blocked is the **institutionalisation** of these words, that is, their coming into general use in the society and so being listed in dictionaries.

Secondly, blocking of this type only applies so long as the word like the ones in (10a) is genuinely synonymous with the word like those in (10b). When Shakespeare talks of the 'ten stealers' meaning the fingers, 'stealer' is no longer synonymous with 'thief'. Similarly, it is quite normal for *batter* and *deliverer* to be available in other uses (for baseball and in a religious sense, respectively), because there they are no longer in competition with the word which would otherwise block them.

Thirdly, blocking appears not to apply in so-called **synthetic compounds**. It is quite possible to speak of a *sheep stealer* even though it would be abnormal to speak of a *stealer*.

Finally, blocking does not always work. There is a general case where the failure of blocking to apply can be explained in a principled way, and then a few individual cases which are far harder to explain. The general case is that blocking frequently fails to work with the most productive morphological processes. The affixation of *-ness* in English is a good example. The existence of *productivity* does not prevent us talking about *productiveness*, even though the two things mean exactly the same thing in morphology. It is true that *-ness* and *-ity* do not always produce synonymous words: most people would probably distinguish between *monstrousness* and *monstrosity*, for example, but there are cases where the two words from the same base are synonymous, and yet are not blocked. If the words were on different style levels, this might also account for lack of blocking. Clipping always provides synonymous words from the same base, but here the different style level (not the different meaning) allows both to co-exist.

As an example of an individual case, consider *normalcy*. *Normalcy* means the same as *normality* (and possibly the same as *normalness*), and yet has become, especially in American English, a perfectly usual word. It has not been blocked by *normality*. In this particular case, *The Oxford English Dictionary* lists first uses for both *normalcy* and *normality* at about the same time, but this cannot be a decisive factor, since the dominance of *normality* in the period since the coining would have been expected to oust *normalcy*. It would not be surprising for two synonymous words created with different affixes to come into being at about the same time, and for one of them eventually to win out over the other, but this is not the whole story in this instance. This is what happened with pairs such as *to doctor ~ doctorise, complemental ~ complementary, expectance ~ expectancy*. In other cases, though, blocking can be seen to have failed. *Coloner* is an earlier word than *colonist, computate* is an

67

earlier word than *compute, conspicuity* is an earlier word than *conspicuousness, heterogeneal* is an earlier word than *heterogeneous.* Current disputes about *disinterested* taking over an area earlier occupied by *uninterested,* and prescriptive debates about *orient* and *orientate, use* and *utilise, adaption* and *adaptation, deduce* and *deduct* show that such changes are still occurring.

Blocking can also be invoked by an embarrassing homonymy, as well as by synonymy. In French there is a productive suffix *-eur,* which is added to verbal bases to produce subject nominalisations like the English ones in *-er* discussed earlier. We find examples like the following:

(11) destruct·eur   'destroyer'
      emprunt·eur   'borrower'
      imitat·eur   'imitator'
      livr·eur   'delivery person/company'

and so on. However, corresponding to English *flier* there is no French word *voleur* from *voler* 'to fly', because *voleur* already exists with the meaning 'thief', and this would cause an embarrassing homonymy. In English you would not expect to find someone who sues called a *suer* (except as a joke) because of the embarrassing homonymy with *sewer.*

In fact, it rather looks as if blocking is not strictly relatable to derivational morphology. Rather there seems to be a restriction on new words from whatever source to the effect that they should not mean the same as existing words or cause an embarrassing homonymous clash. Blocking in this wider sense does not always work, either, as is shown by the existence of synonyms such as *kudos, prestige* and *mana,* or indeed by the existence of synonyms in general. However, many people argue that absolute synonyms rarely, if ever, exist. Blocking because of homonymy can be illustrated without reference to morphological processes in the introduction of *rooster* in many varieties of English to replace the earlier *cock,* or the discomfort many people feel in using the word *sod* to mean 'turf' because of its homonym.

5.5 Defining the productivity of a process
One of the major problems for the linguist who is trying to give a description of some morphological process is to state in a coherent way just what bases may be used in the process. Normally only a limited number of bases, defined by phonological, morphological, syntactic and semantic criteria, are available for any given process. Discovering just what bases are available, and specifying the ways

in which those bases may be defined, are in fact extremely difficult tasks for the linguist.

This leads to problems in discussions of 'full productivity', which have already been mentioned above. Consider two possible definitions of full productivity, one of which is much wider than the other:

(a) A process is said to be fully productive if it applies to every possible base, and those bases are defined solely in terms of their major category (noun, verb, adjective).

(b) A process is said to be fully productive if it applies to every relevant base, defined in terms of a number of specific restrictions of types that will be illustrated below.

Of these, (a) demands much more of full productivity than (b), and is correspondingly far less frequently found (not least because of blocking). Strangely enough, it is (a) that is usually understood as a definition of productivity in the literature, and this is partly why productivity has become the issue it is today.

In the literature, the fact that a particular process virtually never applies completely without exception has been discussed under two headings, both of which are probably misleading. The first is 'limitations on productivity', and the second is 'semi-productivity'.

5.5.1 So-called limitations on productivity. The reason for the label 'limitations on productivity' is fairly clear. Suppose there is a morphological process (call it *p*) which can apply to only a very small number of bases, and another process (call it *q*) which can apply to a very large number of bases. It is probable that a smaller number of forms produced by *p* will be attested than forms produced by *q*. As a result, it appears that *p* does not apply often, and that is taken to mean that *p* has limited productivity. This doesn't necessarily follow. If a process can apply to a limited, finite set of *n* bases, and is actually attested having applied to all of those bases, then that process is fully generalised, and has, correspondingly, been fully productive, whether *n* is equal to 200,000 or to 10. That is, judgements about how productive some process is, or has been, should not be made before it is discovered which bases could provide input to the process. If this is not done, then the term 'productive' is being used in a rather different and, I believe, ultimately misleading way. The fact that virtually no studies of productivity in the sense in which it is being defined here have been carried out is a nuisance for the theorist, but irrelevant to the theoretical discussion.

Although it is not my intention to spend a great deal of time considering individual examples here, it is perhaps worth illustrat-

69

5. Productivity

ing briefly the kinds of ways in which the bases available for certain morphological processes may be restricted. The particular examples chosen are random, illustrating a range of kinds of restriction. In German the suffix -*tum* is now only productive with bases which denote people. Forms such as *Abenteurertum* 'the collection of adventurers', *Bürokratentum* 'the collection of bureaucrats', *Hegelianertum* 'the collection of Hegel scholars', *Ignorantentum* 'the collection of ignoramuses', *Sklaventum* 'the collection of slaves', and so on are found, but forms such as *Altertum* 'antiquity' and *Besitztum* 'property' are **lexicalised** relics, no longer possible formations today. This, then, is a case where there is a semantic restriction on the type of base that is used for this affixation process.

In English, the inflectional suffixes -*s* and -*ing* can be added to virtually all verbs except modal verbs. The few exceptions (such as *beware* and *quoth*) must be specially marked, and genuinely prevent the claim of full productivity for these affixes. Modal verbs are frequently defined in terms of this aberrant morphological marking, but can also be defined in terms of syntactic criteria (they are followed by a verb in the stem form without *to*, they are always the first verb in the verb group, and so on). Here there is a limitation on the bases which are available for these particular affixation processes, and that limitation can be expressed in syntactic terms.

In Russian, the suffix -*ant* can be used to create new words (i.e. it is a Russian suffix, it does not just appear in the borrowed words where it originated), but the base to which the suffix is attached must be a foreign base. The following are examples of Russian-coined words using the suffix:

(12) | kurs | 'course' | kursant | 'student' |
|---|---|---|---|
| diversija | 'sabotage' | diversant | 'saboteur' |
| spekuljatsija | 'speculation' | spekuljant | 'speculator' |

Whether a base is foreign or native is ultimately an etymological question, but it acts synchronically in the same kind of way as declension or conjugation class operate, that is as a morphological feature. This, therefore, is an instance of a morphological restriction on the set of bases available for this affixation process.

In Turkish there is a suffix -*de*- (-*da*- depending on vowel harmony) which is added only to onomatopoeic words ending in /r/ or /l/ to form verbs from imitative words. Some examples are given below, with the final -*mek* (-*mak*) marking the infinitive of the verb.

(13) | gıcır | 'creak!' | gıcır·da·mak | 'to creak' |
|---|---|---|---|
| hırıl | 'growl!' | hırıl·da·mak | 'to growl' |
| horul | 'snore!' | horul·da·mak | 'to snore' |
| kütür | 'crunch!' | kütür·de·mek | 'to crunch' |
| takır | 'tap tap!' | takır·da·mak | 'to tap' |

70

Here there are two types of restriction on the bases available for the process. The first is a semantic one, in that the base must be an onomatopoeic word, the second is a phonological one, in that the segments that the base may end in are specified.

The most common kinds of restrictions on bases are those which specify the part of speech of the base or, for inflectional endings, the declension or conjugation class of the base. These are so common as to require no exemplification: examples can easily be found from English, German, Latin and so on.

The fact that there are so many different possible types of restriction on bases available for morphological processes is just one of the reasons why it is so difficult to say how productive a particular process is. Since many kinds of limitation may apply to the bases available for a single morphological process, and the limitations have to be determined by the analysis of attested forms, the job of the linguist is an onerous one. Indeed, it is not clear whether anyone has ever stated in any clear way all the restrictions applying to the bases for any process: we simply do not know what such a statement would look like, and cannot tell whether all relevant variables might have been taken into account.

5.5.2 So-called semi-productivity. A process is generally said to be **semi-productive** if it does not apply without exception to all bases defined by a certain part of speech. It has just been pointed out, though, that virtually no process applies in this fashion. There are a number of possible reasons for this.

(a) Some bases may not be available for the morphological process for some of the reasons discussed in the last section.

(b) The process may no longer be productive, which is equivalent to saying that the bases to which it can apply can be listed.

(c) The process may be productive, and the base a potential base, and yet the process may not actually be attested with that base. This output of the process might then be said 'not to exist'. This type of argument was discussed earlier in this chapter.

Semi-productivity is frequently taken to be one of the criteria that distinguishes between inflectional and derivational morphology. (See Chapter 2, p. 13 and also below, Chapter 6.) However, the arguments that have been presented here cast considerable doubt on this analysis, and on the notion of semi-productivity as a whole.

REFERENCES AND FURTHER READING

The examples in (1) are taken from Jespersen (1909: 122-7, 139-40). The rule is Chomsky & Halle's rule of Trisyllabic Laxing (Chomsky & Halle, 1968).

The examples in (2) and (4) are all taken from Barnhart *et al.* (1973).

5. Productivity

A reverse dictionary of English is Lehnert (1971). Similar dictionaries exist for Danish, French, German and other European languages, but rarely for other languages. The argument about the productivity of -*ment* can be found in Bauer (1983: 55).

The examples in (7) are taken from Williams (1965), a paper which is interesting in that it shows that the productivity of a suffix may be much greater than one might expect from consulting one's intuitions. However, in the course of citing examples to prove how undesirable the over-use of -*ness* is, Williams also cites as regrettable neologisms some words which have a long history documented in *The Oxford English Dictionary*. In any case, the prescriptivism inherent in this paper should be ignored.

On the comparative productivity of morphology and syntax, see Bauer (1983) and works referred to there.

The main source on blocking is Aronoff (1976). The term 'preemption' is from Clark & Clark (1979). For comments on synonymy, see Lyons (1977).

Homonymics was developed with reference to French by Orr (1962), but this book cannot be recommended to undergraduate students without considerable guidance. There are some brief comments on the subject in Samuels (1972: 67-75) and Trudgill (1974: 29-32).

In section 5.5.1, the data on the German suffix -*tum* is taken from Fleischer (1975), the data on the Russian suffix -*ant* is taken from Townsend (1975: 175), the Turkish example is taken from Lewis (1967: 231). Many more examples of limitations on bases that can undergo various morphological processes may be found in virtually any book that deals with derivational morphology in any detail.

For a more advanced discussion of productivity from a rather different point of view, see Van Marle (1985: Chapter 2). Amongst other things, Van Marle suggests that word-forming processes which demand non-native bases can never be productive, and that processes which require deliberation on the part of the speaker are not productive, even if they can be used to produce new words. According to this, neo-classical compounding in English is not productive despite the numbers of new neo-classical compounds that are formed. Dressler (1981) also stresses that words can be coined for effect which deliberately flout normal rules of word-formation without the processes involved thereby being productive.

6. Inflection and Derivation

As we have already seen in Chapter 2, morphology is traditionally divided into two branches: inflection and derivation. These two are usually visualised as being entirely separate; inflection is a part of syntax, while derivation is a part of lexis. In fact, as was stated in Chapter 2, that is the basis of the distinction: inflection provides forms of lexemes, while derivation provides new lexemes. In recent linguistic theory, this distinction has often been held to have implications for the organisation of the grammar. Rules for inflectional morphology are thought of as being a part of the same system as syntactic rules, while derivational rules are thought of as being in the lexicon, or at least not in the same section of the grammar as the inflectional rules. For example, while several linguists have suggested that the difference between forms of German like *finde* '[I] find' and *findest* '[you, singular] find' might be accounted for in the grammatical derivation of sentences by the use of features such as [+ 1st person], [+ 2nd person] and [+ singular] as markers on the lexeme FINDEN 'to find', it has not to my knowledge been suggested that a form like *Häus·chen* 'house, diminutive' should be accounted for by the use of a feature like [+ diminutive] on the lexeme HAUS 'house'.

All this assumes that it is a fairly simple matter to distinguish between those processes which are inflectional and those which are derivational. This is also the impression that was given in Chapter 2. Now, many of the definitions that allow us to draw the distinction are based on a prior definition of the lexeme. However, most definitions of the lexeme depend on a prior definition of inflection (definitions such as 'an abstract unit of vocabulary which occurs in different inflectional forms', for instance). It would, therefore, be highly desirable to draw a distinction between inflectional and derivational processes without having to make reference to the lexeme; but it is actually very difficult to draw such a distinction. There are a number of criteria which are frequently given as a basis for this distinction, and they will be discussed in this chapter. But we shall see that they are not all easy to apply, and neither do they individually always give the intuitively 'correct' results. They do not even always agree on which processes are inflectional and which derivational.

6. Inflection and Derivation

6.1 Meaning

Basically we are trying to decide when we have a new lexeme and when we just have a form of an old lexeme. On the face of it, this ought to be a fairly simple matter: we probably have reasonably clear intuitions about what are forms of a lexeme and what are new lexemes in any language we speak. However, it is not really as easy as it looks. To see this, consider the data in (1), where causative formations from three languages are put side by side. The second form in each of the languages illustrated means something like 'to make something or someone do what the first form says'.

(1)   *Turkish*
        öl·mek   'to die'
        öl·dür·mek 'to kill'
        Swahili
        chelewa   'be late'
        chelewe·sha 'delay'
        Finnish
        elä·ä   'live'
        elä·ttä·ä   'provide for'

In accounts of the morphology of these languages, the affix in the Finnish example is considered to be derivational, while the affixes distinguishing the two forms in the other two languages are considered to be inflectional. From this it is clear that we cannot rely on meaning to distinguish inflection from derivation. We require some other criteria.

This is a pity. It is otherwise very tempting to say that certain meanings or morphological categories will be inflectional. For instance, we might expect that morphological categories such as number, person, gender, case, tense, aspect, voice and the like will be inflectional where they are marked morphologically at all. This is probably because we expect such categories to be marked on all nouns or verbs as the case may be. It is thus linked to the productivity criterion which was mentioned in Chapter 2 and which will be taken up again below. In fact, this kind of approach would probably work fairly well in the majority of cases. However, there are a number of instances where categories which would be classed as derivational by such a criterion are usually considered inflectional. The Turkish and Swahili examples cited in (1) provide simple examples, and in the Nigerian language Fula, diminutives ('a little ____'), augmentatives ('a big ____') and pejorative diminutives ('a nasty little ____') are apparently inflectional categories. There are also a few cases which would be classed as inflectional by such a criterion but which are usually considered to be derivational. For instance, in Diyari (a South Australian language) and Kwakiutl (a language spoken on Vancouver Island) it appears that the marker of plurality is considered derivational. In Kwakiutl, Keresan (a language of New Mexico) and Quileute (a language spoken in Washington State) aspect is derivational, and in Kwakiutl tense is too.

We thus still need other criteria for distinguishing between inflectional and derivational processes. Three were mentioned in Chapter 2, and they will be considered first.

6.2 Derivation may cause a change of category

If we add the affix -*s* to the form *car* to give *car·s*, we have started out with a noun and finished up with a noun. There is thus a sense in which we have not changed the part of speech or the **category** of the base in the affixation process. In contrast, if we add -*al* to the form *person* to give *person·al*, we have changed a noun into an adjective in the process of affixation, and so have changed the category.

Unfortunately, matters are not quite as simple as this seems to suggest, because we do not have a close enough definition of a category. Categories are determined by distribution: if two items have identical distributions, they will be considered to belong to the same category. But it is not clear just how closely a distribution is to be defined. For example, if we define a distribution as being the frame 'Determiner ____', then all nouns belong to the same category. If, on the other hand, we say that the frame is 'Indefinite Article ____', uncountable nouns are excluded. And if we say the frame is 'a ____' then only countable nouns beginning in a phonetic consonant are included. Each of these might be taken as a category, depending upon the use it was wished to make of the categorisation. Now consider the morphological examples below:

(2)	appear	dis·appear
	bishop	bishop·ric
	boy	boy·hood
	green	green·ish
	king	king·dom
	likely	un·likely
	lingual	tri·lingual
	lion	lion·ess
	Marx	Marx·ist
	poet	poet·ry
	song	song·ster

6. Inflection and Derivation

In all of these examples, the word coined by the affixation process is of the same major category as the word which is its base. Although most of the examples in (2) show suffixation, the same would be true to a much greater extent with prefixation in English. Have the affixes illustrated in (2) caused a change of category, then? On one level, the answer is obviously 'no', but on a more delicate level, the answer is equally obviously 'yes'. After all, *boy* is an animate noun, while *boyʰood* is not, *lioness* is specifically marked as female, while *lion* is not, and so on. Even with the prefixation cases there is a change of distribution and thus of category:

(3)   That is a lingual muscle/*child.
      That is a trilingual *muscle/child.

In fact, on an extremely delicate analysis of what a category is, even the affixes which we consider to be inflectional can be seen to cause a change of category. One of the properties of the set of words of which *person* is a member (which could thus be used to define its distribution) is that it can take an *-al* suffix. Once it has changed category, however, it cannot take that same affix, so that **person·al·al* is not a possible word in English. Similarly, though, one of the things which defines the category to which a word like *car* belongs is its ability to take an *-s* suffix. Since *car·s* cannot take that same suffix (you cannot have *car·s·s*), *car* and *cars* must belong to different categories, and the affixation process must have caused a change of category. On this analysis, it is only the affixes in formations like the German *Ur·ur·gross·vater* 'great-great-grand-father' which do not cause a change of category.

So before we can say that derivational affixes may cause a change in category, but that inflectional ones never do, we need a closer definition of category. If we define category at the coarse level of noun, verb, adjective, then the criterion isolates some derivational affixes, but fails to distinguish between the other derivational affixes and inflectional ones. If we work with an extremely delicate notion of category, it is not clear that the criterion will work at all.

One suggestion is that only derivational processes can change subcategorisation features associated with the base. For example, the derivational prefix *re-* can change subcategorisation:

(4)   They all act parts.
      *They all react parts.

but inflectional affixes can never make such a change, so that the following is a typical pattern:

(5)   They act parts.
       He acts parts.
       Acting parts comes naturally to her.

This allows some way of defining what a change of category means.
       This is not the only problem with this criterion, though. Another
can be seen by considering a form like *shooting*. We would probably
say that in the sentence

(6)   Evelyn was shooting clay pigeons.

the affixation of the -*ing* was inflectional: *shoot* and *shooting* on a
coarse analysis are both verbs. But what about *shooting* in the
following senten es:

(7)   I saw Lee shooting clay pigeons.
       His shooting clay pigeons didn't worry me.
       The shooting of the clay pigeons was dramatic.

Here there is an indefinite borderline between what is a verb and
what is a noun. At some point, however, we would probably agree
that *shooting* had become a noun. Do we then say that the affixation
of -*ing* in that case is derivational, although in other cases it is
inflectional? On the face of it, that is not a particularly satisfactory
solution, since precisely the same affix, with precisely the same set
of allomorphs, is added to precisely the same set of bases in the
two cases, and yet appears to be doing two rather different jobs.
Do we say that there are two homophonous affixes -*ing*, one of
which is inflectional and one derivational? This seems just as bad,
at first glance, since precisely the same set of forms is always
produced by what would then be considered two distinct processes.
The alternative may be to say that at some stage *shooting* has
undergone conversion or zero-derivation and turned into a noun.
That is an analysis which is adopted by some linguists, although it
is open to the theoretical problems involved in conversion (see
section 3.4).

6.3 Inflectional affixes have a regular meaning
All inflectional affixes have a regular meaning, while not all derivational affixes do. The difficulty with this criterion is that many
derivational affixes also have a perfectly regular meaning. This is
particularly true of the most productive affixes – which is probably
not surprising. You have to know what a word is going to mean
before you coin it. So the productive suffixation of -*er*, and -*able*
show quite regular meaning, even though we would probably want
to say they were derivational rather than inflectional.

6. *Inflection and Derivation*

A thornier problem with this criterion, though, is that it is not clear how we specify the meaning of an affix. Consider the affix *-ette* in English. Some examples are given below.

(8)   beaver·ette
      flannel·ette
      maison·ette
      kitchen·ette
      suffrag·ette
      usher·ette

At least three ways of dealing with the meanings are possible here.

(a)   There are three distinct meanings:
        i. small (as in *kitchenette, maisonette*),
        ii. female (as in *sufragette, usherette*), and
        iii. mock material (as in *beaverette, flannelette*).
(b)   There are two distinct meanings here,
        i. mock material and
        ii. diminutive.
      Because women tend statistically to be smaller than men, and because men feel protective towards women, the diminutive meaning is also applied to women, although it is the same meaning. Note that this is stated as a hypothesis, and is not intended to condone such an interpretation.
(c)   There is only one meaning here, diminutive. Diminutive has as its primary meaning 'small in size', but that can, in our society, imply one of two things:
        i. delicacy (as with women) or
        ii. inferior quality (as with the materials and – possibly – with the women).

As a second example, consider the English suffix *-ment*. Under one interpretation, this has a host of meanings, including

(9)   (a) state of being VERBed   employment
      (b) that in which one is VERBed employment
      (c) thing which VERBS   payment
      (d) act of VERBing   encouragement

Each of these meanings is illustrated in the corresponding sentence below:

(10) (a) My employment ceases on the 31st.
      (b) My employment takes me all around the world.
      (c) I enclose payment.
      (d) Her constant encouragement was a boon.

Another possibility is that there is only one meaning for the suffix involved, and that is 'noun formed from a verb', and that everything else is left to the interpretation of the word in context

From these two examples it can be seen that the more delicate the analysis of meaning that is provided, the larger the number of meanings that will be discovered. With the *-ette* example, we might conclude that there was only one meaning, and that *-ette* was therefore at the inflectional end with regard to this criterion, or that there were three meanings, and that *-ette* was clearly derivational with regard to this criterion. More subtly, perhaps, we might claim that there were indeed three meanings, but that each of these meanings was connected with a different suffix, and that there just happened to be three homophonous suffixes *-ette*.

The result is that if we are willing to postulate enough homophonous suffixes, or if we are willing to talk in rather coarse terms when it comes to defining meaning, we can probably claim that every affix has a regular meaning. Under such circumstances, this criterion becomes vacuous. If it is to have some content, then it will first be necessary to establish independently some way of defining the meaning of an affix appropriately.

6.4 Inflection is productive, derivation semi-productive

We have already seen in Chapter 5 that the notion of semi-productivity may rest on some fundamental misconceptions of productivity. The criterion that inflection is productive but derivation only semi-productive is correspondingly under a cloud before we begin. It was in effect argued in Chapter 5 that derivation is more productive than is generally thought.

The reverse is also true. Inflection is less productive than is frequently believed. The phenomenon of 'defective verbs' illustrates this well, and will be familiar to anyone who has studied Indo-European languages, as well as to students of some other languages.

In French, for example, the verb *choir* 'to fall' is only common in the past participle, *clore* 'to close' has no first person singular forms, and is only common in the past participle, *gésir* 'to lie' has no future and no perfect, and is only usual in the third person, *quérir* 'to look for' is only found in the infinitive, and so on.

In Latin, *memini*: 'I remember' and *o:di*: 'I hate' only have perfective forms, *inquam* 'I say' only has third person forms in the imperfect, and *fa:ri*: 'I speak' has no perfective forms.

In English, the modal verbs have no special third person singular present tense form, no present participle, no past participle and no infinitive, and *must* has no special past tense form, either. Verbs such as *abide, beware, pending* and *quoth* also do not have full paradigms.

In Russian, the verbs *pobedit'* 'to conquer' and *multit'* 'to stir up, muddy' have no first person singular of the present tense.

Such examples could be multiplied from other languages.

If it is not true that derivational morphology is semi-productive, and not true that inflectional morphology is fully productive in either of the senses discussed in Chapter 5, then this criterion is not particularly useful as it stands. This does mask the point, though, that on the whole bases for inflectional processes are more likely to be specified simply in terms of their part of speech, and that bases for derivational processes are more likely to require some further specification, of the type that was illustrated in section 5.5.1. A reformulation of the criterion along these lines still does not represent more than a tendency, and is not as strong a statement as the original formulation.

Even this reformulated version might be disputed. When we consider markers of, say, the plural in English, we take it that the three regular markers of plurality, /s/, /z/ and /ɪz/, and the various irregular plural markers such as *-en*, *-ren*, *-im*, vowel change and the like, are all allomorphs of the same morpheme {plural}. When we consider nominalisations of verbs in English, we take it that *-ment*, *-th*, *-ation*, *-age* and so on realise different morphemes, not that they are allomorphs of the morpheme {nominalisation}. This is a direct result of the assumption that a morpheme is defined as much by the form of its morphs as by its meaning: an assumption which seems well motivated when you consider that without it we would be led to the conclusion that *liber* in *liberty* was an allomorph of *free* in *freedom*. Nevertheless, it might well be possible to build up an argument that the plural markers and nominalisation markers ought to be treated in the same way, not in different ways, in which case even the reformulated criterion would fail to hold.

6.5 Derivational affixes are nearer the root than inflectional ones

It is frequently stated that derivational affixes are found closer to the root than inflectional affixes. Across languages, this criterion appears to have a certain statistical validity although, as we shall see, it is no more than a tendency. Despite this, it is not a criterion which allows us to determine whether a given affix is inflectional or derivational. It is simply an observation based on a prior division of affixes into inflectional and derivational. This can be illustrated with the examples below:

(11)   (a) *French*:   arriv·er·i·ons
                      arrive·future·imperfect·1st-person-plural
                      'we would arrive'

(b) *English*:	palat·al·is·ation
(c) *English*:	black·en·ed
(d) *German*:	Forsch·ung·en
	research·nominalisation·plural
	'research' (plural noun)

In (11a) there is a sequence of affixes, of which -*er* is closer to the root than -*ons*, yet all the affixes would usually be classified as inflectional. In (11b) there is a sequence of affixes, of which -*al* is closer to the root than -*ation*, and yet all of these affixes would normally be considered to be derivational. It is only where we have affixes which we take to be inflectional and derivational in the same word, as in (11c and d), that we can see that the derivational one is closer to the root than the inflectional one.

In any case, as was stated earlier, the criterion does not always work. Even in the familiar Indo-European languages we find examples like the following.

(12)	*German*:	Kind·er·chen
		child·plural·diminutive
	Welsh:	merch·et·os
		girl·plural·diminutive
	Dutch:	scholier·en·dom
		pupil·plural·abstract-noun
		muzikant·en·dom
		musician·plural·abstract-noun
	English:	interest·ed·ly
		exaggerate·d·ly
		report·ed·ly
		accord·ing·ly
		lov·ing·ness
		bound·ed·ness
		for·giv·ing·ness
		startl·ing·ness
		speckl·ed·y
		folk·s·y
		new·s·y
		sud·s·y
		better·ment
		less·en
		more·ish
		most·ly
		worse·n

The German example here is no longer productive, but the fact that it was productive at one time shows that this criterion is not necessarily met all the time. The English examples are productive, though it is interesting that the affixes which are most commonly ordered 'wrongly' are the ones involving suppletion, irregular allomorphs, and *-ed, -ing, -ly* and *-ness*: the most derivational of the inflectional affixes, and the most inflectional of the derivational affixes. It might appear that the English examples could be 'rescued' by the use of the zero-derivation option mentioned in section 6.2, but this is not the case. Even if zero-derivation is presumed to change the inflectional form into a different part of speech before the next derivational process applies, the inflection would still be closer to the root than the derivational zero.

6.6 Derivatives can be replaced by monomorphemic forms

The idea of this criterion is that it is possible to replace a derivative in a sentence with a monomorphemic form, and the sentence will still make sense, but it is not possible to do the same with an inflected form. Thus, parallel to

(13)   Patriot·ism is good for a nation.

a sentence like

(14)   Oil is good for a nation.

is also possible, in which *oil*, which is made up of only one morpheme, has replaced *patriot·ism*, and *patriotism* is correspondingly shown to be a derivative and not an inflected form. On the other hand, parallel to

(15)   Lee always arrive·s at noon.

we cannot have

(16)   *Lee always come at noon.

in which the single morpheme word *come* has replaced *arrive·s*, and thus it can be seen that *arrives* is an inflected form and not a derivative.

The first thing to note about this criterion is that it is a test for specific words in context, not a definition. However, it can be rephrased as a definition, since it is more or less equivalent to a statement that inflectional affixes are obligatory while derivational ones are not, where obligatory is to be understood as obligatory to the sentence. More important is the fact that it does not work. It fails in many highly inflected languages because it is hard to find monomorphemic words at all. In Russian, for example, the only apparently monomorphemic form of a feminine noun is the genitive plural (see example (31) in section 3.4). This means that in (17a) there is an apparently monomorphemic form of the noun for 'car' (a monomorphemic feminine noun), despite the fact that it is a genitive plural, while in (17b) it is impossible to replace the word for 'pilot' with a monomorphemic form, despite the fact that it is a derivative (literally 'fli·er').

(17) (a) koljosa maʃin vraʃtʃalis'
       wheel cars'   were-spinning
       'the cars' wheels were spinning'
    (b) on dal ljot·tʃik·u   instruktsii
       he gave pilot·dative-singular   instructions
       'he gave the pilot instructions'

This gives the wrong answers for the test, but in no way denies the obligatoriness of inflections.

In Kanuri, a language of Nigeria, however, nominative and accusative case endings are optional where no ambiguity results. It thus seems that obligatoriness is not always a reliable test.

Even in English this criterion will often give the wrong, or even conflicting, results, as is shown in the following examples.

(18) They always arriv·ed on time.
      They always come on time.

(19) She is bright·er than I am.
      *She is bright than I am.

(20) I bought a dear·er watch.
      I bought a dear watch.

The conclusion must be that this criterion is not very useful.

6.7 Inflection uses a closed set of affixes
It is not generally possible to add a new inflectional affix to a language or to take one away. We could not, for instance, wake up one morning and start using in English a dual marker such as is found in Greek or Maori. Neither could we ignore the singular/plural distinction. It is possible, on the other hand, suddenly to start using a new derivational affix, as is shown by the success of forms in -nomics over recent years (*Nixonomics, Thatchernomics, Reaganomics, Rogernomics* and so on). Furthermore, it is usually said that the set of inflectional affixes will be considerably smaller than the set of derivational affixes.

Firstly, this must be a synchronic statement, although that is frequently not made clear. Diachronically languages do lose and gain inflectional affixes over time. English has lost its second person singular marking on the verb since the sixteenth century (although it is retained sporadically in the language of religion), and Mandarin is commonly said to be in the process of gaining morphological structure, including inflections.

Secondly, it is not clear that all languages can add derivational affixes freely. While it does not have a great deal of derivation to begin with, Maori is a language which does not appear to be adding new derivational affixes, although this could be a result of the fact that there are very few monolingual speakers of Maori left alive, or even speakers for whom Maori is a first language.

Thirdly, it is not clear that inflectional affixes always form a considerably smaller set than derivational affixes. Little research has been done on this aspect of Maori, but again it seems likely that the numbers of inflectional and derivational affixes in that language are much closer to each other than they are in, say, English. At the other end of the scale, it seems that a highly inflecting language like Finnish has far more distinct inflectional affixes than derivational ones.

Although this criterion works, to a certain extent, for English, it may not work for all languages. In any case, if you meet a new affix for the first time, you have no means of telling, from this criterion, whether that affix is inflectional or derivational. This is another observation that depends upon a prior classification.

6.8 Inflectional morphology is what is relevant to the syntax
This is, basically, just a reformulation of the statement that inflection produces forms of lexemes, while derivation produces new lexemes. However, a reformulation can sometimes be useful, in that it allows you to look at the problem from a different angle. In this case, though, it is not as useful as might be hoped.

The main problem is that it is not clear what 'relevant to the syntax' means. If it means 'what is specified in the grammatical word' it is true, but circular, since you only need specify the lexeme and the inflectional morphemes in a grammatical word. It can be made non-circular by saying that anything which marks agreement is inflectional. This is true, but does not define all the processes which we would probably want to call inflectional. It is not even clear that it would show tense affixes to be inflectional, for instance.

In a wider sense, this criterion as worded depends crucially on what the syntax is or does. Many models of syntax have come and gone over the last twenty-five years, and any two of them might define different processes as inflectional if this criterion were taken seriously. For example, if a grammar were developed based on the system used by Jespersen, we might want to say that *extreme·ly* in *extremely tall tower* was the 'adverbial form of *extreme*'. Such a grammar would no doubt have problems associated with it, but it is not an inconceivable way of looking at syntax. And it would have as its result that the affix *-ly*, normally considered derivational, would be seen as relevant to the syntax, and thus inflectional. Similarly, in a different kind of grammar, it might well be argued that *advance·ment* was just the nominal form of *advance*. Such a grammar is, indeed, implied in some relatively recent work on morphology. This would make the affix *-ment* inflectional by the same line of argumentation. A general statement such as 'syntax is concerned with the interrelations of words within larger structures' does not help here, since in both the examples cited this could be argued to be the case: *extremely* is the form of *extreme* required when it modifies an adjective; *advancement* is the form of *advance* which can take articles and adjectives, and function in nominal positions in the sentence.

If the argument in the last paragraph seems too forced to be convincing, a different argument from Eskimo is perhaps clearer. In Labrador Inuttut the marker of the passive is described as a derivational suffix. This classification is based on a number of arguments, including criteria which have been discussed in this chapter. Yet this suffix appears to have an effect on the syntax, as can be seen from the following examples:

(21) angutik   anna·mik   taku·juk
      man-absolutive woman·modalis see·3rd-person-singular
      'the man sees a woman'
      annak   anguti·mut   taku·jau·juk
      woman-absolutive man·terminalis see·passive·3rd-person-singular
      'the woman is seen by the man'

The presence of the passive marker has an effect on the co-occurring case marking, and word order. Here, then, a derivational affix is necessary for the syntax.

Although this criterion is aiming at defining a common and valuable intuition, it is not sufficient as it stands to define the precise area it wishes to capture.

6.9 Conclusion

These are not the only possible criteria for distinguishing between inflection and derivation, but they are probably the most important ones; and the others, in any case, are open to the same kinds of objection. What, then, should be concluded on the basis of these criteria? None of the criteria has appeared satisfactory, so there is certainly no simple way of drawing a distinction.

There are two possible answers to the question. The first is simply to discard the distinction. This is being done by many linguists in contemporary morphological theory. If we discard the distinction, then by implication we also discard the notion of the lexeme, and we are left simply with roots, affixes, and word-forms. This would mean a total reconsideration of the notion of 'lexeme', to see whether we are willing to discard it or not. It certainly has some useful practical applications in terms of lexicography, for instance.

The alternative is to keep the distinction between inflection and derivation, but to view it in another light. In the discussion of the various criteria for distinguishing between the two, it was often the case that the criterion worked in a large number of cases, but failed in others. The criteria were also, in general, less useful as a universal list than in particular languages. One solution to this type of problem has been proposed by language typologists, with the notion of **prototype**. A prototype is what the most typical member of a class is like across languages, and individual languages will be expected to have actual types which diverge from the prototype to a greater or lesser extent. In this sense we might say that a prototypical inflectional affix will not change major category, will have a regular meaning, and be added to every base in the appropriate part of speech; it will be ordered after all derivational markers, will be a member of a small closed set of affixes and be relevant for the syntax in all models of syntax. A prototypical derivational affix will create new lexemes, change major category, have an irregular meaning on a fairly delicate analysis of meaning, especially in established words, come closer to the root than any inflectional affixes, belong to a large open set of affixes, and not play a role in the syntax of the sentence as a whole. Actual inflectional and derivational affixes in real languages will diverge from these prototypes, possibly to such an extent that we can be in doubt as to which class they belong in. However, in any particular language, we would expect to be able to make a distinction based on one or more of the criteria we have listed. It will turn out that the decision made for any particular language will often be related to the notion of paradigm for that language. In highly inflecting languages a derivational affix will predict the existence of a whole paradigm of inflections beyond the derivational affix, while an inflectional affix will predict the existence of a much smaller range of forms, or none at all. For example, in English the fact that a word ends in *-ise* predicts that there will also be forms ending in *-ise·s*, *-ise·d* and *-is·ing*, whereas the existence of a form ending in *-ing* makes no further predictions about the existence of other forms. In languages which are relatively poor, morphologically speaking, this predictive ability is less strik-

6. Inflection and Derivation

ing than it would be in a highly inflecting language, but is still a guide in some cases.

Just how prototypes are to be built into a grammar is an interesting and difficult question – if indeed they are to be seen as parts of the grammars of individual languages. But the notion of prototype allows us to speak of inflectional and derivational affixes in particular languages, and to show how the classes are set up.

REFERENCES AND FURTHER READING

The data on Swahili is taken from Ashton (1944), that on Turkish from Lewis (1967), that on Finnish from Karlsson (1983) and that on Diyari from Austin (1981). Note, however, that it is not absolutely clear from Austin's description why the plural affix in Diyari should be considered derivational and not inflectional. This is stated to be the case, and may well be justified, but it does not appear to be argued for in that book. The information on Fula is from Anderson (1982), that on Kwakiutl, Keresan and Quileute is from Bybee (1985). Kwakiutl is also mentioned by Anderson (1982) under the name Kwakwala.

The argument about category being defined in terms of recursion is from Lyons (1977).

The argument from subcategorisation is from Scalise (1984: 110).

The examples of Russian defective verbs are from Halle (1973).

The distinction in the way in which the markers of the plural and nominalisation are treated, discussed at the end of section 6.4, is directly relevant in some modern writings on morphology. Anderson (1982: 587) draws attention to the anomaly here. Others (e.g. Beard, 1982) have suggested that English plurals may be derivational rather than inflectional.

The example *Kinderchen* is discussed by Fleischer (1975). The Welsh example is from Robins (1964). The Dutch examples are from Booij (1977). The facts about Kanuri come from Lukas (1937: 17).

The comment about the relative numbers of inflectional and derivational affixes in Finnish on page 84 is based on a study of Karlsson (1983). Such a method is, of course, likely to have under-estimated the number of derivational affixes to be found in the language, but the discrepancy in numbers is so great that it does not seem likely that the comment is unjustified.

The title of section 6.8 is a quotation from Anderson (1982). The relatively recent work referred to in section 6.8 in which *advancement* might be taken to be the nominal form of *advance* is, in particular, Chomsky (1970). The definition of syntax provided in the course of the discussion on page 85 is taken directly from Anderson (1982: 587). The examples from Labrador Inuttut are from Smith (1982b).

Works that do not distinguish between inflection and derivation include Lieber (1981). For an introduction to prototypes in typology, see Comrie (1981: 100-4).

I am indebted to Kate Kearns for the notion of paradigm prediction.

For further discussion of the distinction between inflection and derivation, see Anderson (1982), Matthews (1974). For those who read German, a rather more advanced coverage of the topic of this chapter can be found in Plank (1981: Chapter 2).

87

7. The Domain of Morphology

In Chapter 3 it was pointed out that the central domain of morphology is affixation, but that there are a number of other processes which at least impinge on morphology, and may or may not belong to morphology proper. The reason for this is that other processes have certain things in common with affixation processes, while differing from them in other ways. There are thus links of variable strength binding affixation processes to other processes, and the weaker these links become, or the greater the number of intermediate steps in these links, the less likely it is that a particular process should be considered to be morphological. In this section I should like to illustrate this state of affairs. Since it is not clear to me that such an exercise makes any sense in a universalist kind of way, I shall illustrate it purely from English. It may be that other languages display other patterns; though if they do not, this is, of course, a very interesting discovery. Towards the end of this section I shall try to show that some processes are less centrally morphological than others, though no definite conclusion on where to draw the boundaries of morphology will be reached. I shall do this by drawing parallels between various kinds of process, and then trying to summarise them diagrammatically.

(a) Prefixation resembles suffixation because both deal with the addition of obligatorily bound forms to forms which, in the majority of cases, are potentially free.

(b) Prefixation resembles compounding because both prefixes and the first elements of compounds can, under appropriate circumstances, be coordinated in English. This is not the case with suffixes, in particular. This is illustrated below.

(1)   summer and winter holidays
        girl- or boyfriends
        in and out-put
        pro- or anti-vivisection
        psycho- and sociolinguistics
        *adviser and -ee
        *normalcy or -ity
        *aeroplane or -drome

89

(c) Prefixation is like neo-classical compounding because
    i. Many of the same items can act as first elements in neo-classical compounds and as prefixes, such as *socio-* in *sociology* and *sociolinguistics*
    ii. Both prefixes and the first elements of neo-classical compounds can be co-ordinated under some circumstances and not under others:

(2)   pre- and post-natal care
      Anglo- and Franco-philia
      *re- and de-code
      *phon- and graph-ology

        The precise circumstances under which coordination is possible are not well understood, and do not appear to be easily formalised, so they will not be enlarged upon any further here. Suffice it to say, for present purposes, that this similarity exists.

(d) Prefixation is like backformation because both can deal with the same elements: prefixation adds them, backformation deletes them, and the end result may be indistinguishable. In a sentence like *I don't know if Jillian was nonplussed, but she certainly wasn't plussed*, we have a case of backformation, in a sentence like *The PC connectives behave in non-normal worlds precisely as they do in normal ones*, a case of prefixation, but in both instances the same element *non-* is involved.

(e) Suffixation is like neo-classical compounding because the same elements may be used as suffixes and as the second elements in neo-classical compounds, such as *-ology* in *Kremlinology* and *psychology*.

(f) Suffixation is like conversion because they both regularly cause changes to the major category to which the word belongs.

(g) Suffixation is like backformation because the same elements may be involved in both, and the final results may be indistinguishable (see the discussion above with regards to prefixation and backformation). An example is *edit* versus *editor* as opposed to *exhibit* versus *exhibitor*.

(h) Backformation is like conversion because
    i. Neither of them involves overt affixes, yet both can cause changes of major category.
    ii. The two are extremely important ways of forming compound verbs in English, and compound verbs in English are rarely formed except by one of these two processes.

(i) Backformation is like clipping because both involve a shortening of the base.

90

(j) Neo-classical compounding is like compounding because

   i. The same kind of variable meaning relationship holds between the elements in neo-classical and ordinary compounds.

   ii. It can be argued that both are involved with the collocation of roots, even if the roots in the one case are not always English ones.

   iii. The first elements of compounds and neo-classical compounds can (at least under some circumstances) be coordinated; see examples (1) and (2) above.

(k) Neo-classical compounding is like blending because both involve the fusion of two elements neither of which is potentially free, occasionally to the extent that the one is indistinguishable from the other. The form *autocide*, for example, has two meanings: 'self destruction' (neo-classical compound) and 'suicide in an automobile' (blend).

(l) Blends are like acronyms because they are both made up of non-meaning-bearing parts of other words.

(m) Compounding is like syntax because they are both concerned with the collocation of lexemes.

There may well be other possible links that could be drawn, and other reasons for the links that have been made here. These various similarities can be mapped to form a network like the one illustrated in Figure 7.1.

In Figure 7.1 there appears to be a central core of strongly morphological processes, made up of prefixation, suffixation, back-formation and neo-classical compounding. Outside that central core, clipping, blending and forming acronyms appear as processes which are much less morphological. This does not mean that there is a firm line between morphology in the central core and non-morphology outside it. Rather, morphology shades off into other things, and the central core is probably the area which is most clearly within morphology. It should, of course, be remembered that Figure 7.1 is drawn up on the basis of English only, and that other languages (some of which use other processes such as reduplication and infixation) might well give rise to different networks.

This indicates that there are no firm boundaries to morphology. Correspondingly, what is treated as morphology in any particular theory will depend on other facets of that theory. This is made even more complex by the fact that there are, in any case, close links between morphology and phonology on the one hand, and morphology and syntax on the other. The links with phonology are seen in the whole area of morphophonemics. The links with syntax are

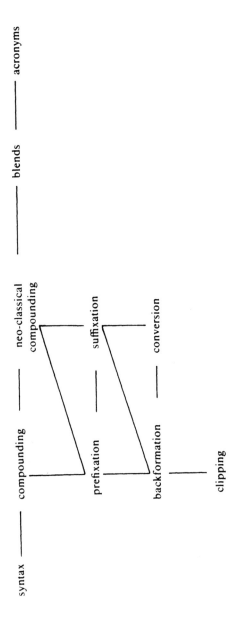

Figure 7.1: Network of various processes in English

shown particularly in clitics and compounds. These three areas will be treated in turn below.

7.1 Links with phonology

What is phonology? The dictionary definition is that it deals with the sound systems of particular languages. There are, however, a number of ways in which this can be done. Consider, for example, the [n] in the word *in* in the two sentences below:

(3)   (a) I read it in the newspaper.
       (b) I saw it in a book.

The [n] in (3b) is an alveolar nasal, while the [n] in (3a) is a dental nasal. Most phonologists would probably agree that this variation is part of the sound system of English, and should be part of the field of phonological study. Now consider the examples below:

(4)   long
       leng·th

We can probably agree that *long* and *leng* are allomorphs of the same morpheme, {long}. Is the phonological distinction between these two allomorphs to be explained as part of the field of phonological study, or is it simply the phonological result of a morphological difference? Different phonologists would give different answers to this question.

The distinction between the two types illustrated in (3) and (4) is not as great as might appear at first glance. If the difference between alveolar and dental [n] illustrated in (3) has a phonological explanation, what about the alveolar and dental [n]s in *ten* as opposed to *ten·th*? Many scholars distinguish between assimilation in the first instance, and similitude in the second, and thus do not equate the two, but it is clear that similar processes account for the dental [n] in both cases. If assimilation like that mentioned above is to be explained phonologically, so presumably is the alternation between [s] and [ʃ] in the word *this* in

(5)   this kind
       this year

Note that the [j] may disappear entirely, giving [ðɪʃɜː]. The same phonetic change is found in the pairs

(6)   express   expression
       regress   regression.

If we assume that *-ion* has a basic phonological form something like /jən/ the same rules can account for both cases. If the forms

93

of allomorphs which depend on assimilation or similitude are to be explained phonologically, presumably alternations due to vowel harmony are also to be explained in that way. So the alternations between *-a* and *-ä*, *-vat* and *-vät*, *-ko* and *-kö* in the Finnish examples below will be given a phonological explanation.

(7) otta·a   's/he takes'   pitä·ä   's/he likes'
     otta·vat   'they take'   pitä·vät   'they like'
     otta·vat·ko 'do they take' pitä·vät·kö 'do they like'

If examples like this, where the segmental form of one part of the word is determined by the segmental form of another part of the same word are to be explained phonologically, what about cases where the segmental form of a word is determined by suprasegmental form? For example the difference in the segmental form of the first morph in *tele·graph* and *tele·graph·y* is determined by the position of the stress. Should this also receive a phonological explanation? And if so, what about the differences between the pairs of English words in (8)? Here the difference between the allomorphs of the root is determined partly by stress, partly by the position of the appropriate vowels in the word, and partly by lexical listing (in that not every word which fits the phonological criteria shows the same alternation, consider *obese, obesity* as a contrast with the examples below).

(8) divine   divin·ity
     obscene   obscen·ity
     profound profund·ity

If such allomorphy is to be given a phonological explanation, then why not the purely lexically determined allomorphy in *long* and *leng·th*?

The dominant approach to phonology over the last twenty years or so has been generative phonology. The standard approach in generative phonology is to see the phonology as a component which links the output of the syntactic component to pronunciation (usually fairly grossly specified). The output of the syntactic component is seen as a series of morphemes, whose precise phonetic shape is to be supplied by the phonology. In the vast majority of cases, each morpheme is given a single deep structure phonological representation, and phonological rules have to apply to this to specify all cases of allomorphy which are observed in that morpheme. The limiting case is suppletion, where two (or more) deep structure phonological representations are specified. The general

7. The Domain of Morphology

trend in phonological studies has been to minimise suppletion, and to derive as much as possible by phonological rules. But consider the situation in Welsh (and comparable data can be found in other Celtic languages). In Welsh, many consonants can undergo mutation, that is a change to another consonant. There are three patterns of mutation, soft mutation (which provides a lenited form of the original consonant), nasal mutation (which provides a nasal corresponding in articulation to the original consonant) and spirant mutation (which provides a fricative at the same place of articulation as an original stop). Each type of mutation can clearly be described in phonological terms, and indeed must be so described. But the conditions under which the various mutations apply have to be described in syntactic and morphological terms. For instance, different prefixes condition different types of mutation in the initial consonant of a base. The initial consonant of an adjective undergoes soft mutation after a feminine, but not after a masculine noun. The initial consonant of a noun undergoes soft mutation after an inflected preposition. The second element of one type of compound also undergoes soft mutation. In all these cases there is a morphological trigger for the phonological process, and any explanation cannot be entirely phonological.

Similar conclusions apply in cases where morphological change is indicated by internal modification of a base. To remain with Welsh, consider the following examples:

(9)   masculine feminine gloss
        byr   ber   'short'
        crwn   cron   'round'
        gwyn   gwen   'white'
        trwm   trom   'heavy'

The feminine forms in (9) will also undergo soft mutation, so that their final form will not be identical with that given above. In cases such as these, it may be possible to give a phonological description of the change of form, but any description of the way in which that change of form operates will also include morphological information. Conversely, of course, any morphological description of the changes illustrated here will involve phonological facts as well as purely morphological ones.

Another example of the way in which morphology and phonology interact is provided by the effect of English suffixes on the stress of derivatives. There are some English derivational affixes which, like all English inflectional affixes, do not affect the stress of the base. For example, when the suffix -less is added to a base, the

95

stress on the new word remains on the same syllable that it was on in the base. This is illustrated below.

(10) 'humour   'humourless
      'meaning   'meaningless
      'character   'characterless
      de'fence   de'fenceless
      re'morse   re'morseless
      ex'pression   ex'pressionless

However, there are other derivational affixes which do affect the stress of the base. They do this either by attracting stress onto themselves (11a) or by attracting stress onto a specific syllable defined in relation to the suffix (11b).

(11) (a) 'journal   journa'lese
          Ja'pan   Japa'nese
          o'fficial   officia'lese
      (b) 'acid   a'cidic
          'poet   po'etic
          'algebra   alge'braic
          'telescope   tele'scopic
          im'perialist   imperia'listic

In either case, the fact that one of these affixes is present has a phonological effect on the base of the new word. Again morphology and phonology can be seen to be closely related.

The extreme view would be that there is no distinction to be drawn between phonological and morphological processes. There are only phonological processes. The actual arrangement of morphs, on this view, is determined syntactically, with the result that there is no separate morphological component of a grammar. This view is implicit in some versions of transformational-generative grammar. More recent theories tend to reject this extreme view, but precisely where the distinction between morphology and phonology is drawn varies from theory to theory. In the light of the close connections, this variation is only to be expected.

There is also a sense in which the effect of phonological processes on morphological strings can make morphological analysis much more difficult. Consider the following data from Sanskrit:

(12) viːna   iːrṣjaja   vinerṣjaja
      without   jealousy   without-jealousy
      saː   uːvatʃa   sovatʃa
      she   spoke   she-spoke

In (12) we see that an open vowel followed by a close vowel across a word-boundary merge as a mid vowel. Which morph does that mid vowel then belong to? Clearly, it belongs entirely to neither, but in some sense to both. We can carry out a morphological analysis in terms of the word-forms as they would be spoken in isolation, but phonological processes then mask the morphological structure. In practice this kind of problem is dealt with in a generative grammar by allowing underlying forms of the morphemes such as {saː} and {uːvatʃa} in (12), and then having phonological rules apply to those underlying forms to produce the **sandhi** phenomena, such as those illustrated above. Some sandhi phenomena are relatively simple, such as assimilation processes mentioned earlier, others far more complex, such as the vowel fusion illustrated in (12). In some cases morphological information is needed to know whether sandhi will occur or not. For example, some speakers of English have an intrusive /r/ in (13a), where a new word immediately follows, but not in (13b), where another morpheme in the same word-form immediately follows:

(13) (a) We want to draw /r/ and paint.
      (b) We are draw*/r/·ing a house.

Different varieties of English have different rules for sandhi at this point. Once again, though, the close relation between phonology and morphology is illustrated.

7.2 Links with syntax
The links between syntax and morphology are at least as close as those between phonology and morphology. In many structuralist grammars (and, following this tradition, in early transformational-generative grammars) the syntax was the part of the grammar which dealt with statements concerning the order of morphs (or morphemes). If the phonology dealt with problems of allomorphy, there was no need for a separate morphological component.

Although this view is unpopular today (for reasons which will be discussed in Chapter 9), there is some evidence to support it. Firstly, there are some languages in which morphs and word-forms are largely co-terminous. In such languages, dealing with an extra component or level of morphology may complicate the linguist's task unnecessarily. Given a sentence like that from Chrau, a language of Vietnam, in (14), a statement of morphology would only complicate the description:

(14) Anh   nhai   nŏq   là   ănh   nhai   nhâng
      I   speak thus is   I   speak true
      'I speak like this, that is truthfully'.

Secondly, syntactic structure appears frequently to give rise diachronically to morphological structure. For example, the French adverbial suffix -*ment* and its cognates in the other Romance languages are derived from the ablative form of the noun meaning 'mind', which could appear as a separate word-form in vulgar Latin. This seems to imply that the distinction between morphs in a separate word-form and morphs in the same word-form is relatively unimportant, and that therefore there is no point in a separate section of a grammar dealing with morphology.

If we are to argue against this point of view, we have to show that words are useful constructs. There are some arguments that seem to show this. However, these arguments do not necessarily show that we must have a level of the word in every language, only that it can be useful in some languages.

First of all, the arguments that were presented in Chapter 4 to show how a word-form can be defined can be turned on their heads. If we have no notion of word, then we cannot state the domains of vowel harmony, cannot state with maximum efficiency the positions where contrastive stress can fall, and so on. There is a danger of circularity here, but not, I think, an insuperable one.

Perhaps the most telling argument, though, is that morpheme ordering in a word can be obligatorily different from morpheme ordering in a sentence. This may be true even where we are probably dealing with the same morphemes. So in English comparatives, mono- and disyllabic adjectives which take the affix -*er* take it suffixed to the adjective, while disyllabic or longer adjectives which take *more* order it before the adjective. Some adjectives may take either form, quite synonymously. Thus the two sentences

(15) Suffixation is commoner than prefixation.
Suffixation is more common than prefixation.

are synonymous, which implies (since the only difference is a difference in the way the comparative has been realised, and the comparative is probably inflectional) that we are dealing with the same morphemes. Nevertheless, the morpheme {comparative} is ordered differently depending on whether it is in the same word-form as *common* or in a different word-form.

Although there are many reasons for seeing morphology and syntax as closely related, and although they may function very largely in similar ways, arguments like this suggest that at least for some languages morphology should be kept separate from syntax.

Nevertheless, there are some areas where it is difficult to draw the distinction. In particular this is true with clitics and compounds.

7. The Domain of Morphology

7.2.1 Clitics. There is a type of obligatorily bound morph which is generally distinguished from an affix. This is the **clitic**, a form which seems to be intermediate between an affix and a word. In the clearest cases (but, unfortunately, not in every case), a clitic is a reduced form of a word with independent existence. The forms *'ve*, *'d*, *'s* and *'ll* as reduced forms of *have, had, has* and *will* respectively are instances of clitics in English.

The problem for the morphologist lies in distinguishing clitics from affixes, since both are bound morphs. There are a number of ways of distinguishing between the two, which will be discussed below. Basically, the distinction is that clitics are more syntactic than are affixes. Since the most syntactic of the affixes are inflectional affixes, the distinction that has to be drawn is between clitics on the one hand, and inflectional affixes on the other.

The criteria for distinguishing between inflectional affixes and clitics, like the criteria for distinguishing between inflection and derivation, do not always define precisely the same set of morphs as clitics, and do not necessarily agree in all cases. Rather, they define the prototypical cases of clitics or inflectional affixes. Actual cases will deviate from the prototype to a greater or lesser extent.

(a) Affixes attach to lexical categories such as nouns, adjectives and verbs. For example, the *-ed* affix which marks the past tense in English attaches to bases which are verbs. Clitics may attach to phrasal categories, although they will always be phonologically attached to a single word in that phrase. The *-'s* formative which marks the possessive in English is a clitic, and illustrates this point. In (16) below, a number of noun phrases are illustrated, each of which contains a possessive noun phrase before the head noun. In every case the *-'s* is attached to the last word in the possessive noun phrase, not simply to the noun.

(16)   a dog's life
         the King of Spain's daughter
         the woman in white's face
         the woman we saw's coat
         the cat which came in's fur
         the man I saw yesterday's hat

(b) As is also evident from the examples in (16), the category of the word to which a clitic attaches itself is usually irrelevant. In the examples above the clitic is attached to a noun, an adjective, a verb and an adverb. Where a clitic is a reduced form of a freely occurring word (such as *'ve* for *have*), the clitic simply occurs wherever the non-reduced word could occur. In contrast, affixes tend to attach to specific categories: the past tense *-ed* marker in

99

English attaches specifically to verbs. This criterion, however, is not always met, since some languages have specific clitic positions where any clitic must be placed. For example, in West Greenlandic, clitic particles usually follow the first sentential constituent, as illustrated in the example below where the particular clitic illustrated indicates that the information expressed was gained at second-hand:

(17) tassa·guuq Kangirlussuatsia·kkut   umiar·passuit
      that-is·clitic (place-name)·case-marker boat·many
      ilummukaa·pput
      move-inwards·3rd-person-indicative
      'Well, it is said many boats came inland by way of K.(fjord)'.

(c) Clitics do not show lexically conditioned allomorphy, while affixes frequently do. The plural in English shows lexically conditioned allomorphy with lexemes such as CHILD, OX, SERAPH, WOMAN and so on. In contrast, the possessive '_s_ does not show lexically conditioned allomorphy. The past tense marker in English is lexically conditioned for verbs such as BE, GO, PUT, SHOOT, SING and so on, but forms of the clitic '_ve_ are not lexically conditioned at all.

(d) Finally, while clitics can attach freely to bases containing affixes or clitics, affixes cannot attach to bases containing clitics. This is illustrated below:

(18) I'd've come
      girls've been seen here
      the dogs' dinners are there, but the cats' 've been eaten
      *cat'ds
      *the man who walk'sed feet

Clitics are divided into **proclitics** which are attached before their base, and **enclitics** which are attached after their base. An example of a proclitic is the French direct object pronoun in sentences like _Claude l'a fait_ 'Claude did it'. An example of an enclitic is Latin _que_ 'and' attached to the second of two conjoined words, as in _Patriam re:gnum· que meum repetere_ 'to reclaim my country and my kingdom'.

7.7.2 Compounds. As was seen in Figure 7.1 on page 92, compounding has links with syntax as well as links with morphology. Some scholars have tried to distinguish, even within English, between those compounds which are the result of morphological processes and those which are the result of syntactic processes. For example, there are some compounds which appear to have a single stress (in the sense discussed in section 4.1.1), while others have two. For example, _apple cake_ is generally agreed to have a single

100

stress, while *apple pie* has two. To a large extent, this coincides with an orthographic distinction between those compounds written as a single orthographic word, and those written as two. There seems to be some feeling, amongst both lay people and linguists, that this orthographic distinction reflects a genuine linguistic distinction of some kind. Since it always comes up in this context, it is worth making the point that hyphenation in English is totally random, and does not necessarily prove anything at all about the linguistic status of strings of elements. To illustrate this, consider the following spellings, found in three different dictionaries:

(19)   girlfriend (Hamlyn's *Encyclopedic World Dictionary*)
         girl-friend (*The Concise Oxford Dictionary*)
         girl friend (Webster's *Third New International Dictionary*).

Presumably we would not want to decide that *girl-friend* is a lexeme for the editors of the Hamlyn's dictionary, but not for the editors of the Webster's. Some linguists seem happy enough to concede GIRLFRIEND (however spelt) as a single lexeme, but are less happy with longer compounds. For example, everyone would probably agree that there is a lexeme TEXTBOOK. What then, about MORPH-OLOGY TEXTBOOK? Is that still a single lexeme? If so, what about MORPHOLOGY TEXTBOOK COVER? And if we have a box that contains these covers, what about MORPHOLOGY TEXTBOOK COVER BOX? Despite conflicting intuitions caused by factors such as the ones just discussed, and despite numerous attempts to provide a scientific basis for these intuitions, it appears that there is no reliable way of drawing distinctions along such lines; for example none of the criteria discussed in Chapter 4 make any distinction between these different kinds of compound. That is not to say that none can be made, and indeed some recent work in Lexicalist Morphology suggests that a distinction between root and synthetic compounds might be drawn on the basis of morphology versus syntax, but this result is not yet generally accepted.

There are at least two arguments in favour of seeing compounding as more closely allied to morphology.

(a) Like derivation, compounding creates new items of vocabulary (that is, lexemes, if this hypothesis is adopted), which appear to be learnt as wholes and used just like any other kind of derived or simplex lexeme. In particular, it is noticeable that speakers do not analyse the internal structure of familiar compounds. To use the noun *hedgehog* you do not have to be aware that its elements imply 'pig which lives in hedges'. In a similar way, to use the derivative *carriage*, you do not have to be able to analyse it as 'nominalisation from CARRY'. Occasionally you get instances

101

where a speaker realises that a compound which has been considered as a unit has an analysable structure, and this is commented on with remarks such as 'I've never thought of that before'.

(b) Like derivatives, compounds provide names for entities, properties or actions. This is opposed to providing descriptions, which is the function of syntax. A derivative like *judo·ist* and a compound like *judo·man* both provide a name for the person concerned, as opposed to a syntactic phrase like 'an expert in judo', which provides a description.

There are other arguments in favour of seeing compounding as being more closely allied with syntax.

(a) Compounds are sequences of lexemes. Any other sequence of lexemes (with the possible exception of idioms, though even they are not totally excluded) is dealt with as syntax and not as morphology. Particularly strong motivation is thus required if one type of lexeme sequence is to be called morphology.

(b) While there are many instances where a compound is remembered and used as an unanalysable unit, as discussed above, there are plenty of other cases where items which are formally indistinguishable are not learned as wholes, but are created on the spur of the moment, and forgotten again immediately. This effect is more noticeable in some languages than in others; for example, it is clearly true of the Germanic languages, but far less true in the Romance languages. A quick glance at any newspaper written in a Germanic language should show the truth of this. An advertisement for a linguistics book on my desk as I write speaks of 'the main issues raised by second language acquisition research', thus coining a compound which is unlikely to be treated as an unanalysable whole.

(c) It is frequently the case that the meaning of a noun plus noun compound is indistinguishable from the meaning of an adjective plus noun phrase. Consider, for example,

(20) atom bomb   atomic bomb
      gold ring   golden ring
      language development   linguistic development
      sea life   marine life
      verb paradigm   verbal paradigm

In cases like those illustrated here, the two constructions appear to be entirely equivalent alternatives. Traditionally, the noun plus noun alternative is seen as part of morphology, the adjective plus noun alternative is seen as part of syntax. While it is possible that there should be such a distinction, it has generally not been as well-motivated as it ought to have been.

102

(d) In other cases, a sequence of noun plus noun is equivalent to a sequence of possessive plus noun. Again similar arguments apply. The latter is usually seen as part of syntax, the former as part of morphology. If there is a genuine distinction, it needs to be well-motivated. Generally, no such motivation is provided. The probability remains, therefore, that they are both structures of the same kind, and that is most likely to mean syntactic structures not morphological ones. Some examples from English to illustrate the parallelism are given below:

(21) birdfoot   bird's foot
      dog house   dog's house
      rat-tail grass   rat's-tail grass
      student evaluations   students' evaluations
      summer day   summer's day
      and contrast, too:
      cat gut   cat's-eye
      cowhide   cow's milk

There are also supporting parallels from other languages. Some of the interfixes used in other Germanic languages are historically derived from (and in some cases are still homophonous with) allomorphs of the morpheme {genitive}. Finnish and Sanskrit both have compounds with genitive first elements.

(e) While it is quite common to find compound prepositions and compounds in other minor categories, it is extremely rare to find prepositions which are created derivationally except by conversion (I know of no such examples). Prepositions may inflect in some languages (e.g. Welsh), but there are no derivational affixes for producing them. Examples of compound forms in minor categories are given below:

(22) *English*   *French*   *Indonesian*
      an·other   le·quel   di·belakang
      because of   the·which   at·back
      any·one   'which'   'behind'
      when·ever   pour·quoi   ke·belakang
      in·to   for·what   to·back
      Finnish   'why'   'behind'
      ett·ei   mal·gré   di·samping
      that·not   bad·liking   at·side
      ell·ei   'despite'   'beside'
      or·not   di·muka
      'unless'   at·front
                                           'in front of'

This suggests that compounding and derivation may be rather different in kind.

There are thus a good many reasons for seeing compounding as being more closely allied with syntax than with derivational morphology. When the linguist builds compounding into a grammar, the relative importance placed on these arguments and the arguments which show the link between morphology and compounding will determine where compounding is dealt with. In current theories, compounding is nearly always dealt with as part of morphology. In either case, the point is made that the dividing line between morphology and syntax is a very fine one, and not necessarily easily drawn.

7.3 Concluding remarks

In this chapter, more questions have been asked than answered. In part this is because many of the questions cannot be answered definitively in a theoretical vacuum, but only in relation to a particular model of grammar. At the moment, as we shall see in the next Part, there are a large number of different models of grammar being used, and a correspondingly large number of ideas about how morphology is to be dealt with in a grammar. In theory, these could range from dealing with morphology entirely as a matter of phonology to dealing with morphology entirely as a matter of syntax. In this chapter it has been hinted that at least for some languages it is going to be far more satisfactory to deal with morphology on its own terms. The models that will be considered in the next Part all do this. What has been shown here is that any morphological component in a grammar cannot be entirely autonomous: it must have close links with both phonology and syntax. How these links are established may well differ from theory to theory. They must exist to account for the rather fuzzy boundaries that morphology seems to have on both sides.

REFERENCES AND FURTHER READING

The matter of when prefixes and the elements of neo-classical compounds can be co-ordinated is dealt with briefly by Quirk *et al.* (1972: 610), where it is discussed in terms of whether the elements concerned are 'loosely' or 'tightly attached'. I know of no research that has tried to pin down this kind of distinction more precisely. It may be connected with lexicalisation, but lexicalisation in itself does not rule out co-ordination, as is shown by the example *ante-* and *post-natal care* given by Quirk *et al.*

The two sentences illustrating the use of *non-* on page 90 are genuine examples, the first from Lawrence Block (1978) *The Burglar in the Closet*, London: Robert Hale, the second is cited in the Supplement to *The Oxford English Dictionary*.

7. The Domain of Morphology

The discussion of Welsh mutation is based on Williams (1980). For further details, and for the syntactic uses of mutations, see that work or any other grammar of a Celtic language.

The matter of affixes and stress is dealt with in considerably more detail in Fudge (1984).

The data on Sanskrit sandhi is taken from Lass (1984). For further discussion of sandhi from a morphological point of view see Matthews (1974: Chapter 6).

The Chrau data in (14) is taken from Thomas (1971). The data from West Greenlandic in (17) is from Fortescue (1984).

The main source on clitics is Zwicky & Pullum (1983). This paper argues interestingly that English *n't* is an inflectional affix and not a clitic. There is also a problem in distinguishing between words and clitics, which is not relevant in the present context. This is treated in Zwicky (1985a). Another useful reference on clitics is Anderson (1985b: 154ff).

The Lexicalist Morphology work on compounds mentioned on page 101 is Botha (1984b).

The point about the lack of distinction between noun plus noun constructions and adjective plus noun constructions is made within Hallidayan grammar, where both count as Classifiers, and is also argued extensively by Levi (1978). She concludes that the appropriate adjective plus noun constructions are types of compound. The alternative conclusion is the one hinted at here: that noun plus noun constructions are syntactic, phrasal constructions.

The data from Finnish is from Karlsson (1983), that from Indonesian is from Kwee (1965).

Part Three: Issues

8. Recognising Morphemes

One of the major problems in morphology is knowing when you are dealing with two realisations of the same morpheme and when two morphs realise different morphemes. At first blush, this may appear to be a trivial matter; the form *cat* realises the morpheme {cat} and the form *dog* realises the morpheme {dog}, and it is intuitively quite clear that these are completely separate morphemes. If one were asked to justify this intuition, one would probably say that the two morphs differ from each other in form and meaning. Unfortunately, this is not enough.

First of all, it must be realised that neither form nor meaning alone is a sufficient criterion. On the basis of form alone we might propose that *cargo* was related to {car} and {go}, that *piety* was related to {pie}, or that *bear* (the animal) and *bare* ('naked') represented the same morpheme. Conversely, on the basis of form alone, we might very well deny that the forms *cacti, cats, caves, cherubim, children* and *mice* realised any common morpheme. On the basis of meaning alone we might propose that forms such as *little, small, tiny, petite, miniscule* shared some morpheme in common. Conversely, we might deny that *escapee* ('one who escapes') and *trainee* ('one who is trained') share any morpheme in common. Yet all these conclusions would be unsatisfactory, if not downright wrong.

More importantly, however, it is not clear how much form or how much meaning must be shared before two morphs can be seen as realisations of the same morpheme. The problem as it relates to meaning has already been illustrated with reference to the suffix *-ette* in section 6.3. The problem as it relates to form will be illustrated repeatedly in this chapter. A simple example is provided by the forms *mother, maternal, matron, mum, mummy* and *mama*. All contain an initial /m/, but they have nothing else in common (although various pairs of these forms have rather more in common). Is this sufficient for us to say that a single morpheme is involved? If not, how many are involved? Problems of this kind become particularly acute where neither the form nor the meaning is unambiguously shared between morphs.

109

The question thus turns out to be far from simple. In the long run, decisions on these matters are likely to be the result of the theoretical approach taken by the individual linguist. However, some guidelines are possible, although the guidelines for affixes and bases are not quite the same.

8.1 Affixes

To make the discussion here more concrete, three sets of data are presented below. In each case a single form is discussed, and in each case it is intuitively fairly clear that the single form represents at least two distinct affixes or morphemes. The clear distinctions are indicated by the columns in which the words are listed. The discussion will then centre on the arguments which support the intuition that we are dealing here with distinct affixes despite the similarity of form.

(1)　(a) earth·en　(b) broad·en
　　　　flax·en　　　damp·en
　　　　gold·en　　　dark·en
　　　　lead·en　　　deaf·en
　　　　silk·en　　　hard·en
　　　　wheat·en　　light·en
　　　　wood·en　　　sick·en
　　　　wool(l)·en　　soft·en

(2)　(a) in·come　(b) in·dependent
　　　　in·door　　　in·direct
　　　　in-house　　in·edible
　　　　in·land　　　in·eligible
　　　　in·lay　　　in·eloquent
　　　　in·put　　　in·equality
　　　　in·set　　　in·sociable
　　　　in·shore　　in·solvent
　　　　　　　　　　in·tangible
　　　　　　　　　　in·transitive

(3)　(a) apple·s　(b) build·s
　　　　cabinet·s　　consider·s
　　　　car·s　　　expect·s
　　　　cat·s　　　hear·s
　　　　curtain·s　　observe·s
　　　　lawn·s　　　provide·s
　　　　pigeon·s　　write·s
　　　　sump·s　　　yield·s

8. Recognising Morphemes

The first, and most obvious, way to distinguish different affixes of similar form is by *meaning*. In (2b), for example, the *in-* means something like 'not, negative', while in (2a), it means something like 'location within'. In (3a) the final *-s* indicates plurality, while in (3b) it indicates '3rd person singular present tense'. A clearly distinct meaning difference, with no possibility of overlap (as in these cases) usually indicates separateness of morphemes. Results are not always so clear, though. In (1) it might be difficult to specify precisely what the meanings are (although something like 'made of' versus something like 'cause to be' seem probable candidates). In other instances, notably in the case of nominalisations of verbs, it can be difficult to specify the meaning of the affix, and to decide what constitutes a distinction in meaning.

A second, again fairly obvious, way to distinguish between affixes is in terms of their *function*. In (1a) the *-en* suffix creates adjectives, while the suffix in (1b) creates verbs. The suffix in (3a) creates nouns, that in (3b) creates verbs. Again this is a useful and fairly easily applied criterion, but again it breaks down in some cases. First of all, the majority of prefixes in English, like the prefixes in (2b) do not have any clear function in terms of creating a particular part of speech: the category of the derivative is the same as the category of the base. This criterion is therefore not always of value when dealing with prefixes in English or languages like it. Secondly, it may not always be clear what the function of an affix is. This can be seen with relation to the *in-* in (2a). *Land* is a noun (possibly a verb, but much more probably a noun in this context) and *inland* is not. The prefix, therefore, has some function in changing category. But *inland* may be an adjective (as in the phrase *inland revenue*), or an adverb (as in *They walked inland for three kilometres*). Should we postulate two distinct morphemes {in-}, one for each of these uses? In general, the answer will be no, as long as the dual function of the derivative is a regular phenomenon. This is the case here with *inboard, inshore*. We might, however, wish to set up other subdivisions of (2a) on the basis of this criterion. Alternatively, we might decide that other uses of these forms were the result of conversion, since English allows widespread conversion.

As well as the category of the new derivative being relevant, the *category of the base* is also a guide. In (1a) the base is in each case a noun, while in (1b) the base is always an adjective. In (3a) the base is always a noun, in (3b) the base is always a verb. The different categories of base help suggest that different affixes could be involved. Again, however, care is required in applying this criterion. In (2b) the prefix *in-* has been applied to adjectives (in the majority of the words listed), but also to nouns. In the case of *inequality*, the most likely analysis is that the prefix has been added to the noun *equality* and not the adjective *equal,* since the established adjective is *unequal* rather than *inequal.* Thus, some affixes may permit classes of base which are wider than a single part of speech. In English this is particularly noticeable with prefixes. In other cases, it may not even be clear what the category of the base is. The prefix *de-* creating verbs such as *delouse, decipher, demast* is generally said to be added to nouns (thus, Marchand, 1969 following *The Oxford English Dictionary*). But in virtually every case a verb homophonous with that noun, albeit rarely as common as that noun, can be found listed in the major dictionaries of English.

It is not only the major category of the base which may be of importance, but also the *restrictions on the base.* For instance, all the bases in (2b) are Latinate, while all of those in (2a) are Germanic in origin. In other cases there may be phonological or semantic restrictions on bases, as discussed in section 5.5.1.

The *range of allomorphs* displayed by an affix can also be relevant. The prefix *in-* illustrated in (2b) has a number of different allomorphs, both in the written and spoken forms (the allomorphs in the written forms do not correspond in a one-to-one manner with allomorphs in the spoken forms, but that is irrelevant for present purposes). In particular, there is an allomorph *il-* (/ɪ/) which occurs before bases beginning in /l/, as in *illegible, illegitimate.* The prefix illustrated in (2a) has no such allomorph, as can be seen from *inland, inlay.* The different range of allomorphs in similar conditioning environments seems to indicate fairly clearly that two distinct affixes are involved here. On the other hand, the parallel sets of allomorphs shown in (3a) and (3b) do not in themselves indicate that the same affix is involved in the two cases.

As well as the range of forms an affix may take, *the form it imposes on the base* can be a relevant criterion. There are two examples of this in (1) and (2), but neither of them is particularly convincing. The first concerns the stress on *in-house.* There is greater stress retained on the second morph of this word, than there is in any of the others listed (*inshore* is the one that comes nearest to it). This difference in the stress pattern apparently caused by the prefix may be sufficient to indicate that this word does not realise the same {in-} as the others in (2a). Indeed, it may be a compound rather than a prefix. The example is not particularly convincing because there could be other explanations for the difference, always assuming that the difference is a consistent one in the first place. The other example concerns the word *earthen* in (1a). The voiceless dental fricative at the end of the base has become voiced here, apparently under the influence of the affix. In words which may contain the same suffix as that illustrated in (1b) (despite the major category of the base) such as *lengthen* and *strengthen*, there is no corresponding voicing of the dental fricative. This suggests that a different affix is involved. In both these cases, the examples would be more convincing if it could be shown that the condition was general over a wide range of examples. Really good examples are hard to find from English, but consider the case of two distinct -*y* suffixes. The first of these forms adjectives from either nouns or verbs, as in *summery, jittery*. The second forms nouns, especially from learned words, and especially from nouns, as in *democracy, diplomacy, spectroscopy*. Now, with this second suffix, the stress shifts away from the place where it would fall on the base (*democrat, diplomat, spectroscope*, respectively). With the first -*y* suffix, the adjective-forming one, this does not happen even in the rare cases where the word becomes long enough to allow stress-shift, as in the forms *coronetty, other-worldy*. This shows a case where homophonous suffixes impose a different form to the base, in that the first does not alter the stress pattern of the base, while the second does. For further discussion of stress in English word-formation see, for example, Fudge (1984).

Different affixes may also *potentiate different subsequent affixation*. **Potentiate** in this context is a technical term which means 'create a base suitable for'. In most cases this potentiation will be a by-product of the major category of the derivative. For example, the suffix in (1b) potentiates subsequent -*ing* affixation because it creates verbs. In other cases potentiation may be more subtle, and correspondingly more useful in distinguishing between affixes. For instance, the prefix *en-* which creates verbs from adjectives as in *endear, ennoble* appears to potentiate -*ment* suffixation (*endearment, ennoblement*), whereas the prefix with the same form, which creates verbs from verbs, such as *enclose, encounter, entreat* does not always potentiate -*ment* in the same way (?*enclosement*, ?*encounterment*, ?*entreatment*).

Finally, different affixes may *show different degrees of productivity*. The negative *in-* illustrated in (2b) is now of very restricted productivity (at least when added to adjectives), and the prefix *un-* tends to be used instead (Marchand, 1969: section 3.26). The prefix or prefixes illustrated in (2a), on the other hand, are still productive, as can be seen by consulting any dictionary of new words. In (3a) and (3b) the two affixes are both extremely productive (possibly fully productive in the more restricted sense of this term, see above section 5.5), without that indicating that they are the same affix.

On the other side of the coin are affixes which are not homophonous, and which at first glance are likely to be judged separate affixes. Homophony in itself, however, is not sufficient to allow a decision to be made one way or another. If homophony were the only reason for judging relatedness, the prefixes in the Indonesian examples in (4) below would have to be seen as realising separate unrelated morphemes.

(4)   men·duga   'to suspect'
       meng·gunting   'to cut (with scissors)'
       mem·buru   'to hunt'

The fact is, that all these prefixes realise the same morpheme. There are thus extra factors which have to be taken into account: *distribution* and *conditioning*.

The general rule is that only forms (putative allomorphs) in complementary distribution can be taken to realise a single morpheme. This is the case for the examples in (4), where *men-* occurs before *d*, *meng-* occurs before *g*, and *mem-* occurs before *b*. The final nasal of the prefix is homorganic with the voiced stop which follows it, and the allomorphs are thus in complementary distribution. Complementary distribution on its own, naturally enough, is not sufficient. The prefix *de-* in English is added only to verbs (*decapacitate, demagnetise*) while the prefix *a-* (*amoral, atypical*) is added only to adjectives. They are thus in complementary distribution, but would not be seen as allomorphs of the same morpheme. For morphs to be viewed as allomorphs of the same morpheme, they must not only be in complementary distribution, but also fit all the other conditions that have already been discussed in this section. It is easier to see forms as allomorphs if the reason for the change in form is apparent; that is, if the allomorphy is phonetically conditioned. Lexical conditioning is possible, but usually restricted to very specific circumstances.

The circumstances where lexical conditioning is generally accepted are also occasions where strict complementary distribution seems not to be required. It is in the case of inflectional systems. Consider the data in (5).

(5)   ?alumnuses   alumni
       brothers   brethren
       bureaus   bureaux
       campuses   *campi
       *childs   children
       fishes   fish
       formulas   formulae
       indexes   indices
       *mans   men

114

octopuses	octopodes
*oxes	oxen
seraphs	seraphim
?stratums	strata
tempos	tempi
*thesises	theses
ultimatums	?ultimata

(for other examples see Quirk *et al*, 1972: 181ff)

In some of the cases illustrated in (5) only a regular plural is in general use, in some cases only an irregular plural is in general use, and in some cases both the regular and irregular plurals are in general use (occasionally distinguished in meaning). Obviously the various affixes that are used to indicate plurality are not completely in complementary distribution. Neither is it the case that the various affixes resemble each other formally. However, because we are dealing with an inflectional (and therefore closed) system, because we have a large majority of regular cases and a well defined meaning which is also carried by the irregular forms, because we have a very general paradigm so that we expect to find the same morpheme marked on the nouns which show (optionally or obligatorily) the irregular affixes, we still say that there is a single morpheme {plural} which is realised by this range of affixes. Note that this distinction makes crucial appeal to a distinction between inflectional and derivational morphology. It seems unlikely that such a disparate range of suffixes would be attributed to a single morpheme if that morpheme was derivational (though Anderson, 1982: 585 does make such a suggestion: see the brief discussion at the end of section 6.4 above). Those scholars who do not distinguish between inflection and derivation are thus likely to face problems in relation to points such as this.

8.2 Bases

It might appear that the problems with bases would be very similar to the problems with affixes. There is a major difference, though, which effectively means that bases are a separate problem: while affixes are generally recognised because they recur with a range of bases, bases are far more idiosyncratic in their behaviour and do not show regular patterns of occurrences with affixes. The same basic point remains true with bases as with affixes: generally speaking a single morpheme will retain a constant shape (or a limited range of related forms) and a constant meaning (or a limited range of related meanings). This, however, is open to a wide variety of interpretations.

115

Interestingly enough, most of the work in this area has been done not by morphologists but by phonologists, since it is of importance to the area of morphophonology, where the two overlap. Discussion of this area therefore demands some basic knowledge in a rather wider area of linguistics than just morphology. Most of the phonologists working in the tradition of generative phonology accept some version of the Unique Underlier Condition (the term is from Lass, 1984). This states that every morpheme has a single underlying morphophonemic representation, except in cases of suppletion. The reasons for this were discussed briefly in section 7.1. This view of the phonology implies that the analyst knows which morphs should be classed together as a single morpheme. In many languages there is no problem here, but English has a particularly complex morphophonology, with the result that many conflicting suggestions have been put forward. These are usually discussed in phonology texts under the heading of **abstractness.** Underlying phonological representations (underliers) which differ from the surface morphs are considered to be more abstract than those which have the same form as the surface morphs. The greater the difference between the underliers and the surface morphs or the greater the proportion of morphs that have abstract underliers, the more abstract the phonology is deemed to be. Underliers which are identical to the surface morphs are said to be **concrete,** in contrast.

The abstract end in this debate is represented by Lightner (1975, 1981, 1983). Lightner's position is basically that the underliers for English morphemes should be at least as abstract as the reconstructed morpheme in Proto-Indo-European, and that more abstract analyses would be permissible if we knew more about the history of the language. As he says (1981: 96):

> To do a synchronic analysis of N[ew] E[nglish] – at least for phonology and D[erivational] M[orphology] – we have to return to 3000 B.C. It is painfully clear that those who thought PIE a primitive form of language were in error. Yet without older texts than we have or without some new concept we cannot go further back.

Yet the reconstruction of underliers as abstract as this is supposed to be based not primarily on etymological knowledge but on a form of internal reconstruction. It will, according to Lightner, become clear to the analyst that there are forms in English which are related in meaning, and also by regular sound correspondences. For example, the pairs listed below would be partial evidence for a correspondence reflecting Grimm's Law.

116

(6)   canine   hound
      cornucopia   horn
      decade   ten
      dental   tooth
      genus   kin
      paternal   father
      pedal   foot
      pipe   fife
      triple   three

Lightner would then build Grimm's Law into his phonology, and
say that morphs like *foot* and *ped* (in *pedal, pedestrian* and the
like) realise the same morpheme. (Note that the fact that *pipe* and
fife are not historically related by Grimm's Law in the same kind
of way as the other examples is irrelevant, since internal and not
historical reconstruction is involved). The result of this position is
that the meaning of morphemes has to be extremely widely specified,
and has to allow for metaphorical extension and diachronic change.
For example, Lightner (1975: 621) suggests that all the words in
(7) below and many others should be derived from a morpheme
{reg} with a meaning something like 'lead straight, guide, conduct'.

(7)   direct
      ergo
      incorrigible
      regal
      regular
      reign
      right
      rule

A position at the other extreme is taken by Vennemann (1974).
He claims that no roots or affixes should be listed in the lexicon
at all, but the smallest item listed in the lexicon as an underlier
should be a word-form. This position is motivated by arguments
internal to the phonological theory Vennemann espouses, but is
basically an attempt to give a specified level of abstraction which
underliers may not exceed.

From the morphologist's point of view, neither of these extremes
appears very attractive. Lightner's extreme abstractness seems to
stretch what is meant by 'morphology' so far beyond its traditional
boundaries that it becomes unrecognisable. In particular, if Lightner's position is accepted it becomes impossible to formulate firm
guidelines on the level of semantic relatedness required before two
morphs can be said to realise the same morpheme. This would

mean that relatedness of form would be the only available criterion, and yet it was argued above that it is not enough to consider relatedness of form without relatedness of meaning. It also seems to be the case within Lightner's view of the grammar that the only way to distinguish the positions in which the various allomorphs of a super-abstract Lightnerian morpheme can occur is by means of lexical listing: there is no phonological or morphological way of distinguishing between a *semidemisemiquaver* and a *hemidemisemiquaver*, for example; the distinction must be marked lexically. This implies that Lightner's lexicon will need a full list of lexemes as well as a full list of morphemes, and the list of morphemes will thus be entirely redundant. Economy (the guideline of linguists such as Lightner) thus argues against such a solution.

On the other hand, Vennemann's extreme concreteness appears to deny morphological productivity by listing productively generated forms on a par with non-productive and suppletive forms. Since it is the basic insight of morphology that word-forms can be analysed into morphs with a consistent form-meaning correlation, this viewpoint seems to negate everything that morphology is concerned with. The morphologist, therefore, is really looking for some degree of abstractness which is intermediate between the two extremes.

The difficulty is that there is no obvious and clearly defined middle ground. In a series of publications, Derwing (1973, 1976; Derwing & Baker, 1979) has shown that there is a cline of relatedness on both phonetic and semantic axes, so that words may be more or less closely related either semantically or phonetically. Abstracting from examples given in the works referred to above, the kind of pattern that can be seen in Table 1 emerges.

Table 1 is not very finely graduated. It would be possible to motivate many more steps on both scales. Yet even with the small amount of data given here it becomes clear that there is no obvious point at which a cut-off line can be drawn, so that the forms on one side of it are said to realise morphemes in common, while those on the other side are said not to. While it might be possible to go through any such list of words and say 'I personally feel that these contain/do not contain realisations of the same morpheme', or even (following Derwing) to test whether a sample of native speakers of English feel that there is a common morpheme involved or not, this does not provide any motivated way of drawing a distinction.

Part of the problem with discussions of this area is that any conclusions depend crucially on the individual researcher's notion

Table 1: Semantic and Phonetic Relatedness of Words

Examples from the works of Derwing cited in the text. The most clearly related words on both axes are at the top left, the least related at the bottom right.

Phonetic relatedness	Clear	Intermediate	Unclear
Semantic relatedness			
Clear	quiet	sheep	father
	quietly	shepherd	paternal
	erase	berry	cat
	eraser	strawberry	kitten
Intermediate	skin	spin	beard
	skinny	spider	barber
	wonder	fable	sister
	wonderful	fabulous	sorority
Unclear	bug	gypsy	lead
	buggy	Egyptian	plumber
	ear	crane	lean
	eerie	cranberry	ladder

of what Linguistics as a whole is doing. Again there are two extreme positions. At one end of the scale there are instrumentalists or 'hocus-pocus' linguists. Such linguists think that their description of a linguistic phenomenon has simply to provide an account of forms that are or have been or could be produced by native speakers of the language, with no implication whatsoever that the account provided will bear any relationship to the way in which speakers actually use the language themselves. Perhaps the extreme formulation of this point of view was Householder's (1966: 100) celebrated (or notorious) remark that 'A linguist who could not devise a better grammar than is at present in any speaker's brain ought to try another trade'. At the other end of the scale are the realists or 'God's truth' linguists, who feel that any description is correct to the extent that it is congruent with the way in which native speakers actually use their language. For such linguists the 'psychological reality' of the units and mechanisms they postulate is of prime importance.

Lightner is fundamentally an instrumentalist, while Derwing, with his insistence on testing the actual behaviour of native speakers, is a realist. Their different approaches to morphology are partly, at any rate, determined by these underlying philosophical attitudes. Any compromise position between the extreme abstractness of Lightner and the extreme concreteness of Vennemann is also going to be conditioned by the philosophical attitude of the linguist. Instrumentalists will search for a compromise which shows maximum generality and theoretical coherence; realists will look for a compromise which can best be shown to reflect native speaker behaviour. The two compromises may have little in common. In addition, not only is a compromise between abstractness and concreteness possible, but also one between extreme realism and extreme instrumentalism. It is thus rather dangerous to attempt to formulate a compromise position for theoretical as well as practical reasons. Nevertheless, this will be attempted in the next section.

8.3 A proposal for limiting abstractness

The proposal to be put forward in this section is one which I have advanced in a number of publications (Bauer, 1978a, 1978b, 1983), and it is controversial. It is basically a compromise solution, and one which suffers the drawbacks of all compromises: it pleases no-one entirely. On the other hand, it does permit a motivated line to be drawn limiting abstractness without going to either of the extremes discussed in the last section.

The proposal is that no underlier may be more abstract than is required to handle productive processes. Only productive processes should be handled by rules. Non-productive processes should not be acknowledged in the grammar, but their products listed separately in the lexicon.

This means that the examples listed in (6) would not be related by the grammar, because Grimm's Law is no longer a productive process in modern English. Forms like *foot* and *ped* would correspondingly not be derived from a single underlier: they would not be considered to be allomorphs of the same morpheme. As a result, FOOT and PEDAL can be considered separate lexemes, related in meaning, but not related in the morphology. On the other hand, the process illustrated in (8) below, is still a productive one. Names with *-on* /ən/ in their last syllable are pronounced with /əun/ rather than /ən/ when the suffix *-ian* is added to produce an adjective from those names. So if a Mrs Robinson left a bequest to fund an art gallery, it might well be called the *Robinsonian Gallery*, pronounced /rɒbɪnsəunɪən/. The underlier for a name like *Robinson* thus has to be abstract enough to allow this allomorphy by rule, and *Robinson* and *Robinsonian* are related by the morphology in a grammar.

8. Recognising Morphemes

(8)   Amazon   Amazonian
       Babylon   Babylonian
       Bacon   Baconian
       Bergson   Bergsonian
       Johnson   Johnsonian

The big advantage of this proposal is that it provides a motivated level of abstractness between the two extremes previously discussed. It was shown in Table 1 on page 119 that there is no obvious way that a line can be drawn between related and unrelated morphs in terms of meaning or phonetic shape, so some other measure is required. Productivity provides this alternative measure. Moreover, any discussion of morphology is going to have to make appeal to productivity for other reasons anyway (as was seen in Chapter 5). For realists there is the added attraction that productivity appears to have correlates in actual linguistic behaviour. Speakers are sensitive to productivity when asked to judge the acceptability of new words (Anshen & Aronoff, 1981; Aronoff, 1980). Aphasics sometimes replace unproductive affixes with productive ones, and one of the signs of language death appears to be a confusion between productive and unproductive processes which are otherwise kept apart (Dressler, 1977).

The major disadvantage of this proposal, from the point of view of the instrumentalist at least, is the loss of generalisation. Many affixation patterns in a language like English are analysable without. being productive (see the discussion in Chapter 5). One example from English is the variations in form of bases arising from the results of the Great Vowel Shift. Some examples are given below:

(9)   chaste   chast·ity
       divine   divin·ity
       jocose   jocos·ity
       profound   profund·ity
       serene   seren·ity

This root allomorphy is widespread in English, and is to a large extent predictable (as witness the discussions in Chomsky & Halle, 1968 and other studies within the same framework), yet it is no longer productive. Correspondingly, if the proposal in this section is adopted, this allomorphy will not be dealt with in the morphology, but each of the words in (9) will be listed separately in the lexicon. Precisely how such words should be treated will be taken up briefly in Chapter 13.

From the realist's point of view, it must also be admitted that there is a certain amount of evidence that language users are not

121

always sensitive to productivity. Wheeler & Schumsky (1980), for example, found that informants failed to segment even forms such as *baker, citizenship* and *kingdom* into morphs, despite the fact that all the suffixes in these words are productive. The evidence is suggestive rather than conclusive, but indicates that even realists might not be completely happy with the proposal being made here.

The discussion in this section has been in terms of limiting abstractness (and thus grammatically acknowledged allomorphy) in bases, but there are also implications in terms of affixes. Affixes which are no longer productive would, on this proposal, no longer be acknowledged as forming separate morphemes. Thus all words containing the nominalisation suffix *-th* (see examples (5) and (6) in Chapter 5) would be listed in the lexicon on a par with monomorphemic lexemes. Note again that the distinction between analysable and productive is crucial here. This may seem counter-intuitive, in that the suffix is clearly analysable in a word like *warmth*. However, it was shown earlier that there are words ending in *-th* where the affix is far less obvious to the naive speaker of English (words like *dearth, month* and so on), and we have also seen in this chapter that it is hard to draw a motivated line between those morphs which should be seen as related to a single morpheme, and those which should be seen as related to more than one morpheme (or indeed as not realising a morpheme at all). Using productivity as a guide allows a clear decision for all these words. It also allows us to explain in some sense why so many of these words should show unpredictable root allomorphy (*long/length*, *moon/month*, *wide/width*). If there is no rule generating a set of alternations and the words are individually listed in the lexicon there is no longer a link in the grammar between the base forms and the variant allomorphs, so that this is no longer grammatically predictable, but only predictable in terms of internal reconstruction; also, it is then possible for the words to change their form diachronically without reference to the form of the original base word.

In conclusion, although it would be naive to suggest that the proposal for limiting abstractness and grammatically recognised allomorphy presented here can solve all the problems associated with this area of enquiry, it does provide a coherent point of view with a level of abstractness that is well-motivated from the morphological side. In that sense, it is perhaps one of the most hopeful developments in the search for a limit to abstractness in grammar.

REFERENCES AND FURTHER READING

The problem of the meaning of affixes, and that of the meaning of nominalisation affixes in particular, is discussed in Bauer (1983: section 6.7).

8. Recognising Morphemes

The discussion of potentiation of *-ment* by *en-* is based on Williams (1981: 250), from where the term 'potentiation' is also taken. However, matters are more complex than is revealed there. Firstly, *en-* added to a nominal base does not always potentiate *-ment* suffixation (*encouragement* is quite normal, but *?enrobement, ?enwallment*). Secondly, it is frequently difficult to know whether the prefix has been added to a noun or a verb (*enlist*). Thirdly, even with adjectives the potentiation does not appear to work all the time: *ensurement* does not seem usual to me. Fourthly, there are problems anyway with *-ment*, which may no longer be productive (Bauer, 1983: 49, 55). This means that we may be dealing with a historical potentiation, which no longer holds. The basic point, however, remains true: if the same form in different uses potentiates different subsequent affixation, it is an argument for seeing two distinct affixes.

Dictionaries of new words include Barnhart *et al* (1973; 1980) and the Supplement to *The Oxford English Dictionary.*

The Indonesian example in (4) is from Kwee (1965). The situation in Indonesian is actually more complex than is illustrated in (4), because base-initial voiceless stops are deleted after the assimilation has taken place, and because [s] is treated for the purposes of the assimilation as a palatal consonant. The basic complementary distribution holds, though.

The question of affixes being recurrent forms is an interesting one. Consider forms of English such as *laugh·ter, bishop·ric.* To all intents and purposes the suffixes here do not recur, and yet we would probably wish to call them suffixes despite that. Words which start off as non-recurrent parts of other words turn into suffixes diachronically: *alcoholic* gives rise to *workoholic, chocoholic, spendaholic* etc. It thus seems that affixes need not be recurrent for us to analyse them as affixes. Precisely what qualities they do need is an open question. Note, though, that if the proposal for limiting abstractness discussed in this chapter is adopted, all unique morphs will only be listed in the lexicon as parts of larger words.

The use of productivity as a guide to what should be listed in the lexicon is also adopted within Functional Grammar (Dik, 1980: 25-8), although in that framework it is not restricted to morphology. I would subscribe to Dik's position here that unproductive syntactic structures should also be lexically listed (for example, *if you please* is not derived by productive syntax, and should be listed in the lexicon as a unit). This takes us beyond what is directly relevant to this chapter. The same position on productivity and the lexicon can be read into the work of Aronoff (1976), but it is not usually specifically allowed for in Lexicalist writings.

9. Lexicalist Morphology

The main reason for the resurgence of interest in morphology in the 1970's and 80's has almost certainly been the amount of attention paid to morphology – especially derivational morphology – by linguists of the Chomskyan school. There is still considerable debate among these linguists about the precise nature of morphological operations, and how they are best treated in a grammar, so it is not possible at the moment to give a clear well-defined outline of their approach to morphology. Nevertheless, most of these linguists appear to share certain assumptions about the way in which morphology should be included in a grammar, and to agree that there are some specific areas which require further elucidation. It is thus possible to outline some of the basic tenets of this school, and to say something about these areas of agreement. For a more complete discussion of the work on morphology that has been carried out by these linguists, the student is referred to Scalise (1984), which gives a clear account of the way in which the study of morphology in this kind of framework has developed. Since the primary tenet of this school is that derivational morphology at least (and possibly also inflectional morphology) must be dealt with in the lexicon, we can refer to this school as the school of Lexicalist Morphology.

9.1 Why the lexicon?

In the early days of Transformational Grammar, it was axiomatic that two sentences or parts of sentences which were related in meaning but differed from each other formally in terms of order of elements or presence versus absence of a few specifiable morphemes were transformationally related to each other. The classic example is the passive transformation, which relates pairs of sentences such as

(1)   The fat cat swallows the milk.
        The milk is swallowed by the fat cat.

These two sentences, obviously related in meaning, were related formally by a series of operations which could be generalised and

125

summarised in a transformational rule of the following kind:

(2)   NP   V + tense   NP
        1   2   3   4 ⟹ 4 BE + 3 2 + ed BY 1

This rule changes the order of the elements numbered 1, 2, 3 and 4, but also specifies the morpheme {past participle} (shown by *ed* in (2)) and the lexemes BE and BY. Given this general approach to such matters, it was inevitable that pairs such as those in (3) which involve morphological considerations should also be treated in the same way:

(3)   Robin is devoted to her mother.
        Robin's devotion to her mother.

Pairs such as these were also derived from a common underlying structure by different sets of transformational rules. This is the approach that was taken in Lees (1960).

However, it gradually became clear that there were problems with this kind of approach, some of which were discussed in Chomsky (1970). Chomsky considered the case of derived nominalisations in English such as *destruction, marriage, trial*. He argued that such nominalisations were irregular both semantically and morphologically. They were irregular semantically in that there was not precisely the same change of meaning between the verb and the nominalisation in each case. That is, the semantic relationship between *destroy* and *destruction* is not the same as that which holds between *marry* and *marriage* or *try* and *trial*. Yet it was fundamental to the Chomskyan approach that transformations do not change meaning (a corollary to the position that paraphrases are related by transformation). If these derived nominalisations were to be created by syntactic transformation, they would thus be breaking a constraint on such rules. Thus it was argued that the rules which create nominalisations are not just like other transformations.

This conclusion is supported by the fact that for some verbs there are two nominalisations which do not mean the same thing:

(4)   approve   approval   approbation
        commit   committal   commitment
        employ   employ   employment
        join   junction   juncture

In pairs like these there is no fixed correlation between the meaning and the form of the nominalisation, so that any transformation that tries to link form and meaning will prove impossible, even without considering the more general constraint.

Chomsky also pointed out that further problems arise from the transformational analysis of derived nominalisations because there are many sentences which do not have a corresponding derived nominalisation. For instance, although (5a) corresponds to (5b), there is no (5d) to correspond to (5c).

(5)   (a) Kim was amused at the children's antics.
      (b) Kim's amusement at the children's antics.
      (c) Robin amused the children with stories.
      (d) *Robin's amusement of the children with stories.

To this we can add that there are a number of nominalisation affixes whose distribution is not predictable, that there are verbs which have no derived nominalisation at all (verbs such as *come, eat, open, see*), and that some words which look like nominalisations have no corresponding verb: *exigency, invultuation, notion, tutelage*.

All of this makes it very difficult to postulate any transformations which have general applicability. Yet one of the aims of writing transformational rules should be precisely to make sure that they apply to as many potential input strings as possible (ideally all potential input strings). Again the conclusion is that these nominalisations should not be generated by ordinary syntactic transformations.

There are also other reasons for saying that the rules of morphology are different in kind from the rules of syntax. It is generally accepted that rules of syntax do not make appeal to phonological structure, and do not need to make reference to the output of phonological rules. In contrast, there are many instances of morphological rules requiring phonological information before they can apply. One example was given in section 5.5. Another concerns the German diminutive suffix *-chen*, which is not added to bases ending in /x/ or /ŋ/ (Fleischer, 1975: 179). Siegel (1974: 163ff) gives several similar examples from English, including a particularly nice example (although a rather marginal one in terms of the English system as a whole) involving formations including *-bloody-* or other expletives. The expletive is always added immediately before a stressed syllable (sometimes a secondary stress, but never before a zero-stressed syllable). Thus *absobloodylutely* is perfectly normal, but not *abbloodysolutely, absolutebloodyly*. This example is striking because most generative phonological theories would see stress as being generated by a series of phonological rules. In such theories, therefore, the stressed syllable cannot be identified until after the appropriate phonological rules have been processed. This is then a very clear case of rules for word-structure depending crucially

127

on phonological structure, and thus being markedly different from syntactic rules.

If nominalisations are not to be derived from their corresponding verb by a syntactic transformation, then some other way must be found of stating in the grammar the relationship between strings such as those in (3) and (5a, b). Clearly there are at least semantic relationships which hold between the members of such pairs. There are also close parallels of subcategorisation of a type which were traditionally captured in the transformational relationship. If we consider a verb and its corresponding nominalisation it is frequently (though not always) the case that the same kind of subject and object can occur with both, and that where the verb takes a direct object, the nominalisation takes the preposition *of* (this is a typical pattern, but not an exceptionless one: Bauer, 1983: 81). This is illustrated below:

(6)   (a)   Kim caroused until the stars faded from the sky.
       (b)   Kim's carousal lasted until the stars faded from the sky.
       (c)   *Kim caroused the whole bottle/his friends.
       (d)   *Kim's carousal of the whole bottle/his friends.
       (e)   Pat refused entry to everyone.
       (f)   Pat refused to come home.
       (g)   *Pat refused that he would come home.
       (h)   Pat's refusal of entry to everyone.
       (i)   Pat's refusal to come home.
       (j)   *Pat's refusal that he would come home.
       (k)   Sam laughed at the joke.
       (l)   *Sam laughed the joke.
       (m)   Sam's laughter at the joke.
       (n)   *Sam's laughter (of) the joke.

Relationships like these need to be captured somehow, and Chomsky's answer is that they should be captured in the lexicon. He suggests that there should be a 'neutral lexical entry' which is neither completely specified as a verb nor as a corresponding nominalisation, and that such matters as subcategorisation should be dealt with in this neutral entry. In such a system, it seems natural that the rules relating the form of the verbs to the form of the nominalisation should also be somewhere in the lexicon, possibly as redundancy rules as suggested by Jackendoff (1975).

Most subsequent work in Lexicalist Morphology appears to have by-passed the suggestion for a neutral lexical entry, while adopting the suggestion that derived nominals should be dealt with in the lexicon. In either case, there does not seem to be any pressing need to handle nominalisations in the lexicon rather than, say, in a separate morphological component of the grammar. There may not be any distinction between these two suggestions: it is perfectly possible to have a morphological component which is relatively autonomous and yet seen as being within the lexicon. There are various possibilities here for alternative ways of organising the grammar. The alternatives may look extremely different from each other without differing substantially, or making any different empirical claims. What is crucial is that (a) the rules which form nominalisations are not ordinary syntactic transformational rules and (b) they must still allow generalisations to be made about verbs and their nominalisations.

It should be noted that this discussion has been carried out purely in terms of verbs and their nominalisations. The assumption is made in Lexicalist Morphology that the argument extends to all derivational morphology. This could be seen as controversial, given that the morphology of nominalisations (at least in English) is considerably less regular than that found in other constructions; but generally this assumption has been accepted without comment.

9.2 The function of a morphology

The goal of a morphology is set out by Aronoff (1976: 17-8) in the following terms:

> Just as the simplest goal of a syntax is the enumeration of the class of possible sentences of a language, so the simplest task of a morphology, the least we demand of it, is the enumeration of the class of possible words of a language

or, in rather different terms, (1976: 19):

> It [is] the task of a morphology to tell us what sort of new words a speaker can form.

This means that theoretically (although regrettably not always in practice) the study of actually attested words is, for the Lexical Morphologists, only a guide to potential words, the real subject of their study. This is precisely the view-point that was espoused in section 5.3. In the jargon of Lexicalist Morphology, this means that we need an **overgenerating morphology** (Allen, 1978), i.e. one which generates more words than are familiar to any particular individual, or than are to be found in any particular reference book, even words which are not likely to be found because of blocking. The basic idea behind an overgenerating morphology is that it should allow everything to be generated that is not excluded by some principled restriction on the form of a rule.

129

9. Lexicalist Morphology

9.3 Full entry theory

Despite (or perhaps rather, because of) the acceptance of the idea of an overgenerating morphology, most Lexicalist Morphologists seem to operate with some version of a **full entry theory** of the lexicon. According to this, every word which 'exists' is listed in the lexicon. For some Lexicalist Morphologists (e.g. Lieber, 1981; Selkirk, 1982) stems and affixes are also listed in a lexicon (not necessarily in the same list as the 'existing' words), while for others this is not a requirement (e.g. Aronoff, 1976). Precisely how the full entry lexicon is used varies from scholar to scholar. For Halle (1973) the lexicon is preceded by a filter on the output of word-formation rules (usually abbreviated as WFRS), and makes sure that only 'existing' words are entered in the lexicon, and thus used in sentences. For Jackendoff (1975), the full entry lexicon acts as a domain in which lexical redundancy rules operate, linking verbs with their nominalisations in non-generative ways, for example. For Aronoff (1976) the WFRS act as 'once only' rules, generating forms which are then listed in the lexicon. According to this theory WFRS are distinct from syntactic rules, in that while syntactic rules apply every time the appropriate construction is used, WFRS do not: they apply only when a word is originally coined. The full entry theory of the lexicon has certain advantages if it is considered in realist terms, since it explains why it is perfectly possible for an individual speaker to know two words and be able to use them without being aware of the derivational relationship that holds between them. *Dear* and *dearth* would come into this category for many people (see the discussion in section 8.2 in general). Even if no realist claims are to be made for the model, this remains a very sensible approach to dealing with non-productive morphology. But what about productive uses of morphology?

Jackendoff (1975) is not primarily concerned with productive morphology, but he does make some relevant comments. For example he admits (1975: 667) that

> it is quite common for someone to invent a new compound noun spontaneously and to be perfectly understood

and yet from there he goes on to state that

> the normal mode for syntactic rules is creative, the normal mode for lexical rules is passive.

Jackendoff's idea is that morphology is used productively so infrequently that the few occasions when this does happen can be dismissed as exceptional cases of analytical redundancy rules being turned on their heads and used abnormally. The norm is for morpho-

130

logical rules to be used to analyse 'existing' forms. This deserves further comment. It is ironic that Jackendoff should have cited compound nouns as his test case, since some figures are actually available on these in German, and they do not support his contention. Thiel (1973) reports on a count of compound nouns from the weekly paper *Die Zeit*, where in a corpus of 1331 compound nouns only 37.9% were found listed in dictionaries, while 62.1% were neologisms. This scarcely supports the notion that the creative use of compounding rules is in some way not normal. It has, of course, been shown that there are reasons for saying that compounding is a very syntactic kind of process (see above, section 7.2.2). Jackendoff's point would undoubtedly be more effectively made with respect to derivatives. Even here, though, Jackendoff appears to be dismissing the quite considerable productivity that various types of affix show. This is striking enough in English, but even more striking in a language like Eskimo, where derivational affixes abound and the chance of a speaker having heard or used a particular derivative in his or her previous experience becomes vanishingly low. Consider, for example, a West Greenlandic example like the following, where all the affixes except the last one are derivational (Fortescue, 1984):

(7)   puu·ssa·qar·ti·nngil·ara
        bag·future·have·causative·negative·1st-singular-3rd-
        singular-indicative
        'I have no bag for it'

This dismissal of productivity is even more striking with reference to inflectional affixes. Following Halle (1973) Jackendoff (1975: 665) suggests that

> paradigmatic information should be represented in the dictionary. As a consequence, the lexical insertion rules must enter partial or complete paradigms into deep structures, and the rules of concord must have the function of filtering out all but the correct forms, rather than that of inserting inflectional affixes.

For a language like English such a proposal seems entirely plausible. In Finnish, however, the maximal nominal paradigm contains about 2,000 distinct forms, and the maximal verbal paradigm over 12,000 when cliticised forms are included, and 150 and 850 respectively if cliticised forms are excluded (Karlsson & Koskenniemi, 1985: 210-1). In a case like this, Jackendoff's proposal seems computationally inefficient, whether it is intended as a psychologically real statement of speaker behaviour, or simply as an instrumentalist

131

model. It is worth quoting Karlsson & Koskenniemi (1985: 212) at length in this context:

> For analytic languages such as English, [the Full Entry Hypothesis] is perhaps possible to defend, the main reason being that lexemes have so few forms. Now consider the situation in morphologically rich languages like Finnish. It makes little sense to claim that all the 150 nominal and 850 verbal paradigm members (of all nouns and verbs, respectively) would be independent lexical entries. First, this would amount to the strange claim that the Finnish lexicon is hundreds of times larger than the English one. Second, there would be no convincing account of how language users are capable of acquiring, understanding and producing forms of new words they have not heard before. One would have to hypothesize e.g. that it happens by internally generating and storing all the core forms. But this would imply storing some 850 forms upon learning a new verb. Only a handful of these are likely to be used at all. Some 800 forms would be strange inhabitants of the lexicon: never heard and never used in speech production.

It thus seems that the Lexicalist model needs to be modified to deal appropriately with productive morphology, perhaps particularly in languages like Finnish, but probably in general.

9.4 Strata in the morphology

It is a well-known fact about English that it contains two distinct types of affix. The first type, generally Germanic in origin, does not affect the stress-pattern of the base to which it is attached. This type of affix is therefore sometimes termed 'neutral' (Chomsky & Halle, 1968). In generative phonology it is associated with a strong '#-boundary'. The other type of affix is called 'non-neutral' and associated with a weaker '+-boundary'. It is generally Latinate in origin and is associated with a change in stress-pattern in the base to which it is attached. This difference is exemplified below:

(8)	base	neutral affix	non-neutral affix
	'curious	'curious#ness	curi'os+ity
	pro'ductive	pro'ductive#ness	produc'tiv+ity
	'patriarch	'patriarch#y	patri'arch+al
	'finite	non#'finite	'in+finite

Notice, too, in (8) that only the non-neutral affixes have an effect on the segmental form, and this can also be seen in:

(9)	base	neutral affix	non-neutral affix
	profane	profane#ness	profan+ity
	organ	organ#ise	organ+ic
	expend	expend#able	expens+ive

132

Also, only non-neutral affixes appear to show obligatory phonetically conditioned allomorphy:

(10)　in+　il+legal, ir+relevant
　　　　un#　un#lawful, un#reasonable

The best way to account for these differences seems to be to order the phonological rules (including, crucially, the stress rules) after the rules introducing affixes with +-boundaries, but before the rules introducing affixes with #-boundaries. In that way, the phonological rules will determine the segments and stress pattern of *curious*, for example, before {#ness} is added, so that the segmental shape and stress of *curious* remains the same in *curiousness*. However, {+ity} is added before the phonological rules apply, so that the segmental form of *curiosity* and its stress pattern are determined in the presence of the whole string, and not just by the base. Siegel (1974) therefore suggests that these various processes are ordered in the following way:

(11)　　　　　　　Roots
　　　　　　　　　　|
　　　　Rules for addition of
　　　　　+-boundary affixes
　　　　　　　　　　|
　　　　Appropriate phonological
　　　　rules, including stress
　　　　　　　　rules
　　　　　　　　　　|
　　　　Rules for addition of
　　　　　#-boundary affixes

Since no inflectional affix in English affects stress or regularly causes segmental changes in a base, all inflectional affixes have a #-boundary. The organisation of rules in (11) thus predicts that all +-boundary affixes (which are all derivational) should occur closer to the root than inflectional affixes. This is in fact the case. There are words of the form *formal+iti#es* but none of the form **pro-fane#s+ity*. The model in (11) also predicts that there should be strings of the form *root+affix#affix* but not of the form *root#affix+affix*, where both affixes are derivational. This is less clearly true, but it is certainly true that there are innumerable words which fit this constraint and relatively few which break it. For example all words which end in +al#ly (e.g. *industrially*), +al#ness (e.g. *exceptionalness*), +ive#ness (e.g. *prescriptiveness*), fit the constraint, and there are no established words ending in, for
133

example, #*ness* + *al* (Lehnert, 1971), despite the fact that other nominalisations occur before -*al* (*sculpt* + *ur* + *al*).

I have discussed this ordering hypothesis purely in terms of English, and it might appear that the ordering of the types of affix is a result of the very mixed history of English and has ultimately an etymological explanation which would be uninteresting cross-linguistically. It is thus important to note that similar differences have been found in a wide range of languages, including Dutch, Italian, Japanese, Kannada, Malayalam, Russian, and Tagalog (see the references in Aronoff, 1983: 363 and Scalise, 1984: 99). The classes of affixes appear to behave in similar ways to the English ones, having similar phonological effects and ordering restrictions. In most, possibly all (I have not access to all the appropriate papers) of these cases, the distinction is a result of etymologically diverse sources of vocabulary. It is interesting that this kind of language mixture should have such similar effects in so many different languages.

The ordering hypothesis presented in (11) is extended by Allen (1978) to include compounds. Allen argues that compounding is carried out in a third stratum, which applies after the two strata given in (11). This predicts that there will be no cases of derivational affixes using compounds as their base. That is, there will be no derivatives of the form *[[war-hero] ic], *[[street-music] al], *[mis [fuel-injected]] (Allen, 1978: 215). Such an analysis implies that inflectional affixes must be separated from other #-affixes, since inflectional endings occur regularly outside compounds. In English this can only be illustrated clearly with compound nouns (compound adjectives never take synthetic comparison in -*er*, and so are never inflected; compound verbs, which do carry inflections, are usually formed by conversion or back-formation, which might be seen as providing an intermediate step, distancing the inflection from the compound), but it could be illustrated with other types of compound in other languages. The plural marker comes outside the compound in forms like [[text·book] s] and [[red·skin] s]. This can be seen particularly clearly with the last example. *Redskins* are not a number of skins which are red (i.e. the plurality is not applied purely to the *skin*-element), but a number of the entities each of which would individually be a *redskin*. Secondly, if we consider a compound such as *Walkman*, it seems that most speakers make the plural by adding -*s*. If the morpheme {plural} were added directly to the element *man*, internally, the result would be *Walkmen*. The more usual plural form demands the bracketing [[Walk·man] s].

Given this conclusion, the form of the ordering constraints on the rules must be:

(12)   Roots
                 |
Rules for addition of   Stratum I
  + -boundary affixes
                 |
Appropriate phonological
  rules, including stress
        rules
                 |
Rules for addition of   Stratum II
  #-boundary derivational
        affixes
                 |
Rules for compounding   Stratum III
                 |
Rules for inflectional   Stratum IV
        affixes

9.5 Heads and feature percolation

As was seen in section 3.6, endocentric compounds in English are hyponyms of their righthand element. A *sea-bird* is a type of bird, a *heffalump trap* is a kind of trap, if you *trickle-irrigate* some land, then you are irrigating it, and so on. This means that the semantic information associated with the righthand element in the compound is also associated with the compound as a whole (although the compound as a whole will focus on some special type of entity denoted by the righthand element). The same is true of some information which can be seen as grammatical rather than, or as well as, semantic. For example, if we consider *sea-bird*, we find that the compound as a whole, like its righthand element *bird* is animate, countable, and a noun. In a language like German it is the righthand element which determines the gender and declension class of the compound as a whole. This is illustrated below:

(13)   *def* sing   *indef* sing   *gender*   *gloss*
       der Beamte   ein Beamter   m   'official'
       der Staats·beamte ein Staats·beamter m   'government official'
       der Tag   ein Tag   m   'day'
       der Geburts·tag   ein Geburts·tag   m   'birthday'
       das Brot   ein Brot   n   'bread'
       das Butter·brot   ein Butter·brot   n   'sandwich'
                                                        lit. 'butter bread'
where *Staat* is masculine, *Geburt* and *Butter* feminine, and where data for plural forms would provide similar results: see any good German grammar.

135

The element which determines such matters for the whole compound we can term the **head** of the compound. There is a generalisation here, namely that the compound as a whole must be marked for many of the same features as the head of the compound. That is, given a tree such as

(14)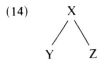

where X is an endocentric compound and Y and Z are the two elements that make up the compound, and where Z is the head of the construction X, X must carry many of the same grammatical features as Z.

This is ensured by a principle known as **feature percolation**. There is more than one version of it in the Lexicalist literature, but a simple picture of how it works can be given quite easily. In any tree, features from all the daughters are available to the mother node. In some cases those features will be in agreement, in other cases they will conflict. For example, in the compound *sea-bird* the features on both *sea* and *bird* will agree in that the parts are nouns, but conflict in that *bird* is animate whereas *sea* is inanimate. Where there is no conflict, the mother node is marked for the features in common. Where there is conflict, the mother node takes the feature of the head element. In two-element compounds, this means that all grammatical features from the head are taken for the mother node. If we consider a German compound such as *Butter-brot* this will give the following picture:

(15)

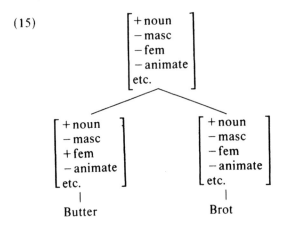

All the agreeing features are the same on all three nodes, and where there is disagreement, as in the value for the feature [feminine], it is the value for the head which is repeated on the mother node.

Purely semantic features (if, indeed, meanings are represented in terms of features) do not work in precisely the same way, since the meaning of the compound is a function of the meaning of both parts of the compound, and it is not simply a matter of agreement or conflict.

It is suggested within Lexicalist Morphology that the notion of feature percolation is generalisable from endocentric compounds to all cases of word-formation, and possibly to all morphological processes, including inflectional ones. Exocentric compounds provide a problem, but they are frequently assumed by Lexicalist Morphologists all to be lexicalised, and not generated by productive rules. They will accordingly not be considered further here. In derivational morphology, though, it is fairly clear how feature percolation will work. The head in a suffixal derivative will be the suffix, because it is the suffix which determines, for example, which part of speech the derivative as a whole belongs to. In most cases of prefixal derivation in English the base will be the head, because the prefix does not determine the part of speech of the derivative as a whole, but there are a few exceptions such as *be·witch, de·plane, en·train* where the prefix does determine the category of the entire derivative, and thus is the head. We therefore have trees like the following:

(16)

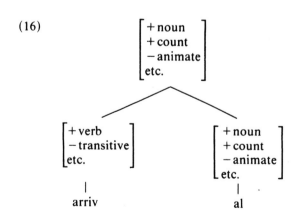

(17)

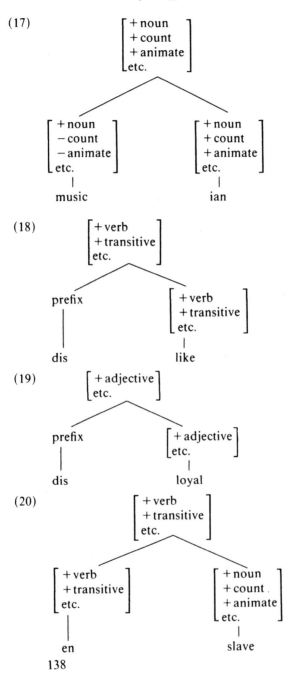

(18)

(19)

(20)

9. Lexicalist Morphology

In cases of inflectional morphology it is less clear what the head is, and this is a matter of some disagreement; but if we assume that it is the stem we can generalise feature percolation in the following kind of way (a French example is used to make the point more clearly):

(21)

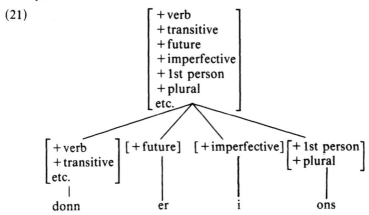

There is a certain amount of dispute in the literature on how to recognise a head element. The main paper on this topic is Williams (1981), where it is argued that, at least for English, this can be decided in the unmarked cases by the Righthand Head Rule. This states that (other things being equal) the head in an English word is the righthand element in that word. There is plenty of evidence that such a rule is not suitable across languages, and it is not even clear how valuable it is in English, given the number of exceptions to it (words like *bewitch* and so on, cited above, exocentric compounds, compounds including particles such as *by-pass* and *in-put* and also a few other compounds like *who(m)ever*). A full discussion of this topic would go far beyond the bounds of this book. It is an important area for Lexicalist Morphology, and one that requires serious consideration. But it seems likely that any final answer to this problem will be far more complex than the Righthand Head Rule.

9.6 Other considerations

I have outlined in this chapter those facets of Lexicalist Morphology which seem to me to be most central to that school of thought and also those facets where there seems to be a reasonable amount of agreement between different scholars. Lexicalist Morphologists have dealt with far more topics than have been included in this brief survey, some of which are still extremely contentious. For instance, there is still a great deal of discussion on the topic of whether inflectional rules are to be found in the lexicon with other morphological rules, or whether they rightly belong in the syntax. Another topic on which there does not yet seem to be general agreement is the way in which WFRS interact with subcategorisation rules (that is, rules which state what syntactic environments words can occur in). In particular, there are a number of attempts to constrain WFRS, so as to rule out, by some general principle, large numbers of non-occurrent constructions. This book does not allow space to explain all the arguments that lie behind such constraints, and all the arguments against them. Nevertheless it is, I think, worth listing some of the postulated constraints, to show the kind of work that is being carried out in Lexicalist Morphology. These have the status of working hypotheses, which may require considerable modification in the light of further data, and many (if not all) of them are contentious.

The Word-Based Hypothesis (Aronoff, 1976: 21):
All regular word-formation processes are word-based. A new word is formed by applying a regular rule to a single already existing word. Both the new word and the existing one are members of major lexical categories [defined as adverb, adjective, noun and verb].

There are a number of constraints implicit in this one, one of which has been rephrased as

The No Phrase Constraint (Botha, 1981: 18):
Morphologically complex words cannot be formed (by WFRS) on the basis of syntactic phrases.

Another constraint is

The Unitary Base Hypothesis (Aronoff, 1976: 48):
The semanticosyntactic specification of the base, though it may be more or less complex, is always unique. A WFR will never operate on either this or that.

In other words, an affix may be added to a nominal base or to a verbal base, but it will not be added to either a nominal or a verbal base. In such cases, Aronoff claims, it will always be the case that there are two affixes, presumably distinguishable on other grounds.

Multiple Application Constraint (Lieber, 1981: 173):
No word formation process ... can apply iteratively to its own output.

140

This constraint prohibits the formation of words such as *person·s·s* or *king·dom·dom* with the same affix repeated. This constraint will be considered again in section 12.3 below.

Generalised Lexicalist Hypothesis (Lapointe, 1981: 22):
Syntactic rules are not allowed to refer to, and hence cannot directly modify, the internal morphological structure of words.

This constraint says, for example, that it can never be the case that an underived noun can take part in a syntactic transformation while a morphologically complex noun cannot do so. Also, the form of a word cannot be determined by its syntactic environment. The second part of this is controversial (see e.g. Anderson, 1982), but not the first.

The Adjacency Condition (Allen, 1978: 155):
No rule of word formation can involve X and Y, unless Y is uniquely contained in the cycle adjacent to X.

This constraint says that it is never possible to have a morphologically complex word of the form

(22)   [[[[root] affix W] affix X] affix Y]

where the form of affix Y is determined by any property of the root or affix W; only affix X can affect affix Y.

This list of postulated constraints, which is far from exhaustive, gives some idea of the type of work being done in Lexicalist Morphology, in particular the level of abstraction at which the work is being carried out.

9.7 Some criticisms
There are a number of problems with the Lexicalist framework. Where these are subjects of current dispute within Lexicalist Morphology, they do not matter, since it is clear that an attempt is under way to solve them. Where they are not recognised as problems within Lexicalist Morphology they are potentially more serious. I shall deal here very briefly with just two: productivity and its links with lexicalisation and overgenerating morphologies, and the stratal theory of morphology.

The goal of morphology was said above (section 9.2, see also section 5.3) to be the description of the possible words of a language. This implies that the actual words of any language have only a restricted role to play in a morphology. That role is mainly concerned with providing a data-base which can be used as a basis for a grammar of words. The grammar of words will then predict that other words than those in the original data-base are possible. If subsequent new words attested fit the predictions of the grammar, the grammar is at least observationally adequate. (In fact, this is a simplification, since new rules can be added to a grammar at any time, but it will suffice for present purposes.) But not all existing words can be used as a basis for working out what the WFRS are, because some of them may be lexicalised; that is, the WFR which produced them is no longer productive (see Chapter 5). The database thus has to be considered with great care.

There can, I think, be little doubt that the Lexicalist Morphologists are right that the lexicalised words have to be listed in the lexicon. The question then arises as to what should be done with those words which are established in the community and those potential words which are not established in the community, whether they are attested or not. Is there any difference in principle between *unleadedness*, which I have just this moment invented, *scaredness*, which is attested, but not in, for example, *The Oxford English Dictionary* (Williams, 1965), and *boundedness* which is listed in the *OED*? Such difference as there is seems to be a difference between the number of people in the community who are familiar with the words, rather than a difference inherent in the words themselves. It thus seems to me that any theory which gives a particular status to *boundedness* as opposed to other *-ed·ness* words is to that extent misleading. Lexicalist Morphology falls into this category. The particular status is given to *boundedness* because only *boundedness* is listed in the permanent lexicon. In Aronoff's version of Lexicalist Morphology, *scaredness* and *unleadedness* are treated in the same way: the WFRS generate *scaredness* and *unleadedness* when the words are first used by means of once-only rules; the two new lexemes are then stored in the user's lexicon on a par with other lexemes; both are thus part of my personal lexicon (since I have just used these words) though other people's will be different. This too seems misleading. It implies that if I do not use the word *unleadedness* for the next two years, but then get involved in a discussion of whether petrol should be leaded or not, I will not have to generate *unleadedness* from scratch for that discussion, it will already be listed in my personal lexicon as a familiar item. It is hard to see just how this claim could be tested empirically, but *a priori* it does not seem to be correct, at least not for a real native speaker of this language as opposed to the ideal speaker-listener. For real speakers, there seems to be some link between familiarity (based on regular exposure) and the possibility of something becoming established in the lexicon. *Hapax legomena* are not established words.

This is linked with the fact that regular new words are coined all the time without being listed in dictionaries. Evidence of this can be found in the numerous articles in the journal *American Speech* which list attested words which have some formative, or method of formation, in common. It is rarely the case that all such words later appear in standard dictionaries. If we are talking about real speakers of the language, it is quite clear that they cannot have all these words in their lexicons. If we are talking about the ideal speaker-listener, who might be expected to have all these words in the lexicon, the only way to ensure that they are all there is to include the maximum potential output from all WFRs. If that is done, there should be no distinction between *unleadedness, scaredness* and *boundedness*. I therefore conclude that some further clarification of the role of the permanent lexicon within Lexicalist Morphology is required.

Turning now to the stratal theory of ordering of processes, it too has a number of problems associated with it, the most important of which is that it appears to be contradicted by the data. To see this, it is important to ask first how it is possible to tell what the structure of a word is.

The most obvious clue is meaning. Consider the following passage from the Dr Seuss book *Fox in Socks*, which is aimed at pre-school children:

> What do you know about tweetle beetles? Well ...
> When tweetle beetles fight it's called a tweetle beetle battle.
> And when they battle in a puddle it's a tweetle beetle puddle battle.
> AND when tweetle beetles battle with paddles in a puddle, they call it a tweetle beetle puddle paddle battle.
> AND ... When beetles battle beetles in a puddle paddle battle and the beetle battle puddle is a puddle in a bottle they call this a tweetle beetle bottle puddle paddle battle muddle...

Consider the compound from this *tweetle beetle puddle paddle battle*. This compound describes a kind of paddle battle, so 'paddle' and 'battle' belong together. We know that the creatures having these battles are tweetle beetles, so those two elements must belong together. This is a special kind of paddle battle, so the element which tells us what kind must go closely with paddle battle, and we have, as a result, the following structure:

(23)

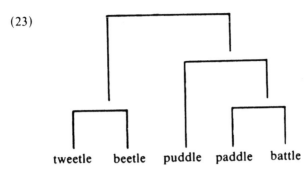

tweetle   beetle   puddle   paddle   battle

There is no reference in this compound to a beetle puddle or a puddle paddle, and this is shown by the structure, which reflects the meaning. The same kind of exercise can be carried out with derivatives. If we consider *encouragement* we can see that it contains three morphs, *en·courage·ment*. These could be structured [[en·courage]ment] or [en[courage·ment]]. The first of these is supported by the semantics. *Encouragement* means 'act of encouraging', and *encourage* means something like 'put courage into'. The second is excluded for semantic reasons, and also on distributional grounds: although the prefix *en-* is added to nouns (as the existence of *encourage* shows) none of the patterns that this process regularly gives rise to are ones which are relevant here. This prefix added to nouns can have one of the following meanings:

(a) 'Put into NOUN', as in *encage, entomb*. *Encouragement* does not mean 'put into couragement'.

(b) 'Make into a NOUN', as in *enslave*. *Encouragement* does not mean 'make into a couragement'.

(c) 'Put a NOUN on a person or thing', as in *encrown*. *Encouragement* does not mean 'put a couragement on a person or thing'.

(Meanings taken from Marchand, 1969: 162f.) Thus the meaning of an affix or affixation process is relevant: other things being equal, we expect to find an affix having one of a fairly restricted number of possible meanings, otherwise the notion of a WFR will not make sense. Furthermore, if it is the case that *-ment* affixation is no longer productive (and there is some evidence that this is so: see Bauer, 1983: 55), then the fact that *couragement* is not an established form in its own right may also be relevant. There is nothing else available which could have been the base for the *en-* prefixation if the structure [[en·courage]ment] is rejected. We also have the evidence that *-ment* has probably never been used as a suffix on a noun base (Marchand, 1969 says that all the words like *devilment* which appear to come from nouns are actually formed on the basis of obsolete verbs). We thus expect *-ment* to be added to a verb, such as *encourage*, but not to a noun, such as *courage*. All these reasons support the analysis in (24).

(24)

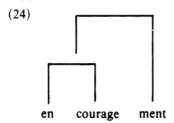

en   courage   ment

There may still be cases where it is difficult to make a decision about the structure of a derivative. Consider the cases of *enliven* and *misshapen*. The prefix *en-* is regularly added to adjectives, as in *enable, enlarge, enrich* with the meaning 'make ADJECTIVE', so it could be added to *live*. But the suffix *-en* is only added to adjectives, as in *darken, straighten* and not to verbs. The prefix *en-* can be found added to verbs (although this use seems not to be productive), as in *enclasp, enclose, entrust*, but then it means 'VERB in', which is not appropriate for *enliven*. The only structure that can really be motivated for *enliven* is

(25)

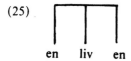

en   liv   en

The problem with *misshapen* is that there is no regularly occurring form *misshape* (verb) or *shapen* in current English. Only the extra etymological information that *shapen* was the past participle of the verb *shape* up until the fourteenth century, allows us to assign the following structure to *misshapen*:

(26)

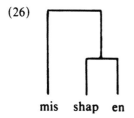

mis   shap   en

If the use of etymological information is excluded in making a synchronic decision, there is no strong evidence to indicate that
145

the structure is anything but

(27)

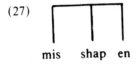

mis   shap   en

Examples like this are unusual, since in most cases it seems to be perfectly possible to assign a structure to English words where every branch in the tree is binary. Dvandva compounds with more than two elements such as *Cadbury-Schweppes-Hudson* are the only regular exceptions to this principle.

On the basis of this, we can now turn to consider the stratal ordering hypothesis. The problem here is that the hypothesis is apparently not supported by the data. It seems to be possible to find ordering relations amongst elements from the four strata put forward in (12) which are not predicted by the stratal ordering hypothesis. This is shown in Table 2, where the kind of analysis discussed in the preceding paragraphs has been undertaken. It can be seen that of the possible orderings of the strata set up in (12), only one does not seem to occur. The patterns predicted not to occur by the stratal theory in (12) are marked with two asterisks in Table 2.

It should be noted that the Lexicalist Morphologists themselves are aware of problems with the stratal ordering hypothesis, and have tried to overcome them in many ways. As a result, the form of the hypothesis presented in (12) is not the only form to be found. Other versions merge strata III and IV, allow suppletive forms to

Table 2: Possible Orders of Four Classes of Rule

non-neutral derivational inside neutral derivational	[[im + [[pi] + ous]]#ness] [[[mysteri] + ous]#ness] [[[commerc] + ial]#ism]
**	
non-neutral derivational outside neutral derivational	[[[govern]#ment] + al] [[[develop]#ment] + al] [[un#[[[grammat] + ic] + al]] + ity] [[[arch#[angel]] + ic] + al] [[[profess]#or] + ial]
non-neutral derivational inside inflectional	[[[quant] + ifi]#ed] [[[quant] + iti]#es] [[[oper] + ate]#d]

146

Table 2: continued

**

non-neutral derivational outside inflectional	NO EXAMPLES FOUND IN ENGLISH
non-neutral derivational inside compounding	[[job] [[secur] + ity]] [[[satur] + ation] [point]] [[[quant] + ity] [surveyor]]

**

non-neutral derivational outside compounding	[[[set] [theoret]] + ic] [[[party]-[[polit] + ic]] + al] [[[[common][sens]] + ic] + al]
neutral derivational inside inflectional	[[[develop]#ment]#s] [[[walk]#er]#s] [[[[comput]#er]#is]#ing]

**

neutral derivational outside inflectional	[[[accord]#ing]#ly] [[[interest]#ed]#ly] [[[lov]#ing]#ness] [[[folk]#s]#y] [[more]#ish] [[most]#ly]
neutral derivational inside compounding	[[[govern]#ment] [offices]] [[[lectur]#er] [scale]] [[[own]#er]-[[occupi]#er]]

**

neutral derivational outside compounding	[ex#[[frog][man]]] [un#[[self]-[sufficient]]] [[[laid][back]]#ness] [[[skate][board]]#er]

**

inflectional inside compounding	[[[universiti]#es] [yearbook]] [[[suggestion]#s] [box]] [[[shoot]#ing] [stick]] [[least][ways]]
inflectional outside compounding	[[[black][bird]]#s] [[[bath] [towel]]#s] [[[test]-[market]]#ing] [[[hang]-[glid]]#ing]

be introduced in Stratum I, suggest that the stratal ordering applies only to the affixes on one side of the root, so that a + -boundary prefix outside a #-boundary suffix does not constitute a violation, and so on. And there are a number of sub-regularities among the violations. For example, most of the cases of derivational endings occurring further from the root than inflectional endings involve the derivational affixes -*ness* and -*ly,* which are extremely productive and very much at the inflectional end of the cline of derivational affixes, and the inflectional affixes -*ed* and -*ing,* which are very much at the derivational end of the cline of inflectional affixes. In fact, many scholars argue (notably Allen, 1978) that the suffixes -*ed* and -*ing* are derivational in some of their functions, so that examples involving them do not constitute violations of the stratal ordering hypothesis. Even when such cases are taken out of consideration, however, there remain some unexplained violations of the hypothesis. The ordering hypothesis may explain the majority of cases in English, but these exceptions still jeopardise it as a general explanation of the facts. The actual word-forms we can attest in English do not support simple adherence to the stratal ordering hypothesis. If this were merely a research strategy, acknowledged as an overgeneralisation, this might not matter. But it is often taken as a fixed point of reference. In one case (Williams, 1981) it has even been suggested that other principles should be abandoned to allow the ordering hypothesis to be maintained. This seems to be methodologically unsound, as well as a distortion of the basic data.

9.8 Review: Lexicalist Morphology

Lexicalist Morphology has brought about a new era in the study of morphology. Because of work done within this school it is now generally accepted that at least derivational morphology is quite distinct from syntax. More and more people also seem to be coming to see morphology as distinct from phonology. There are very few linguists who would still wish to see those lexemes which can be analysed in terms of non-productive processes generated by rule rather than listed in the lexicon. Lexicalist Morphologists have also started a search for formal universals in word-formation processes of a very different kind from anything that has gone before. The abstract principles and conditions that they operate with and attempt to elucidate are very clearly influenced by the type of work that has been done in syntax over the last ten years or so. As yet the results of their search for universals and abstract principles have been rather disappointing, in that there is data readily available to show that the conditions do not hold. It is to be hoped, however, that successive refinements will lead to a more exact picture of the kinds of abstract universals that can be maintained in morphology. However, a fundamental review of their position on productivity and the permanent lexicon, a rather more realistic approach to the stratal ordering hypothesis, and a clarification of some other prin-

9. Lexicalist Morphology

ciples such as rules for determining headedness in derivatives would seem to be essential if this theory of morphology is to have a sound foundation.

REFERENCES AND FURTHER READING

The best introduction to Lexicalist Morphology is Scalise (1984). The only other source is the original works. The paper which gave the main impetus to Lexicalist Morphology is Chomsky (1970). Halle (1973) was the first important article stimulated by the ideas there, and that was followed by Jackendoff (1975), although much of the content of these two papers has not become part of the accepted basis of Lexicalist Morphology. Three theses, Siegel (1974), Aronoff (1976) and Allen (1978) form the real basis of Lexicalist Morphology, and since their appearance there has been an explosion in the amount of work done in this framework. For a review of the work done by Lexicalist Morphologists on compounding, see Botha (1984b).

The 'general acceptance' that syntactic rules do not require access to phonological information mentioned on page 127 is rather overstated, although as a very broad generalisation it holds within writings in the Chomskyan tradition. For some suggestions as to where it might fail to hold, see W. Bauer (1982: 334ff) and Plank (1984).

In (8) the prefix *non-* is listed with a #-boundary. Allen (1978) argues that it must actually contain a sequence of two such boundaries. This does not in fact influence the points made about the data in (8). The general principle holds.

Although the examples in (10) are presented in the text in more or less the terms in which they are usually presented by Lexical Morphologists, they require further comment. On the face of it, it is quite simply wrong that {in +} has phonetically conditioned allomorphs and {un#} does not. Pronunciations like *u*[ŋ]#*kind, u*[m]#*moved* are common, if not the norm. It looks as though the Lexicalist Morphologists are misled by the orthography. However, there is a difference between the two types, in that the phonetically conditioned allomorphs of {in +} are obligatory in all styles, while those of {un#} are optional in some styles. It is in this much more abstract sense that only +-boundaries demand obligatory phonetically conditioned allomorphy.

For fuller discussion of headedness in morphology see Anderson (1980), Baldi (1983), Zwicky (1985c), and some brief discussion in the notes to Chapter 13.

The criticisms presented in section 9.7 with reference to productivity are not as true of the model presented in Allen (1978) as they are of other versions of Lexicalist Morphology. Allen's model does not appear to have been universally adopted, however, and even it is not immune to criticism. Allen suggests that as well as the permanent lexicon there should be a conditional lexicon. The conditional lexicon contains the output of all WFRs which has not yet become lexicalised (i.e. made unpredictable in some way, phonologically, morphologically or semantically). This makes the conditional lexicon infinite in extent since, for example, N + N compounding is recursive and there is therefore no longest compound in the English language. A grammar with an infinite component in it is not particularly explanatory: if the grammar is infinite, it could simply contain a list of forms which are stated without explanation to be grammatical.

10. Word-and-Paradigm Morphology

If Lexicalist Morphology deals primarily with derivational morphology, Word-and-Paradigm morphology concentrates on inflectional morphology. While it seems reasonably clear that the methods of Word-and-Paradigm (henceforth WP) could be extended to cover derivational morphology as well (and statements are occasionally made to that effect by the proponents of WP, e.g. Robins, 1959: 125), WP has been developed to deal with the inflectional morphology of morphologically complex languages, and it is here that its strengths are most apparent. As will appear below, the focus of theoretical attention in WP morphology is also rather different from that in Lexicalist Morphology. Some versions of Lexicalist Morphology and WP approaches are perfectly compatible with each other, and may indeed supplement each other.

In the discussion in this chapter I have avoided the specialised terminology used in WP in favour of the terminology already introduced in this book. Some translation will thus be required to read the original works in this area.

10.1 The distinctiveness of WP

The WP approach to morphology is a reaction to the usual simplistic notion that words can be analysed into sequences of morphs each of which is in a one-to-one correspondence with a morpheme. While such a model of morphology may be largely applicable in some languages, there are many more where it is grossly inadequate. This has already been seen in the discussion of empty morphs and portmanteau morphs, for example. In the case of the empty morph there is a formative which does not correspond to any morpheme, in the case of the portmanteau morph there is more than one morpheme which is realised in the morph. The situation also arises (and this too, has already been illustrated) where a single morpheme is realised by a number of morphs, which may be discontinuous. All of this is illustrated in the diagram in (1), which shows the patterns of realisation involved in the Italian word-form *canterebbero* '[if] they would sing'. The -*bb*- occurs only with forms which are both third person and conditional, the stressed -*e*- following the -*r*- occurs consistently only in conditional forms, the -*ro* occurs

151

10. *Word-and-Paradigm Morphology*

only with the third person plural, the *-r-* occurs with futures and conditionals (Matthews, 1970: 107-8).

(1)

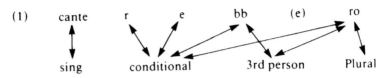

In a situation of this kind there can be no equation of morph and morpheme, and words cannot be seen as realising ordered sequences of morphemes. Rather the abstract morphemes have an influence on the way in which the word-form is made up, either individually or in combination with other morphemes.

In WP morphology the word-form is therefore taken as the basic unit of syntax, even though it is not minimal. The word-form is derived by a number of processes or operations which apply to the lexeme. The morphemes other than the lexeme which influence the form of the word-form determine which processes apply. The linguist as analyst can deduce what these processes are by consideration of the entire paradigm in which the lexeme appears, and by contrasting the word-forms which appear in that paradigm. In this way syntax and morphology are kept clearly distinct, which is not necessarily the case in a system which takes the morpheme as its basic unit.

Morphologists working with WP point in particular to two advantages of the theory. Firstly, there are many cases where a single formative appears to realise different morphemes in different parts of a paradigm. As an example, consider the *-b-* which occurs in Latin *ama:bo* 'I shall love' and *ama:bam* 'I was loving'. It appears to be a function of either the future tense or the imperfect, since it is missing in the present *amo*: 'I love', the perfect *ama:vi*: 'I loved', the future perfect *ama:vero* 'I shall have loved', the pluperfect *ama:veram* and all tenses of the subjunctive. It is not simply a non-present marker, because other non-present tenses do not show it. There is no reasonable analysis according to which it realises a single morpheme. Rather than say that there is a single morph which realises two distinct morphemes, it seems preferable to say that the *-b-* is generated by operations in the two partial paradigms, but is not related, that is, it represents two homophonous morphs. In other cases, the position of a formative relative to others can define the value of the formative. In Finnish the suffix *-in* can indicate the superlative nominative singular of an adjective, or be an allomorph of the illative case. Thus in (2a) *-in* means 'superla-

152

tive', but in (2b), where it occurs after another affix, it means 'illative' (i.e. 'into') (Karlsson, 1983):

(2)   (a) selv·in
           clear·superlative
           'clearest' (nominative singular)
    (b) selv·imp·i·in
           clear·superlative·plural·illative
           'clearest' (illative plural)

Since WP is concerned with the word-form as a whole rather than with the shape of individual formatives within the word-form, it can easily deal with features such as this. It should be noted, however, that any theory which allows homophonous morphs to belong to different morphemes can also cope with such data. WP is not the only possibility.

The second advantage of WP is that it can cope with **cumulation** of morphemes in a single morph (i.e. with portmanteau morphs). For example, the Latin *bon·us* shows the number, gender and case of the adjective 'good' in the *-us* suffix, and these various morphemes (singular, masculine, nominative) cannot be analysed within the affix. Any theory which demands that each morpheme should be spelt out in turn independently of others cannot deal with this type of realisation. WP, however, allows clusters of morphemes to determine the shape of the word-form as a whole, and can thus deal with such data (we shall see precisely how in the next section).

Anderson (1977: 30ff) provides an example from the Algonquian language Potawatomi to show the necessity for a WP type of approach to the morphology of at least some languages. Later (1982) he provides a similar example from Georgian, so the problem is not isolated. In Potawatomi the paradigm for a transitive animate verb with first and second person subjects is, in part, as follows:

(3)   n·wapm·a   'I see him'
        k·wapm·a   'you (singular) see him'
        n·wapm·a·k   'I see them'
        k·wapm·a·k   'you (singular) see them'

In this paradigm, the *n-* prefix marks the first person singular, the *k-* prefix the second person singular, the *-a* suffix marks a transitive verb, and the *-k* suffix marks the third person plural object. The root is *wapm*. However, when the subject is in the third person, the initial prefix marks the object of the verb, not the subject, and the final suffix marks the subject, not the object:

(4) n·wapm·uk   'he sees me'
     k·wapm·uk   'he sees you (singular)'
     n·wapm·uko·k   'they see me'
     k·wapm·uko·k   'they see you (singular)'

Here the -*uk*(*o*)- appears to mark the changed status of the verb. The *n*- and *k*- prefixes still mark first and second person singular respectively, but these are objects in (4) while they were subjects in (3). Anderson claims that any system of morphology that assigns morphs to morphemes (or meanings to forms) and then provides formulae for combining morphs will be in grave difficulty in describing this kind of phenomenon. Only in WP, which allows the cumulation of morphemes to determine the shape and order of affixes will such a language not create difficulties of description.

WP, it should be clear, is a morphological theory which has its origins in the traditional grammatical treatment of the classical languages. This is (or used to be) seen as a disadvantage by some scholars, who attributed to WP the lack of formalness and lack of universality that were associated with traditional grammar. Morphologists working within WP have been quick to argue that for the traditional style to have remained dominant for so long, it must at least have reflected something of the way in which speakers felt their languages functioned. These morphologists thus feel that it is worthwhile providing the formalness that traditional grammar lacked in an attempt to bring this approach to morphology up-to-date.

The biggest potential disadvantage of WP is that it may not be the most suitable model to apply to all languages. For example, although Turkish has quite complicated morphology, it seems that it can be explained without any of the complexities of WP. That is because in Turkish there is generally a one-to-one relation between morpheme and morph; cumulation, the kind of situation illustrated in (1), or the inversion shown in (3) and (4) are not found. At the other end of the scale, a language like Chinese has very little inflection at all. Robins (1959: 123) argues that even in a case like this, WP may have some contribution to make in allowing compounds, for instance, to be treated as single word-forms. He claims that even in such cases,

> the word as formally established is the most profitable unit to be taken as basic in the statement of ... sentence structures.

This is obviously open to empirical verification. While it looks as though WP may not have much to offer in such languages, this cannot simply be presupposed.

10.2 An example

As an example of the way in which WP morphology works, I have taken the forms of neuter nouns in German, although many of the rules I shall mention would also be used in generating the forms of nouns of other genders. German noun morphology is not nearly as complex as, say, Italian or Latin verb morphology, so the full extent of the way in which WP works cannot be illustrated using this example. Enough detail can be given, however, for it to be reasonably clear how such extensions would work. For a full discussion of Latin verb morphology in this framework see Matthews (1972). In several places in this exposition it will be seen that there is more than one way to deal with a given phenomenon within WP. This is not necessarily a disadvantage for the theory. In some cases a decision about which of two competing ways is best could be taken on the basis of a larger sample of data. In other cases decisions would, in the long run, be made in terms of the relative economy of the options – something which cannot be seen from such a small section of the morphology of a single language.

German has several distinct classes of neuter noun from a morphological point of view. Some of these classes are extremely large, some are restricted to a single noun. Nouns typifying these classes are listed below in their nominative singular and plural forms. Other forms will be considered subsequently. The numbers attributed to the classes are entirely random.

(5)

Class	Singular	Plural	Gloss
1	Mädchen	Mädchen	'girl'
2	Ufer	Ufer	'bank (of a river)'
3	Kloster	Klöster	'monastery, convent'
4	Kind	Kinder	'child'
5	Bein	Beine	'leg'
6	Bett	Betten	'bed'
7	Buch	Bücher	'book'
8	Floss	Flösse	'raft'
9	Herz	Herzen	'heart'
10	Auge	Augen	'eye'
11	Konto	Konten	'account'
12	Prinzip	Prinzipien	'principle'
13	Auto	Autos	'car'

Even a superficial glance at the forms in (5) makes it clear that a number of processes are involved in specifying the forms of German

155

neuter nouns. These processes can be expressed as a number of rules, as in (6):

(6) Rule 1 Suffix *-e* to the base.
     Rule 2 Suffix *-er* to the base.
     Rule 3 Suffix *-en* to the base.
     Rule 4 Suffix *-n* to the base.
     Rule 5 Suffix *-s* to the base
     Rule 6 Suffix *-i* to the base.
     Rule 7 Delete the final vowel in the base.
     Rule 8 Umlaut rule (discussed below).

Each of these rules could be stated more formally, using some suitable notation, but the prose versions are sufficient for present purposes. The Umlaut rule requires further discussion, however. In orthographic terms, it takes as its input *a*, *o* and *u*, and turns them into *ä*, *ö* and *ü*, except where there is a diphthong *au*, which is changed to *äu*. (This last case is not illustrated in (5), but is shown by *das Haus*, *die Häuser* 'house'.) No other vowels are affected by Umlaut. The phonology of this operation is complex for a number of reasons, but the complexity is not enlightening for the morphology. It is easier simply to stick with the orthographic version (as was implicitly done in the other rules in (6)), and say that the Umlaut rule is

(7) $$\begin{Bmatrix} a \\ o \\ u \\ au \end{Bmatrix} \rightarrow \begin{Bmatrix} ä \\ ö \\ ü \\ äu \end{Bmatrix}$$

It is now necessary to consider a format for morphological statements within the WP model. For any statement of a morphological process, it is necessary to know the following:

(a) the type of base to which the statement applies (abbreviated below as B);
(b) what limitations there are on the base, if it applies only to a subset of the possible bases (abbreviated L);
(c) what the process is (abbreviated P);
(d) what the form produced by applying the process P to the base B is. Matthews (1972) terms this the Reference, which will be abbreviated R.

While all this information is necessary in order to give a complete morphological statement, it is quite possible for L or P to be blank: that is, for there to be no limitations on the base or for there to be no processes distinguishing between the input and the output. This will be the case in instances of conversion, for example, or where classes of base that are distinguished in some cases are not distinguished in others. This will be illustrated below.

In this example we will use the following features/morphemes: nom[inative], acc[usative], gen[itive], dat[ive], sing[ular] and pl[ural]. A capital N stands for noun. Since we are only dealing with neuter nouns, a marking for gender is implicit rather than explicit. The form of the lexeme which is basic in the lexicon we will call the lexical base (LB). Other bases will be randomly numbered.

To begin with, we can say that the nominative singular form is always identical with the lexical base. In other words, the lexical entry for any of these nouns is a representation (however structured) of the 'singular' column in (5). In the WP format we can write this as follows:

(8)   B   L   P   R

     LB

$$\begin{bmatrix} N \\ +\text{nom} \\ +\text{sing} \end{bmatrix}$$

In other words, the nominative singular is derived from the lexical base with no process (it is identical to the lexical base) and without limitations (that is, it is true of all the nouns). Generally speaking, . the nominative plural is derivable directly from the singular by the rules in (6), but in two cases (Classes 11 and 12) other changes are made first: in one case vowel deletion, in the other vowel addition. There are two ways of dealing with this: either an intermediate step is set up, which is obtained without any process for a significant number of nouns, or two rules are permitted to apply in sequence to derive an output from an input. The two are virtually equivalent, but the former actually requires slightly less space to write out, and is adopted here.

(9)	B	L	P	R
(a)	LB	Classes 1, 2, 4, 5, 6, 9, 10, 13		Base2
(b)	LB	Classes 3, 7, 8	Rule 8	Base2
(c)	LB	Class 11	Rule 7	Base2
(d)	LB	Class 12	Rule 6	Base2

(e) Base2 Classes
1, 2, 3

$$\begin{bmatrix} N \\ +nom \\ +pl \end{bmatrix}$$

(f) Base2 Classes   Rule 2
4, 7

$$\begin{bmatrix} N \\ +nom \\ +pl \end{bmatrix}$$

(g) Base2 Classes   Rule 1
5, 8

$$\begin{bmatrix} N \\ +nom \\ +pl \end{bmatrix}$$

(h) Base2 Classes   Rule 3
6, 9, 11, 12

$$\begin{bmatrix} N \\ +nom \\ +pl \end{bmatrix}$$

(i) Base2 Class 10   Rule 4

$$\begin{bmatrix} N \\ +nom \\ +pl \end{bmatrix}$$

(j) Base2 Class 13   Rule 5

$$\begin{bmatrix} N \\ +nom \\ +pl \end{bmatrix}$$

It would be possible to simplify this list of statements further if, for example, classes 4 and 7 could be merged. This could be done if it were assumed that the Umlaut rule does apply to Class 4, but because the input conditions to that rule are not met, it simply applies vacuously. Classes 5 and 8 could not, however, be merged in the same way, since the plural of *Mal* 'time' which belongs in Class 5 is *Male* and not *Mäle*. It might also be possible to merge Rules 3 and 4, and see them as phonetically conditioned variants of each other. Generally *-n* occurs after a vowel, and *-en* after a consonant, but there are sufficient examples where this is not so (including *Prinzipien*) for the rule to be rather difficult to write. In particular, either *-n* or *-en* may follow an *r* or an *l*, depending on whether the syllable in which it occurs is stressed or not (but again with some exceptions).

We turn now to other case forms of the nouns. The accusative is always precisely the same as the nominative for neuter nouns both in the singular and in the plural. This can be written as follows:

(10)   B   L   P   R

$$\begin{bmatrix} N \\ +nom \end{bmatrix} \qquad\qquad \begin{bmatrix} N \\ +acc \end{bmatrix}$$

Similarly, the genitive plural form of the noun is always the same as the nominative plural, so we can write:

(11)   B   L   P   R

$$\begin{bmatrix} N \\ +\text{nom} \\ +\text{pl} \end{bmatrix} \qquad \qquad \begin{bmatrix} N \\ +\text{gen} \\ +\text{pl} \end{bmatrix}$$

The dative plural form ends in *-n*, except in Class 13. Where the plural already ends in *-n*, the nominative plural and the dative plural are identical. Otherwise an *-n* is added to the plural form.

(12)   B   L   P   R

  (a) $\begin{bmatrix} N \\ +\text{nom} \\ +\text{pl} \end{bmatrix}$ Classes 1, 6, 9, 10, 11, 12, 13 $\begin{bmatrix} N \\ +\text{dat} \\ +\text{pl} \end{bmatrix}$

  (b) $\begin{bmatrix} N \\ +\text{nom} \\ +\text{pl} \end{bmatrix}$ Classes 2, 3, 4, 5   Rule 4 $\begin{bmatrix} N \\ +\text{dat} \\ +\text{pl} \end{bmatrix}$

For most of the classes, this could be simplified to a certain extent by allowing Rule 4 to apply anyway, and then having a phonological rule which turns a sequence of two *n*'s into a single *n*. This appears unobjectionable from a theoretical point of view, but would still leave Class 13 isolated. It is thus not clear which solution is the more economical. The use of phonological rules to rescue the output of morphological rules is widely accepted as normal. In any case, some of the morphological rules are clearly phonological in content – in the case in hand most notably the Umlaut rule. This indicates that a clear-cut distinction between morphology and phonology is not really possible (see the discussion in section 7.1). The two interact. Other alternatives to the rules in (12) would be possible: for example, an entry under L demanding a final /n#/ would capture the real phonological generalisation from (12a), and would force us to see Class 13 as the exception it really is. Using phonological rather than morphological limitations on rules is perfectly acceptable within this framework; indeed, it is to be expected (see the discussion in section 5.5.1 above).

To turn now to the dative singular forms. In most cases these are identical with the nominative singular forms. However, in some cases the dative singular may end in *-e*. This is optional, and is less usual than it used to be except in a few fixed expressions. We can

159

allow for it by marking an optional process. Class 9 is exceptional in this regard, anyway.

(13) B   L   P   R

(a) LB Classes $\begin{bmatrix} \text{N} \\ +\text{dat} \\ +\text{sing} \end{bmatrix}$
        1, 2, 3, 10,
        11, 12, 13

(b) LB Class 9   Rule 3 $\begin{bmatrix} \text{N} \\ +\text{dat} \\ +\text{sing} \end{bmatrix}$

(c) LB Classes   (Rule 1) $\begin{bmatrix} \text{N} \\ +\text{dat} \\ +\text{sing} \end{bmatrix}$
        4, 5, 6, 7,
        8

The genitive singular, the last remaining form, ends in *-s* or *-es*. In most cases the *-e-* is optional in precisely the same way as it is for the dative singular. The obvious solution is thus to have the following statement:

(14) B   L   P   R

$\begin{bmatrix} \text{N} \\ +\text{dat} \\ +\text{sing} \end{bmatrix}$ Rule 5 $\begin{bmatrix} \text{N} \\ +\text{gen} \\ +\text{sing} \end{bmatrix}$

The only problem with this statement is that while the dative *-e* on the end of *Floss* is optional, the *-e-* is obligatory in the genitive singular *Flosses*. Again, the best way to solve this is probably to have a phonological rescue rule which inserts an *-e-* between two *s*'s (or rather, more generally, between two sibilants). This would also allow for cases such as *Mass* 'measurement' which belongs to Class 5. Again other alternatives would no doubt be possible, though the obvious ones are less economical.

It would probably be possible to simplify the statements that have been given here even further. For example, note that in the plural forms only the dative is distinctive. This could be captured if it were possible to have an R specification of the following type, where [-dat] implies either [+nom] or [+acc] or [+gen]:

(15) $\begin{bmatrix} \text{N} \\ -\text{dat} \\ +\text{pl} \end{bmatrix}$

Such simplifications may be more imagined than real, since the implication is still in some sense a part of the rule.

In any case, the point of the example is not to provide a definitive description of the morphology of the German noun, but to illustrate the kind of way in which wp morphology works. The notation is capable of handling far more complex examples than this one. While the case has been illustrated where a single morpheme makes two changes to a base, cumulation of two morphemes within a single form has not been so clearly shown. The great advantage of wp is that it can deal with such problems, as well as with the intermingling of rules of affixation with rules making internal phonological modifications to the base. This last case has been illustrated here with Umlaut.

10.3 Synopsis

The wp approach to morphology is mainly concerned with providing a theoretical framework, and with that a notation, for escaping from a simplistic view of morphology in which there is a one-to-one correspondence between morph and morpheme. In doing this, its practitioners have concentrated mainly on the inflectional morphology of a small number of morphologically highly complex languages. Derivational morphology, and the morphology of other, morphologically simpler, languages have tended to be ignored. However, there is no reason to suppose that the general approach taken in wp could not account for derivational morphology. It does seem likely, however, that precisely those facets of wp descriptions which make them so well suited to languages such as Latin or Potawatomi would remain largely unexploited in the description of languages such as Turkish or Yoruba. There is a suggestion that wp may nevertheless provide useful insights in the description of such languages, but it remains to be clearly exemplified.

wp descriptions are most useful

(a) in cases where there is a regular paradigm;
(b) in cases where there are cumulative realisations of meaning (portmanteau morphs);
(c) in cases where a single morpheme is realised by a number of formatives, possibly not even contiguous formatives;
(d) in cases where an analysis into morphs is complicated by the many-to-many realisation rules involved;
(e) in cases where there is morphological inversion, as in the Potawatomi example discussed earlier;
(f) in cases where rules of affixation and rules with phonological content (such as vowel lengthening, Umlaut, etc.) are used side-by-side with similar effects.

The major disadvantage of wp morphology is that the mechanisms it employs appear to allow almost anything as a morphological

161

10. Word-and-Paradigm Morphology

operation. Like transformational grammar, therefore, it probably requires constraining in some way in order to exclude rules which are universally impossible. At the moment it is probably not possible to proceed far in this direction, since we have too little knowledge about precisely what is possible in language. The way forward in WP morphology lies in attempting to discover what constraints are possible, and this involves WP descriptions of rather more data than we currently have available.

REFERENCES AND FURTHER READING

For the background to WP morphology, see Hockett (1954) and Robins (1959). Most of the recent development of WP, and in particular the development of a notation, has been undertaken by Matthews, see especially Matthews (1972). Even more recently, WP morphology has been taken up by Anderson (1977, 1982) within what is basically a Lexicalist framework. A number of papers by Anderson's students have come out in working papers, but are not generally available. Another version of basically similar ideas, although with some additions, is put forward by Zwicky (1985b).

My exposition of WP differs from the originals in a number of ways, but particularly in matters of terminology. In keeping with the terminology used elsewhere in this book, I have talked in terms of realisation, where the usual term in WP is **exponence**. Similarly, what I have termed formatives are usually called **exponents** of the various morphemes, or in Matthews' terminology, of the morphological **properties**. I have simply used the term morpheme, as elsewhere in this book. Hence the need for the term 'feature/morpheme': in the work of Matthews these would be treated as properties, and neither as features nor as morphemes. It seems to me that the more customary feature notation is equivalent to Matthews' notation here, and nothing is gained by the extra notation or terminology. I have totally ignored here the notion of morphological **categories,** which is actually an extremely useful one. A morphological category is a class whose members are morphological properties. For example, in some languages the morphological properties of present, past and future may be the options within the morphological category of Tense; the morphological properties singular, dual and plural may be the options within the morphological category of Number, and so on. Morphological categories are then such things as Person, Number, Gender, Case, Aspect, Mood, Tense, etc. (Matthews writes categories with a capital letter to distinguish them from properties, but this usage is not general.) One use of these categories will be seen in Chapter 11. As far as notation is concerned, I have basically adopted that used by Matthews, although with a few minor amendments which have no theoretical import. For example, I have altered the order of B, L, P, R in an attempt to make the process more easily comprehensible (Matthews puts R first and B last). I have also changed the labels slightly. Anderson (1977, 1982) has his own notation, which is perhaps more easily comprehensible to the outsider. A rule such as (12b), namely

$$\begin{bmatrix} N \\ +nom \\ +pl \end{bmatrix} \quad \begin{matrix} Classes \\ 2, 3, 4, 5 \end{matrix} \quad Rule\ 4 \quad \begin{bmatrix} N \\ +dat \\ +pl \end{bmatrix}$$

162

would be formulated by Anderson as follows:

$$\begin{bmatrix} N \\ +\,dat \\ +\,pl \\ \begin{Bmatrix} Class\ 2 \\ Class\ 3 \\ Class\ 4 \\ Class\ 5 \end{Bmatrix} \end{bmatrix}$$

$$/X/ \rightarrow /X + n/$$

This actually provides slightly less information than Matthews' type of notation used in the chapter, in that there is no specification corresponding to B. This information has to be provided by rule ordering, which is thus an extra complication in Anderson's version of WP. Zwicky's notation is different again, but is transparent to anyone familiar with that of Matthews. Both Zwicky and Anderson work with a system of what Zwicky calls 'defaults': values which apply if no other stipulation is made. In the example given in the chapter, the default for dative plurals is a final -n, and only Class 13 would have to be separately specified, since the dative plural in that class ends in -s.

11. Morphological Typology and Universals

There is considerable irony in the fact that although we have available morphological descriptions of numerous languages we know very little about morphological typology or morphological universals. No doubt there are good reasons for this. The study of morphological typology appears to have become stuck in a rut, historically, and the study of language universals is, in any case, quite new; and so far syntactic universals have received more attention than morphological ones. Furthermore, when researchers start looking for morphological universals, it seems that they are extremely difficult to formulate precisely (Carstairs, 1984b). Thus, however much we may suspect that morphology is potentially a rich field for typological and universalist studies, we are in no position to demonstrate it. This, of course, means that the potential for research in these areas is enormous. Before we go on to look at typology and universals in more detail, a few comments on each are required.

Language typology is concerned with possible patterns of co-variation throughout the languages of the world. Suppose, for example, that in the languages of the world there are two ways of marking syntactic relation A, call them A1 and A2, and two ways of marking syntactic relation B, B1 and B2. If it is the case that languages which use A1 always use B2, and languages which use A2 always use B1 this is a possible domain for a typological statement. Typology is specifically not interested in genetic language relationships, but in links which exist despite the lack of any known common source for the languages concerned. The idea is that a typological statement should express a limitation on the range of possible variation which can occur in the structures of languages. Perhaps the most successful known language typology is in terms of the order of the elements Subject (S), Verb (V) and Object (O) in a sentence. Languages which have the basic order VSO all seem to use prepositions and not postpositions (there is a postposition in the Turkish *adam için*, literally 'man for', 'for the man' as opposed to the preposition *for* in the English equivalent).

It can be seen, therefore, that typological studies can lead us to formulate statements of implications which are believed (we can never be absolutely sure) to hold for all languages. Such statements are called **implicational universals.** An implicational universal is a statement of the the form 'If a language has feature *a*, then it also has feature *b*', without any implication that the reverse is also true unless this is specifically stated.

The term 'universal' itself looks as though it refers to things which are true in all languages. There are such statements, such as 'All languages have vowels' which are true of all languages (as far as we know, but, of course, in this case omitting sign languages). Such statements are called **absolute universals.** But there are also, perhaps more commonly, **universal tendencies.** A universal tendency is a statement such as 'If a language has only one fricative it is /s/' which is true for the vast majority of languages, but not for all. In the case in point, it is not true for Maori, whose only fricatives are /f/ and /h/. A universal tendency, then, is a statement which we expect to be true, and which we know to be true of most languages, but one to which we know there are exceptions. Such statements are still important, because they are statements of ways in which actual language structures differ from purely random patternings, even if there are known cases which contravene them. Tendencies may or may not also be implicational. An example of an implicational tendency is 'If a language has SOV basic word-order, it will have postpositions' which is not true of Persian, for example.

Armed with this small amount of terminology, we can now go on to consider the details as applied to morphology. We shall deal with typology first, and then with universals.

11.1 Morphological typology

Morphological typology is fraught with confused terminology, inconclusive results, and the emotive appeals of linguistic imperialists, who were convinced that the language they favoured represented some kind of linguistic or aesthetic ideal. Yet students of linguistics tend to come across the terms **isolating, agglutinative** and **fusional** early in the study of the subject, and they are part of the standard and widely-used terminology of linguistics. Accordingly, they are discussed here, though not without a kind of Editorial Health Warning: morphological typology, in the present state of the art, should be taken in small doses, diluted with a great deal of scepticism. Illustrating the terminological confusion of this area, it should be noted that 'agglutinating' is sometimes used in place of 'agglutinative', and 'inflective', 'flectional', 'inflecting' or 'inflectional' (despite the possible confusion) are sometimes used in place of 'fusional'. Some authors use the terms 'analytic' and 'synthetic' as meaning 'isolating' and 'non-isolating', for others these terms have different implications.

The three-way division of languages into isolating, agglutinative and fusional goes back to the work of Friederich and August von Schlegel in the early years of the nineteenth century. Their ideas were developed by others in the course of that century, frequently in an attempt to show that the fusional languages, such as the Classical, were the acme of human linguistic endeavour. It was this type of misuse which led this *trop fameuse classification* (in the words of Meillet) into disrepute, and led Sapir (1921: 124) to make the following acerbic statement:

> A linguist that insists upon talking about the Latin type of morphology as though it were necessarily the high-water mark of linguistic development is like the zoologist that sees in the organic world a huge conspiracy to evolve the race-horse or the Jersey cow.

Sapir (1921) and, following him, Greenberg (1954) attempted to rehabilitate the typology, but without any notable success. Indeed, part of the confusion in terminology appears to stem from their disparate attempts to clarify and enlarge on what they felt to be misused labels.

What, then, do the categories refer to? A pure isolating language would contain no obligatorily bound morphs, so all words would be invariable. Languages usually cited as being close to this ideal are Chinese and Vietnamese. A pure agglutinative language would have obligatorily bound morphs, each of which realised a single morpheme, and ideally where the obligatorily bound morphs always appeared with precisely the same form. Turkish is frequently cited as a fairly typical agglutinative language, although the obligatorily bound morphs there are not of fixed form. Swahili is another example. A fusional language does usually contain obligatorily bound morphs, but there is no simple one-to-one correspondence between morphs and morphemes. Examples are the Classical languages: Greek and Latin.

To this three-way division, some scholars of American Indian languages felt the need to add a fourth category, the category of **polysynthetic** languages. This is one in which there is a high density of obligatorily bound morphs and these are semantically more important than would be expected of an affix, even a derivational one, in other language types. For example, in West Greenlandic there is a single word-form meaning 'You simply cannot pretend

167

not to be hearing all the time' which is made up as follows (Fortescue, 1984):

(1)   tusaa·nngit·su·usaar·tuaannar·sinnaa·nngi·vip·putit
       hear·negative·intransitive-participle·pretend·all-the-
       time·can·negative·really·second-person-singular-indicative

The Eskimo languages are usually cited as the main examples of polysynthetic languages, but others such as Kwakiutl are also included. Some authors are quite scathing about this category. Sapir (1921: 123) calls it

> an uncomfortable 'polysynthetic' rear-guard to the agglutinative languages;

and Bazell (1966) is dismissive, saying that the category

> deserved the self-contradictory definition of the Oxford Dictionary: 'characterized by combining several words of a sentence [...] into one word'.

However difficult this category may be to define, and however awkwardly it fits into the system of classification, it is again a term in current use.

One of the important things to notice about this typology is that there are very few pure types, if any. Consider, for example, a sentence of English like:

(2)   Obscenity can be found in every book except the telephone directory.

In this sentence, many of the words appear to present an isolating type of morphology: *can, be, in, book*, for instance. Others appear to show agglutination: *obscen·ity, direct·ory*. And *found* shows the fusional type, since there are two morphemes but no simple analysis into morphs. This result is typical, not only of English but perhaps of all languages. Sapir stresses that it is even possible to mix isolating and polysynthetic types in the same language. We are thus not dealing with absolutes when we speak of these types, but with tendencies.

In fact, it is probably possible to break the three main types down into two simpler parameters: the ratio of morphemes to word-forms, and the number of morphemes to morphs (especially, but not necessarily exclusively, obligatorily bound morphs). This is illustrated in Table 3 on page 169. In this table the qualitative terms 'high' and 'low' are used rather than any precise quantities to show that we are dealing with tendencies. The number of morphemes per word-form may be high or low in an fusional language, since

led is fusional (realising the two morphemes {lead} and {past tense})
just as much as *regentur* (Latin, 'they will be ruled', realising the
morphemes {rule}, {3rd person}, {plural}, {future}, {passive}).
Nevertheless, fusional languages are usually considered to have a
relatively high number of morphemes per word-form. The polysynthetic category does not fit easily into Table 3 since it is distinguished
from agglutinative largely by the semantic importance or density
of the elements involved.

Table 3: Breakdown of three main types into two parameters.

		number of morphemes per morph	
		low	high
morphemes per word-form	low	isolating	fusional
	high	agglutinative	

The average number of morphemes per word does seem in general
to distinguish isolating languages and polysynthetic languages from
others. The following figures are given by Greenberg (1954) on the
basis of passages of running text one hundred words long:

Vietnamese	isolating	1.06
English	mixed	1.68
Old English	fusional	2.12
Swahili	agglutinative	2.55
Eskimo	polysynthetic	3.72

My own figures over smaller samples are broadly comparable:

Yoruba	isolating	1.09
English	mixed	1.69
Turkish	agglutinative	2.86
Russian	fusional	3.33

The average number of morphemes per morph, on the other hand,
does not appear to give the same kind of spread:

Yoruba	isolating	1.00
English	mixed	1.37
Turkish	agglutinative	1.31
Russian	fusional	1.58

169

This seems to be because the number of morphs which show cumulative exponence, even in an fusional language, is in fact a rather small proportion of the total, because of the number of indeclinable prepositions and particles, and the number of roots and derivational affixes which do not allow cumulation. The English total is boosted by a few very common words such as *has, is, him,* etc., which are portmanteau morphs.

Once we have set up a typology of this type (however satisfactory or unsatisfactory it may be) we are left with the vital question asked by Kroeber (1954: 297):

> What do we do with a morphological classification of the world's languages when we have it?

Basically, a typology is not of much value unless it predicts other things about the various types of language. For instance, a typology in terms of the relative order of Subject Verb and Object is useful since it allows you to predict (not with total accuracy, but with a fair degree of success) the relative order of nouns and adjectives, of main verbs and auxiliaries, of adpositions and noun phrases, and so on. Now as far as can be discovered from most of the research specifically in this area, a typology in terms of isolating, agglutinative and fusional does not correlate with anything else in the morphology at all. There is some slight correlation with syntax, in that isolating languages use word-order to distinguish subjects from objects more centrally than do fusional languages, and the languages with the freest word-order tend to be of the fusional type. It also seems that agglutinative languages tend to be SOV languages. It should however be noted that there are fusional languages with fairly fixed word-order, and isolating languages can use adpositions to indicate function. The value of the typology *qua* typology is thus very much in doubt.

Nevertheless, the categories may say something useful about the type of grammar required to deal with languages which belong to them. Hockett (1954) distinguished between three 'models' of grammar (morphology and syntax): Item and Arrangement (IA), Item and Process (IP) and Word-and-Paradigm (WP). Hockett saw these as reflecting a different approach on the part of the linguist to the data to be described. He pointed out that a description given in terms of one of these models can (with a certain amount of contrivance) be reformulated in terms of one of the others. While this is true, the models do not all allow the same statements to be made with the same degree of ease. IA allows only statements of lists of items and the positions in which the items can be found; IP allows dynamic statements in terms such as adding one thing to another or turning one thing into another; wp allows statements of much greater complexity in terms of operations, input conditions and the like. Generally speaking IA is the simplest type of model, IP is rather more complicated, and wp the most complicated. It seems in general that isolating languages can be dealt with adequately with an IA type of grammar. Some facets of agglutinative and fusional languages are more easily dealt with in terms of an IP grammar. And some facets of fusional languages require the power of a wp grammar to be dealt with most effectively.

To illustrate this, let us start with a sentence of English which is made up of monomorphemic word-forms, and is thus isolating in type.

(3)   The dog can see the rabbit.

In an IA grammar we can say that this sentence is made up of three constituents, a noun phrase, a verb group and another noun phrase, that the noun phrases are made up of determiners and nouns, that verb groups are made up of auxiliaries and main verbs, and that determiners are words like *the*, nouns are words like *dog* and *rabbit*, auxiliaries are words like *can*, and main verbs are words like *see*. Using this set of statements, we can see that we have accounted for the distributions of the various items that occur in sentence (3). In an isolating language there is, of course, no need to make any morphological specifications, because there are no obligatorily bound morphs.

Now consider a partial paradigm for a Turkish noun EL 'hand'.

(4)

	Singular	Plural
accusative	el·i	el·ler·i
genitive	el·in	el·ler·in
locative	el·de	el·ler·de
ablative	el·den	el·ler·den

This partial paradigm can also be described perfectly well using an IA grammar. The root is the leftmost item in the word-form, following that comes the plural marker (if the word is plural), and following that comes the appropriate case marker. If we add that the morph realising {3rd person possessive} is *-in-*, and it comes before the case marker, we can work out that other words of Turkish must be *elinde* 'in his/her/its hand', *ellerinden* 'from his/her/its hand', and so on.

But now consider the following partial paradigm from Turkish, which shows the same case forms, but this time of a word whose root ends in a vowel, GECE 'night'.

171

(5)

	Singular	*Plural*
accusative	gece·yi	gece·ler·i
genitive	gece·nin	gece·ler·in
locative	gece·de	gece·ler·de
ablative	gece·den	gece·ler·den

Here the sequence of two vowels in the accusative and genitive singular has been broken up by a consonant: *y* in one case, *n* in the other. We can of course still describe this in terms of an IA grammar, by saying that there are two forms of the accusative and genitive endings and the first occurs after a consonant, the second after a vowel. If we go further, though, we see that this is a regular feature of Turkish. The third person singular possessive marker after a vowel is *-sin-* so that 'of his/her/its night' is *gece·sin·in* but 'in his/her/its nights' is *gece·ler·in·de*. And so far, we have not taken vowel harmony into account, which makes the ablative plural of TARLA 'field' *tarla·lar·dan*. At this point, rather than listing all the possible allomorphs and the places where they occur, it might seem simpler to use a dynamic notation and say that the plural marker becomes *-lar-* when it follows a back vowel, that a consonant is introduced if adding a suffix gives rise to a sequence of vowels, and so on. At this point, we have started using an IP type of grammar.

Now consider the following two nominal paradigms from Russian, GAZETA 'newspaper' a feminine noun and STOL 'chair' a masculine noun:

(6)

Singular		
nominative	gazet·a	stol
accusative	gazet·u	stol
genitive	gazet·ɨ	stol·a
dative	gazet·e	stol·u
instrumental	gazet·oi	stol·om
prepositional	gazet·e	stol·e
Plural		
nominative	gazet·ɨ	stol·ɨ
accusative	gazet·ɨ	stol·ɨ
genitive	gazet	stol·ov
dative	gazet·am	stol·am
instrumental	gazet·ami	stol·ami
prepositional	gazet·ax	stol·ax

The problem with describing a paradigm like this is that the inflectional suffix *-e* can realise {feminine dative singular} or {prepositional singular}, the suffix *-u* can mark {feminine accusative singular} or {masculine dative singular} and the ending *-y* can mark

172

{nominative plural}, {accusative plural} or {feminine genitive singular}. This can still be done in an IA grammar, by listing all the possible affixes and all the classes of base to which they can attach and under what circumstances, but it is extremely cumbersome. It could be done with an IP grammar by saying which affixes can be added to which bases to produce which forms. But a WP grammar is specifically designed to cope with the case where the presence of a number of morphemes together triggers a specific (but non-unique) affix (see Chapter 10). In a WP grammar the list of morphemes which create the input conditions are listed, the base which is required and the operation which is carried out on that base. Of course, this model could be applied very easily to the paradigms in (4) and (5) as well as to the type of structure illustrated in (3), but it would no longer be efficient, since more information would be demanded by the rule format than is strictly necessary.

We can thus conclude that while the classical typology in terms of isolating, agglutinative and fusional languages does not appear to be helpful as a typology of the languages of the world, it may be helpful in determining the complexity of the grammar that is required to provide an account of that type of language.

11.2 Universals concerning order

We shall begin this section with a list of a few putative universals concerning order in morphology, and then go on to consider what generalisations can be drawn on the basis of these. The discussion is based primarily on Bybee (1985). The universals listed here are not in any particular order, and those which are known to be tendencies and not absolute universals are marked with a parenthesised T.

(7) Number is marked closer to the root than case (T).

(8) Aspect is marked closer to the root than tense.

(9) Aspect is marked closer to the root than mood.

(10) Aspect is marked closer to the root than person (T).

(11) Tense is marked closer to the root than mood (T).

(12) Tense is marked closer to the root than person (T).

(13) Imperative markers (where these occur) come closer to the root than person/number markers (T).

(14) Interrogative affixes occur as the final suffix on a verb (T).

(15) Languages which are exclusively suffixing use postpositions.
173

(16) Languages which are exclusively prefixing use prepositions.

Most of these universals can be condensed into a statement that there is a tendency for the following ordering of morphs in a word-form:

(17)   Verbs: root - aspect - tense - mood - person
        Nouns: root - number - case

or the precise reverse in prefixing languages. This is assuming, of course, that all of these categories are realised morphologically, which they may very well not be. But those which are realised morphologically, and which are realised consistently on one side of the base, will tend to show this ordering. (The case where, say aspect is realised as a prefix but tense as a suffix is not directly covered by this generalisation.) The question is whether there is any particular reason for this tendency.

Bybee (1985) makes a convincing case for this being governed by principles of relevance and lexical generality. By relevance she understands the degree to which the morphological category affects the lexical content of the base (1985: 15). For example, if we compare aspect and person agreement with reference to a base which is a verb, we can see that verbs typically show actions or states, and aspect represents ways of viewing the internal make-up of the action or state: this is clearly extremely relevant. Person agreement, on the other hand, is far less relevant, since it refers to an argument of the verb, and not to the verb itself. By lexical generality is meant low semantic content, so that the category can apply to a large class of bases. The more relevant a category is the more likely it is to be expressed either by forming a completely separate lexical item, or by derivation, or by inflection, and these three show a decreasing level of perceived relevance (relevance being, in the final instance, a cultural property). The more lexically general a category is, the more likely it is to be shown by inflectional morphology. There is thus a tension between these two factors, which between them determine how a particular category is marked.

This can be illustrated with the notions of number and case. The case marking on a noun shows its relationship to other elements in the sentence, the role that noun plays, and so on. This is of low relevance to the noun, since it does not directly affect the lexical content of the noun base. It is, however, of high lexical generality, since it can apply to virtually any noun. Number, on the other hand, is of far greater relevance. It has a much greater effect on the lexical content of the noun, while still being of high lexical generality. We would therefore make the prediction that number would occur closer to the root than case does, and this is precisely what is observed (see (7) above). One result of this is that even in English we can find some words with a special form (probably a separate lexeme) for the plural or collective: words such as *people, cattle* and possibly, nowadays, *brethren.* Other languages do this far more commonly. Note also that according to Greenberg (1963) all languages mark plurality on at least some nouns. Not all languages mark case.

The same principle can be argued to be operating in the ordering of elements within the noun phrase in English. The difference between *a pretty little girl* and *a little pretty girl* is a matter of whether we are dealing with a group of little girls or a group of pretty girls. Culturally, it seems to be more normal to deal with a class of little girls, so that the first order is the more natural out of context. Similarly, Greenberg (1963: 68) notes that the order of items in the noun phrase across languages tends to be

(18) Demonstrative Numeral Adjective Noun
OR
Noun Adjective Numeral Demonstrative

Bybee is able to argue convincingly that on the basis of relevance, one would expect precisely the order given in (17). While she lists several examples of languages which break this pattern to a greater or lesser extent, the weight of the evidence is overwhelmingly on her side.

If this principle has general applicability, it ought to be possible to extend it quite simply. For example, we would predict that causation would have a greater lexical effect on the verb base than aspect does, and that it would thus occur closer to the root than any of the other categories mentioned so far. In English causatives are shown either by lexical paraphrases, by the use of separate lexemes or by derivation, as is shown below:

(19) (a) He made the horse swallow the pill.
(b) She killed the fly. [caused it to die]
(c) He ran the horse round the field.
(d) She lightened my load.

If we consider what happens in languages with overt morphological causative markers, this is what we find. In some languages like Kanuri and Swahili the causative marker is not on the same side of the root as the other affixes under consideration, so these do not provide any relevant data. In Finnish, the causative marker is considered to be derivational, and occurs inside all inflectional markers. In Hixkaryana (a Carib language spoken in Brazil) the causative affix is closer to the root than the cumulative affix which marks tense, aspect and (to some extent) person. This is illustrated in the following example:

(20) w·eny·ho·no
      1st-sing-subject-3rd-sing-object·see·causative·immediate-
      past
      'I showed it'.

In Diyari, which does not mark aspect, the causative morph occurs closer to the root than the tense morph:

(21) ṭana ṇari·ŋanka·ṭadi·yi
      they dead·causative·reflexive·present
      'They kill themselves'

And in Turkish, the morph realising causation also occurs closer to the root than the morphs for tense, mood, and so on:

(22) tanı·ş·tır·ıl·ay·dı·k
      know·reciprocal·causative·passive·subjunctive·past·1st-
      person-plural
      'Would that we had been introduced to one another!'

Thus Bybee's hypothesis about relevance is again vindicated in this random sample of languages from very different language families.

One important fact about Bybee's hypothesis here is that it allows her to account for the frequently noted tendency (not, *pace* Greenberg, 1963, absolute universal: see above section 6.5) for derivational affixes to be closer to the root than inflectional ones. In fact, many of the characteristics of inflection and derivation discussed in Chapter 6 can be explained with reference to Bybee's principles of relevance and generality. For example, the regular meaning of inflectional affixes is related to their generality; the fact that derivational affixes are frequently category-changing indicates relevance, and so on.

This leaves us with (15) and (16) to discuss. There is a tendency for the use of prepositions to correlate with the following ordering of elements:

(23) noun – modifying genitive
      verb – object
      noun – adjective

and for the use of postpositions to correlate with the reverse orders. In each case, the order of modifier and head is the same for all four constructions (the three in (23) and prepositional/postpositional phrases). The universals in (15) and (16) can be seen as related to this. If affixes are heads of words (a hypothesis discussed within Lexicalist Morphology, see also below, Chapter 13), the same generalisation can be seen to be applying within the word and outside the word: heads either precede their modifiers or follow them.

11.3 Implicational universals

There are a number of implicational universals discovered by Greenberg (1963), most of which concern the existence of various categories or the places in which the categories are marked. Again the same procedure will be adopted as in section 11.2, with the universals being listed first, and then discussed.

(24) The presence of inflectional morphology implies the presence of derivational morphology.

(25) The presence of morphological gender marking implies the presence of number marking.

(26) The presence of a special property of trial number marking implies the presence of a dual, which in turn implies the presence of a plural.

(27) If a verb agrees in gender with either its subject or its object, then adjectives agree in gender with the noun they modify.

(28) If a verb agrees with either its subject or its object in gender, it also agrees with it in number.

(29) If a language marks gender on a noun, it marks gender on a pronoun.

(30) There are never more gender categories in a non-singular number than there are in the singular.

(31) If the pronoun is marked for gender in the plural, it is also marked for gender in the singular.

(32) If a language marks gender on a first person pronoun, it always marks gender on a second and/or third person pronoun.

(33) Morphological marking of either person/number or gender on the verb implies morphological marking of tense/mode on the verb.

Some of these universals can be explained with reference to Bybee's notion of relevance discussed in section 11.2. For example, (24) can be reformulated to state that if less relevant categories are marked morphologically on a base, more relevant ones will be

177

marked morphologically, too. This is not actually necessary: it would be possible to imagine a case, for instance, where aspect was always shown by using a different lexeme, while tense was marked morphologically. If we assume that Greenberg's universal holds, and this type of language is never found, it is presumably because it would be a very uneconomical way of dealing with aspect, because of the lexical generality of aspect. (33) can also be explained in terms of relevance, since person/number and gender are both less relevant for a verb than tense/mode, and a less relevant category is unlikely to be marked if a more relevant one is not. (28) can also be explained by the same principle. The gender of a subject or object has less direct effect on the lexical content of the verb than the number of entities involved in the action. If the less relevant category is marked on the verb, it would be expected the more relevant category would be marked. Since number is lexically general, it would be expected that number on the verb would be marked inflectionally.

(30), (31) and (32) can all be explained in terms of another general principle, but this requires some preliminary discussion of the notion of markedness. The terms **marked** and **unmarked** are used in a number of slightly different ways. Firstly, a property can be said to be marked with relation to another one if it is shown by some morphological marker in the language under consideration. In this sense the English plural *cats* is marked in relation to the singular *cat* by the presence of the -s. This sense of marked is translated into German as *merkmalhaft*. Secondly, something can be said to be unmarked if it has a wider distribution than another category with which it contrasts minimally. In this sense, the English singular is unmarked with reference to the plural since it is also found in generic sentences such as

(34)   The tiger is a ferocious beast.

which actually refer to more than one tiger, and in the first elements of compounds, even if more than one is implied:

(35)   He spends his days sewing up trouser legs.
       She has built hundreds of possum traps.

Related to this (but not always identical with it) is that the most commonly occurring form is frequently said to be unmarked with regard to a less commonly occurring partner. These last two senses are translated into German as *markiert*. It is sometimes inconvenient that English does not allow us to distinguish between the various meanings of 'marked'. As can be seen, these three meanings actually coincide with the English singular/plural distinction, where plural is marked in all senses; and this is frequently, but not always, the case. Now consider the three universals under discussion. In each case the universal can be explained by a meta-universal which states that a more marked category will never show a finer division for other categories than its less marked counterpart. This holds in (32) because the 1st person pronoun is generally the one with the most restricted usage (despite royal plurals, and editorial *we*) and the 3rd person is, across languages, generally the least marked.

(26) can be seen to be due to another application of the same meta-universal, since you do not have special marking for specific numbers greater than one unless you have a marking for the less marked notion of plural, and while there are several natural phenomena that occur in twos (eyes, ears, legs etc), phenomena that occur in threes are rarer, and the use of a trial is correspondingly rarer.

(29) may be a result of the same meta-universal if pronouns can be said to be less marked than nouns, but this is less clear.

This leaves (25) and (27). (25) appears to contradict the principle of relevance. Gender has a bigger direct effect on the lexical content of a noun than number does. Amongst other things, this can be seen by the number of instances in English where gender is shown by a separate lexeme (*cow, bull*; *man, woman*; *king, queen*; *hen, rooster/cock*; etc.) or a derived form (*lion, lioness*; *prince, princess*; *usher, usherette*; etc.), while it is never shown by inflection, though number is shown predominantly by inflection. (27) does not fit neatly into either category. It is clear that gender is more relevant to nouns than it is to verbs, but it is not clear that gender is more relevant to adjectives than it is to verbs. This may be partly explained by a closer link between an adjective and a noun than between a verb and the noun, but this is hard to prove without some suitable survey of the way in which languages operate.

11.4 Paradigm-centred universals

So far no attempt has been made to define the notion of paradigm. This is deliberate, in that a precise definition of the relations embodied in a paradigm is extremely difficult (see Carstairs, 1984b: 167ff for one attempt). This is despite the fact that it takes very little experience of paradigms to allow you to recognise one. We can make some attempt to be more precise, though.

First of all, paradigms are usually inflectional (although some writers do use the term in a rather broader way). This is because a paradigm implies regularity and predictability. The word derives etymologically from a Greek word meaning 'pattern, example', and the idea is that the word-forms for other lexemes should be predict-

179

able according to the pattern of the paradigm lexeme. While a few lexically conditioned exceptions to the paradigm are possible (see section 6.4), very few exceptions are usually accepted in a paradigm, which is why it is relatively rare for derivational morphology to be discussed in terms of paradigms. A paradigm, then, lists all the word-forms of a lexeme, or those word-forms of a lexeme which are related in sharing a particular morpheme (the term appears to be used with both meanings: in the one case we would talk about the verb paradigm, in the other, the paradigm for the present indicative). In fusional languages it is usual for a paradigm to list all the possible word-forms of a lexeme. In an agglutinative language, it is usually impossible to list all the word-forms, so only those which contain obligatory morphs occurring more peripherally (further from the root) than the morph realising the morpheme under consideration are given. Thus a Finnish paradigm for case endings does not include all the word-forms with more peripheral, but not obligatory, possessive markers. That is, a partial paradigm like (36) ignores possible word-forms like those in (37):

(36) *nominative*   auto
      adessive   auto·lla
      inessive   auto·ssa
      elative   auto·sta
      genitive   auto·n

(37) auto·nsa
      car·3rd-person-possessive
      'his/her car'
      auto·lla·ni
      car·adessive·1st-person-singular-possessive
      'in my car'
      auto·sta·si
      car·elative·2nd-person-singular-possessive
      'out of your car'

Isolating languages do not, of course, have paradigms.

Since not all the lexemes of a language necessarily follow the same pattern of inflectional endings, we find various inflection classes (conjugations, declensions, etc.), such as those in (6) above. Each conjugation or declension shows its own paradigm.

What then can we say about paradigms, and the way in which lexemes fit into them? It seems that there is always a basic form in a paradigm from which other members of the paradigm can be deduced (Bybee, 1985). In verbal paradigms there is a tendency cross-linguistically for this basic form to be the third person singular of the present indicative, each of these properties being realised by zero more commonly than its more marked counterparts. This fits with Greenberg's (1963: 74) observation that plurality is always marked formally somewhere in a language, while singularity may not be. Children learning inflected languages appear to learn this basic form first, and create other forms by applying processes to the basic form. While they may make mistakes in arriving at other, more marked, forms, they do not generally make mistakes with the basic form. In some languages, the paradigms may be so complex that there are in fact, several basic forms in this sense. In these cases, there is always one which is less marked than the others, and again, mistakes are only made in creating the more marked forms. Bybee (1985) illustrates this from a number of languages, and also shows how this principle may constrain historical change.

There also appears to be a Paradigm Economy Principle (Carstairs, 1983, 1984c) in operation. To understand this principle, consider the following hypothetical example. Suppose there is a language with four cases, and different marking for singular and plural. Suppose further that for each of these bundles of morphemes there is more than one affix attested in the language. The affixes might be something like the following:

	Singular	Plural
nominative	-∅, -s	-n, -ad
accusative	-∅, -m, -u	-n, -ud
genitive	-a, -r	-ri, -e
dative	-e, -en	-ru

Now, in theory, it might appear that any given noun could 'choose' its case affixes at random from the list given for each of the cases. If that were true, one noun might take the first option for every case/number combination except the accusative singular, where it took the third option, another the last option for every case/number combination except the nominative plural and genitive singular, and so on. In fact, one would then have to learn the case/number endings for every noun with the noun itself, because there would be 192 different possible combinations of case endings, far too many to make any other system feasible. In fact, of course, languages do not work like that. In its strongest form, the Paradigm Economy Principle states

> the inflexional resources of a given word-class must be organized into as few paradigms as is mathematically possible (Carstairs, 1984c: 119).

In the hypothetical case illustrated above, the language would have to have no more than three paradigms. While it may not be possible to maintain the Paradigm Economy Principle in this extremely strong form (Carstairs, 1983), it does seem that there is an extremely strong tendency operating here, which has the effect of reducing memory load in the learning of paradigms (however unlikely that seems in the light of your own experience of learning highly inflected languages!).

It seems that there are also constraints on syncretism in paradigms. **Syncretism** is homonomy between two forms of a lexeme caused by neutralisation. In the Russian example in (6), for instance, there is syncretism between the dative and prepositional singular of GAZETA. (6) is repeated here for convenience:

(38) *Singular*
nominative	gazet·a	stol
accusative	gazet·u	stol
genitive	gazet·i	stol·a
dative	gazet·e	stol·u
instrumental	gazet·oi	stol·om
prepositional	gazet·e	stol·e

Plural
nominative	gazet·i	stol·i
accusative	gazet·i	stol·i
genitive	gazet	stol·ov
dative	gazet·am	stol·am
instrumental	gazet·ami	stol·ami
prepositional	gazet·ax	stol·ax

Carstairs (1984a) points out that under certain circumstances syncretisms lead to a reduction in the number of forms that have to be learned. For instance, in the Russian example there is a syncretism between dative and prepositional which is conditioned by the morpheme singular, and all three are realised in the same portmanteau morph. These are precisely the circumstances where there is a reduction in the number of forms that have to be learned: instead of having to learn two distinct forms of the lexeme GAZETA for the two cases, there is only one form, *gazete* to be learned. In instances where there is no portmanteau morph involved, the situation is rather different. Consider the Turkish paradigm in (4), repeated below for convenience:

(39)
	Singular	*Plural*
accusative	el·i	el·ler·i
genitive	el·in	el·ler·in
locative	el·de	el·ler·de
ablative	el·den	el·ler·den

If the locative and ablative plurals were to be syncretised as, say, *el·ler·di*, this would not reduce the number of forms to be learned, since you would still have to know that ablative is marked by *-den* in the singular, locative by *-de* in the singular, and then the extra form *-di* in the plural. It turns out that this type of syncretism is indeed extremely rare, and that there may be some further generalisation to be captured concerning the few cases where it does occur. If the locative and ablative plural were syncretised as *el·ler·de*, with *-de* marking both locative and ablative in the plural, but only locative in the singular, there would be no extra forms to learn, and this type of syncretism is correspondingly more common.

It thus seems that part of the function of paradigms is to reduce the memory load involved in learning a morphologically complex language, and that this is done in a number of ways including paradigm economy and efficient use of syncretism.

To see how some of these constraints function, consider the following data on Tamil noun declensions (Asher, 1982). The set of endings in the noun declensions is as follows:

(40) | | |
|---|---|
| *nominative* | -∅ |
| *accusative* | -e |
| *dative* | -ukku |
| *instrumental* | -aale |
| *comitative* | -ooʈe |
| *locative* | -kiʈʈe, -ile |
| *ablative* | -kiʈʈeruntu, -ileruntu |
| *genitive* | -ooʈa, -u |

Note that the ablative affix could be divided into two morphs, although the form given here is apparently the normal one listed by Tamil grammarians.

Given that there are maximally two choices in any particular slot, the Paradigm Economy Principle predicts that there will be two different declensions. This is in fact the case. Plurality is marked by a suffix -(a)ŋka(ɭ) where the presence of the /a/ is phonetically conditioned by the previous sound (the /a/ is present after a consonant, but not after a vowel) and the presence of the /ɭ/ is partly phonetically and partly grammatically conditioned: the /ɭ/ is present only before a vowel in the same word-form. The plural suffix, which is obligatory for one declension and optional for the other, occurs before the case suffix, in accordance with the statistical universal (7) above. Since number and case morphology is agglutinative, it is not surprising to find that there is no syncretism in the paradigm. The basic form of the paradigm is clearly the nominative form, which has no ending. For some nouns the stem is not identical with the nominative singular form, but the change in form is always predictable from the form of the nominative (although the rules of allomorphy are peculiar to noun stems, and do not apply to other classes). Complete paradigms for the singular of nouns PAYYAN 'boy' and MARAM 'tree' illustrating the two declensions are provided below. The forms of the plural can be worked out from the discussion above.

(41)

nominative	payyan	maram
accusative	payyan·e	maratt·e
dative	payyan·ukku	maratt·ukku
instrumental	payyan·aale	maratt·aale
comitative	payyan·ooʈe	maratt·ooʈe
locative	payaŋ·kiʈʈe	maratt·ile
ablative	payyaŋ·kiʈʈe(·)runtu	maratt·ile(·)runtu
genitive	payyan·ooʈa	maratt·u

From this it can be seen that it is not quite true, as was once thought, that 'languages [can] differ from each other without limit and in unpredictable ways'. There are restrictions on the way in which the morphological structure of languages is arranged, although these restrictions are not necessarily obvious at first glance.

REFERENCES AND FURTHER READING

For an introduction to universals and typology in general, and to morphological typology too, see Comrie (1981).

On the history of morphological typology, see in particular Greenberg (1954) and the works he refers to. For a text-book introduction, see Lyons (1968). A brief, but more modern, introduction is provided by Anderson (1985a), who also provides an outline of how the polysynthetic language Kwakiutl works.

Greenberg (1954), as well as calculating the number of morphemes per word for eight different languages, also calculates a number of other statistics, designed to give measures of isolation, agglutination, etc. The match between my figures and Greenberg's own seems to be coincidence. He cites figures for other passages which are more different than the figures I came up with, but which are still in the region of 1.6.

On Item and Arrangement and Item and Process approaches to grammar, see Hockett (1954) and Matthews (1970). For a discussion of Word-and-Paradigm morphology see Chapter 10, and for references, see the section at the end of that chapter.

The data from Turkish comes from Lewis (1967). The position of the extra consonants is somewhat fudged in the presentation here. They could be seen as empty morphs, separate from the morph to which they are marked as belonging in the text. The *n* in the third person singular possessive is also a problem, since it is missing in the absolute case. It, too, might be seen as an empty morph, or possibly a subtractive morph. The analysis of these points (and indeed of which morph these should be attached to if they are not separate empty morphs) depends on the wider analysis of Turkish, and is not of immediate concern here. Note also that a case might be made for dividing the ablative suffix into a locative -*de*- followed by an ablative -*n*. This would fit well with localist theories of grammar, but is not generally done in discussions of Turkish. Again, it makes no difference to the points being put forward in this section.

The list of universals in section 11.2 comes from Greenberg (1963) and Bybee (1985). The data on various languages is derived from the following works: Diyari, from Austin (1981), Hixkaryana, from Derbyshire (1979), Kanuri, from Lukas (1937), Swahili, from Ashton (1944), Turkish, from Lewis (1967).

In example (21) in section 11.2 it can be seen that the Diyari reflexive affix comes further from the root than the causative affix. In (22), the reciprocal affix comes closer to the root than the causative affix. In Turkish, the reflexive affix is also placed closer to the root than the causative. It thus appears that there is a conflict between the ordering of reflexive and causative in these two languages which might be counter-evidence to the hypothesised principle of relevance. This would, however, be an ungenerous conclusion to draw, since the notion of relevance is stated to be culturally dependent. There may simply be a different cultural perception of the relative relevance of these two features. If that is so, we might expect to find them in apparently random order across a number of unrelated languages. The principle of relevance requires further elaboration.

The 'meta-universal' discussed in section 11.3 derives from the work of Jakobson, and is discussed very briefly by Waugh (1976: 97) under the title 'non-accumulation of marks'. The use of the principle is illustrated in Jakobson (1960).

12. Natural Morphology

Natural morphology is not a theory of morphology in the same way that Lexicalist Morphology or Word-and-Paradigm Morphology are theories. Whereas those two theories are concerned with building up a formalism which will allow the description of the morphology of individual languages, natural morphology is concerned with providing a partial explanation for patterns of morphological behaviour. As such it is concerned with morphological universals, and the way in which these universals interact with general cognitive or semiotic principles. While Lexicalist Morphology and even WP might be said to be concerned with linguistic universals in one sense, there is a difference. Lexicalist Morphology and WP deal with formal universals concerning the way in which a grammar is built up and the types of rule involved. Natural morphology deals with substantive universals such as the range of possible morphological patterns and the categories that are necessary in morphology. The difference is that between the Chomsky and the Comrie approach to the whole question of language universals. Thus, while Lexicalist Morphology and WP tend to concentrate on detailed deliberations of the way in which individual languages work, natural morphology is far more centrally involved with the range of possible variation within morphology. As a result, the study of natural morphology is perfectly compatible with either Lexicalist Morphology or WP or both; but it often provides a different perspective on the data.

It is unfortunate that much of the material on natural morphology has until recently not been easily available. Not only has most of the work in this area been written up in German (which ought not to be an excuse for its being virtually ignored), but it has appeared in publications which are not readily available in university libraries, even within Europe. One of the major books in the area has also been announced as forthcoming for several years, its contents only familiar to a small number of insiders. It is to be hoped that recent publications such as Dressler (1985, 1986) will help to overcome these problems.

187

12. Natural Morphology

12.1 Naturalness

Natural morphology came into being in 1977, directly influenced by the then fashionable movement in natural phonology (Dressler, 1985: 321). In phonology 'naturalness' was often ill-defined, with the result that although scholars could agree that naturalness was a desirable thing, they could not agree on what it actually entailed (Dressler, 1982: 72; Lass, 1984: 198). A problem for natural morphology, therefore, was that if it was to be given any solid core content, naturalness had to be properly defined.

Naturalness is defined in natural morphology as the converse of markedness (see above, section 11.3 and, in more detail, Zwicky, 1978). That is, a particular morphological phenomenon is natural if

(a) it is widespread in the languages of the world;
(b) it is itself relatively resistant to language change;
(c) it arises relatively frequently through language change, particularly analogical change;
(d) it is acquired early by children learning languages in which it occurs;
(e) it is left relatively unaffected by language disorders such as aphasia;
(f) it is relatively unaffected by speech and language errors;
(g) it is maintained in pidginisation and introduced early in the process of creolisation;
(h) it has a high frequency and wide distribution in individual languages.

(Mayerthaler, 1980: 29; 1981: 4-5; Wurzel, 1980: 104; 1984b: 165). The appeal to evidence external to the language system itself is striking in this list.

As was mentioned above, naturalness is also determined by general cognitive or semiotic principles. Of these the most important is the principle of **constructional iconicity** (also called **diagrammaticity**). An **icon** is a linguistic sign which shows a similarity of some kind between its structure and the object the sign represents. In the case of constructional iconicity that similarity is simply a matter of amount: an extra amount of meaning is represented by an extra amount of form. In the words of other researchers: 'formal complexity corresponds to conceptual complexity' (Haiman, 1985: 147), or 'what is semantically "more" is formally symbolized by "more"' (Wurzel, 1984b: 167). Precisely how semantic 'more-ness' is to be determined is discussed in some detail by Mayerthaler (1980), but is in most cases relatively clear from a purely intuitive point of view. Thus plural is seen as being 'semantically more' than singular. The addition of an affix to mark plurality, as in *car·s* is thus maximally constructionally iconic. An internal modification as in *mice* as the plural of *mouse* is far less iconic, because although there is a mark of the change in status, it is not an additional mark to reflect the additional semantic structure. An unmarked plural such as *sheep* as the plural of *sheep* is non-iconic, since there is no marker of the additional semantic structure. A subtractive morph to show plurality as in the German dialect form *hon* 'dogs' from the singular *hond* is counter-iconic, in that less formal structure reflects more semantic structure. There is a scale of naturalness here from the most iconic = most natural, down to the least iconic = least natural. The prediction is that if any language only uses one technique it will be the most iconic one, and that the most iconic one will be the most common kind in any language, independent of whether it also uses other kinds (Dressler, 1982: 74).

12.2 Conflicts of naturalness

There will, inevitably, be cases where there is a conflict between what is natural on one parameter and what is natural on another. Perhaps the most obvious cases of this are those where what is natural in phonological terms is unnatural in morphological terms. For instance, it seems to be fairly natural for a word-final unstressed vowel to be deleted, particularly if that vowel is a close vowel. In some cases, though, this will mean that a whole suffix is deleted. It might then be the case that as a result of this natural phonological rule, the situation arises where what was once constructionally iconic is no longer so. It seems, in fact, that a great deal of 'unnatural' morphology arises in precisely this way. For example, the feminine plural genitive in Russian, which is striking because it has no overt marker, arose precisely through the deletion of unstressed [u] (Wurzel, 1980: 109). In this particular case, then, it seems that phonological naturalness is more potent than morphological constructional iconicity in determining the outcome of language change. But general statements are required as to what will happen in any given conflict of criteria for naturalness, or at least, of the type of condition which will affect the outcome.

As an example of a case of morphological conflict, consider the naturalness of transparency on the one hand versus the unnaturalness of extremely long words on the other. Transparency is the extent to which there is a clear match between meaning and form. To the extent that the relationship between the two is obscured, the construction is said to be opaque. Dressler (1985: 330-1) gives the following hierarchy of transparency:

(1) I Only allophonic rules interfere   excite·ment
         between form and meaning

189

II	Phonological rules such as resyllabification interfere between form and meaning	exis$t·ence
III	Neutralising phonological rules such as intervocalic flapping interfere between form and meaning	rid·er (in American English)
IV	Morphophonemic rules (but with no fusion) interfere between form and meaning	electri[s]·ity
V	Morphophonemic rules with fusion interfere between form and meaning	conclu[ʒə]n
VI	Morphological rules, such as rules reflecting the Great Vowel Shift interfere between form and meaning	dec[ɪ]sion
VII	Suppletion creates opacity	be → am

I is the most transparent, VII the least. I is accordingly seen as the most natural option, and is expected to be the most common option across languages. Suppletion is predicted to be (and is) the least common option.

Conflicting with the naturalness of transparency, we have the naturalness of words that are not too long. It is claimed that the optimal size of an affix is a syllable, and that the optimal size of a lexical base is one or two syllables (Kilani-Schoch & Dressler, 1984: 52). The source of these generalisations about the size of words and affixes is not clear. Kilani-Schoch & Dressler (1984) cite Ohlander (1976) and Stein (1970). Neither of these is particularly specific, and in any case Ohlander is dealing specifically with Old English, Stein with English, French, and German. The range of languages on which the generalisation appears to be based is thus extremely small, and typologically unrepresentative. Dressler (1982: 76) admits that 'thorough typological studies are necessary' in this area. In the absence of such studies, we may accept the general statement for the sake of the argument, although it should be noted that at least the precise values quoted are open to question. On this basis, we can conclude that the ideal length of a word-form is somewhere in the region of three syllables, plus or minus two.

In agglutinative languages, where there is in general a one-to-one relationship between form and meaning (see above, section 11.1), transparency is maximised. As a direct result of this, however, word-forms often tend to become long. Fusional languages keep their word-forms relatively short at the expense of transparency.

12. Natural Morphology

Compare the translations of the phrase 'of our hands' in (2) below, where the citation form of the lexeme for 'hand' in Turkish is EL, and in Icelandic is HÖND.

(2) Turkish (agglutinative):
     el·ler·imiz·in
     hand·plural·1st-person-plural·genitive
     Icelandic (fusional)
     vor·ra hand·a
     1st-person-plural-possessive·genitive-plural
     hand·genitive-plural

The difference between agglutinative and fusional languages can thus be seen partly as a difference in the way various parameters of naturalness have affected particular languages.

One particularly interesting set of conflicts occurs between system-independent and system-dependent naturalness. The factors that have been discussed so far all deal with system-independent naturalness, that is, they may be expected to apply equally in all languages. System-dependent naturalness, on the other hand, applies only to a single language, and is determined by patterns peculiar to that language. To exemplify this, we shall consider the plurals of German nouns as discussed by Wurzel (1984a, 1985). First, however, a further terminological digression is required.

In fusional languages a distinction can be drawn between stem inflection and base form inflection. In Russian, for example, masculine nouns show base form inflection, where the affixes are added to the whole word, as is shown in the following partial paradigm:

(3) | CHAIR | singular | plural |
     | --- | --- | --- |
     | nominative | stol | stol·i |
     | dative | stol·u | stol·am |
     | prepositional | stol·e | stol·ax |

Feminine nouns, on the other hand, show stem inflection, because the affix is added to the stem, as shown in the following partial paradigm:

(4) | BOOK | singular | plural |
     | --- | --- | --- |
     | nominative | knig·a | knig·i |
     | dative | knig·e | knig·am |
     | prepositional | knig·e | knig·ax |

While the distinction looks perfectly clear in these terms, it is not necessarily as clear-cut as it has been made to appear here. As far as I can make out, the term 'base form inflection' is used when the affixes are added to the citation form of the lexeme, and 'stem

191

inflection' means they are added to only the base in the citation form of the lexeme. However, in the example quoted, *knig* is a word-form realising the genitive plural of KNIGA, and could be reinterpreted as the basic form in the paradigm. The feminine nouns in the Russian example might therefore be something closer to base form inflection. Stem inflection would be better illustrated with the Latin DOMINUS, where every case singular and plural is marked by an affix. The distinction is thus clear at each extreme, but there may be some mixed cases in between.

Now German plurals are mainly marked by base form inflection.

(5)
Singular	Plural	Gloss
der Tag	die Tag·e	'day'
der Uhu	die Uhu·s	'owl'
das Brot	die Brot·e	'bread'
das Kind	die Kind·er	'child'
die Hand	die Händ·e	'hand'
die Uhr	die Uhr·en	'clock'

There is, however, a small class of nouns in German which show stem inflection. Some examples are:

(6)
Singular	Plural	Gloss
die Firm·a	die Firm·en	'firm, business'
der Radi·us	die Radi·en	'radius'
das Stadi·on	die Stadi·en	'stadium'

Since base form inflection is the rule in German and stem inflection is very much a minority case, there is pressure to change the stem inflections in German to base form inflections. Thus, while no new words seem to be being added to the class of stem inflections in German, words which previously showed stem inflection are changing class so that they show base form inflection. In some cases these changes are well established, in others they are still limited to informal style levels, non-standard varieties, and so on.

(7)
Singular	Old Plural	Innovative Plural	Gloss
das Konto	die Kont·en	die Konto·s	'account'
das Aroma	die Arom·en	die Aroma·s	'aroma'
die Junta	die Junt·en	die Junta·s	'junta'
die Tuba	die Tub·en	die Tuba·s	'tuba'
der Globus	die Glob·en	die Globus·se	'globe'

This change is brought about because one of the **system-defining structural properties** of modern German is the property of using base form inflection. This is a property of modern German, but not, say, a property of Russian or Latin, or even of Old High German. It is clearly not universal. Neither is this a rule, in the generative sense of the word 'rule'. The system-defining structural property is a generalisation available to speakers of a language concerning the morphology of their language. Such generalisations tend to produce unity in the morphological structure of individual languages. They tend to force change in a language even in the face of what would be seen as natural from a system-independent viewpoint.

This can be seen even more clearly with another facet of German plural formation. As was shown above there is a hierarchy of iconicity such that the addition of an affix is more iconic than internal modification. It would therefore be predicted from a system-independent viewpoint that plurals created by internal modification would tend to yield to plurals created by affixation. Despite this, there is a group of plurals in modern German where affixation is yielding to internal modification (Umlaut). Examples are:

(8)

Singular	Old Plural	New Plural	Gloss
der Mops	die Mops·e	die Möpse	'pug'
der Strand	die Strand·e	die Strände	'beach'
der Zwang	die Zwang·e	die Zwänge	'compulsion'

The important point to note about the words in (8) is that they are all masculine. Neuter nouns, for instance, show changes in the other (more generally expected) direction:

(9)

Singular	Old Plural	New Plural	Gloss
das Boot	die Böte	die Boot·e	'boat'
das Rohr	die Röhre	die Rohr·e	'pipe'

The point, according to Wurzel, is that most masculine nouns now have this kind of Umlaut plural, while most neuter nouns do not. A criterion of **inflectional class stability** tends to lead to changes which support this pattern. As a result, he says (1984a: 73), incorrect plurals such as *die Hünde* instead of *die Hunde* from *der Hund* are more acceptable than incorrect plural forms with no Umlaut (for example, an incorrect *die Flüsse* instead of *die Flusse* from *der Fluss*). This criterion of inflectional class stability is clearly language specific, not universal, and it appears to take precedence over universal natural patterns. That is, where universal and language specific naturalness criteria conflict, the language specific ones seem to take precedence.

In similar ways it seems that feminine plurals in German are gradually changing so that they are marked with an -*n* plural, while masculine nouns that used to have an -*n* plural are losing it (Wurzel,

193

1985: 594-5). Similar factors might explain the resistance to loss of the final -*e* on German feminine nouns (Ohlander, 1976: 170).

12.3 Implications

Perhaps the most important feature of natural morphology is that it attempts to give some kind of explanation of morphological universals in terms of semiotic, and perhaps ultimately cognitive, principles. This is the same kind of approach as that we saw taken by Bybee in Chapter 11, but generalised far beyond the two principles that Bybee proposes.

Care must, of course, be taken not to get into a vicious circle such that something is claimed to be universal because it is natural, and natural because it is universal. It is for this reason that there is stress placed on the need for external evidence of naturalness. This was seen in the list on page 188. It is also the reason that the semiotic background is seen as important by natural morphologists (Dressler, 1985: 323).

So, for example, Mayerthaler (1980: 30; 1981:28) gives a list of tendencies in morphological marking that look very much like Greenbergian statistical implicational universals. Some of these are repeated below in (10). Mayerthaler says that it is natural for there to be no marking on the category in the first column, but for there to be one in the category in the second column. We can reformulate this in Greenbergian terms by saying that a marking for the category in the first column implies a marking for the category in the second column. The difference between the two is that Mayerthaler's list has as an 'explanation' the principle of constructional iconicity, a semiotic principle based in turn upon cognitively defined ideas of what 'more meaning' is.

(10) | Singular | Non-singular |
| --- | --- |
| Active | Non-active |
| Indicative | Non-indicative |
| Nominative | Non-nominative |
| Cardinal number | Non-cardinal |
| 3rd person sing. | Other persons |

Clearly, any universals arising from such a list are only statistical, not absolute: the English 3rd person singular present tense -*s* suffix is a notorious counter-example to the last item on the list, for instance. But natural morphology does not expect to find absolute universals of this type.

The whole notion of constructional iconicity can be taken even further. For instance, Haiman (1985: 137) notes the following 'nearly universal' property of the contrast between what he terms the direct cases (nominative/accusative or ergative/absolutive) and the oblique cases (all others):

> In no language will the morphological bulk of a direct case affix *exceed* that of the oblique case affixes, as a general rule. There will be languages, however, in which the morphological bulk of oblique case affixes exceeds that of direct case affixes.

Haiman estimates bulk simply in terms of syllables, although some more subtle way of counting could no doubt be used. This might be extended to endings within a paradigm of oblique cases, too. In Latin, for instance, the dative and ablative plurals show a di-syllabic case ending (*-ibus*), and they are doubly marked. Moreover, it would be worth examining whether similar facts hold true (or how far they hold true) for all the pairs listed in (10). Is it the case that where the indicative is overtly marked, its marker is at most the same size as the marker of the subjunctive? If all affixes in the language under consideration are of the same 'size' (however computed) this may not mean anything, but where there are affixes of different 'sizes' the implication may be found to hold more widely.

Since the general constraints introduced by the Lexicalist Morphologists (see section 9.6) are also statements that are presumed to be universal, they should also fall within the purview of natural morphology. The universals are often of a rather different kind, as was discussed earlier, but this is not necessarily crucial. It is important, though, that whereas universals in Lexicalist Morphology tend to be formulated as though they were absolute universals, within natural morphology they would rather be seen as statements of relative naturalness. For example, The Word-Based Hypothesis (Aronoff, 1976: 21) is stated as follows:

> All regular word-formation processes are word-based. A new word is formed by applying a regular rule to a single already existing word. Both the new word and the existing one are members of major lexical categories [defined as adverb, adjective, noun and verb].

In natural morphology this would have to be modified. Dressler (1982: 76) suggests that the lexeme is a manageable unit for perception: it must be listed in the speaker's lexicon, while formatives smaller than the word may not be; items larger than the word are not recurrent in the same way that the lexeme is (unless they are idiomatic). He suggests that is why word-based morphology is preferred. But there is plenty of evidence that not all morphological processes are word-based (for some discussion see Bauer, 1980;

1983: 174ff; Botha, 1981; Carroll, 1979; Scalise, 1984: 71-6). Where Lexicalist Morphology is concerned, this simply indicates that the constraint has been incorrectly stated. In natural morphology, this state of affairs would be expected, but it would also be expected that the deviations from word-based morphology would be the exceptions and should, in some sense, cost more in terms of the description or language processing.

Similarly, consider the Multiple Application Constraint (Lieber, 1981: 173):

> No word formation process ... can apply iteratively to its own output.

That this constraint is not universal can be seen from Afrikaans diminutives such as *kind·jie·tjie* 'nice little child', Italian diminutives such as *car·in·in·o* 'very nice little' (Scalise, 1984: 133 and note), German forms such as *Ur·ur·gross·mutter* 'great-great-grand-mother', and a few English prefixes such as those in *meta-meta-rule, re-rewrite.* Consider also the following data from Zulu:

(11)   umu·ntu   'person'
       um·ntw·ana   'child'
       um·ntw·any·ana   'small child'
       um·ntw·any·any·ana   'very small child'

Such examples simply contradict the constraint as put forward by Lieber, but again such examples would be trivial if the constraint were reformulated as a markedness convention within natural morphology. Under such conditions it would simply be expected that such reapplication would be exceptional in any language (which appears to be the case) and costly in terms of the description required and the processing time required by speakers coping with it. Both of these seem to be true as far as the English prefix *re-* is concerned. There is a brief discussion in Bauer (1983: 68) of the difficulty in deciding which forms in *re-re-* are acceptable and which not, and the processing difficulty is suggested by the fact that the sequence *re-re-* is usually avoided in terms of a paraphrase with *again* (Stein, 1977: 225).

Similar implications for relative cost apply also to Word-and-Paradigm morphology. One way to simplify a WP rule is to make the operation it describes null. According to the principle of constructional iconicity, however, this should make the morphology less natural, since it would lead to a greater amount of conversion. There is thus conflict between what appears to be simplification in a WP rule schema, and what should be simplification in the sense of likely language change (that is, becoming more natural). In an ideal grammar these two would coincide.

There are also implications to be drawn from natural morphology about various questions of description at all levels. For instance, it seems that discontinuous morphs are less natural than continuous ones. This implies that circumfixes, transfixes and infixes should be less usual than other types of affixation. We have seen that this is the case. Most cases of circumfixes can probably be analysed as being made up of a prefix and a suffix (this is true of the German example cited in section 3.1.3, where the *ge-* prefix is not used on all verbs). Infixation, which gives rise to a discontinuous base, is, in any case, extremely rare in the languages of the world. Transfixation should be doubly unnatural: not only does it involve discontinuous affixes, but also discontinuous bases. We know that it is virtually restricted to the Semitic languages, so its general rarity is confirmed. Furthermore, it is not completely generalised there: Semitic languages also have large numbers of suffixes and prefixes. Nevertheless, transfixation is notably dominant in these languages. Even if we assume that this is a system-defining structural property of these languages, the question remains as to why it should be so unnatural in system-independent terms. Kilani-Schoch & Dressler (1984) suggest that transfixation is, in fact, so unnatural that it does not exist, and that so-called transfixes are the result of misanalysis. They suggest that a better analysis for Classical Arabic is in terms of a basic form and multiple internal modifications (Ablaut and/or consonant gemination). They base their argument on the patterns that are actually attested, as a proportion of the possible forms if transfixes could have any form. Their argument no doubt needs to be evaluated by a competent scholar of Semitic, but is at least superficially persuasive. If their analysis is adopted, the Semitic languages are still not maximally iconic, but they are much more natural than they appear using a transfixal analysis.

At a much more trivial level, consider the problem of the multiplication of homophonous affixes discussed in section 6.3. It was said there that the suffix -*ette* might be seen as one, two or three affixes, depending on one's position with regard to the meaning of a suffix. Haiman (1985) provides a means of solving such quandaries. He gives what he calls the Isomorphism Hypothesis, which states (1985: 19)

> Different forms will always entail a difference in communicative function. Conversely, recurrent identity of form between different grammatical categories will always reflect some perceived similarity in communicative function.

197

12. Natural Morphology

This hypothesis is formulated for application to syntax, but it can be modified for morphology, too. In morphology it is questionable whether 'different forms always entail a difference in communicative function': do the various nominalisation affixes really have a different 'communicative function', for example? But within natural morphology, Haiman's hypothesis could be seen as representing the unmarked, and therefore natural case. If the converse is applied to morphology, then we are under some obligation to take the three meanings of *-ette* as being meanings of the same suffix, unless there is overwhelming evidence to the contrary. In the case of English plural, possessive and third person singular present tense morphemes (all of which have the same allomorphs), I take it that the facts discussed in section 8.1 would constitute such overwhelming evidence.

12.4 Conclusion

As yet very little descriptive work has been done using natural morphology. It is to be expected that further research will lead to modifications in the theory, and to greater detail in some of the many areas which are currently rather obscure. Of these, perhaps the most notable is the prediction of which parameter will win out under what circumstances in the cases of naturalness conflicts. Also, researchers in this area will have to beware of the temptation to provide *ad hoc* 'explanations' of apparently unnatural phenomena. It may be that what appears 'unnatural' in one place is actually a lot less unnatural when a lot more data is considered. At this stage a statement that certain features are currently inexplicable within the framework would be preferable to appeals to loosely-formulated and badly-understood intuitions. Future research will have to concentrate not only on the linguistic side of the predictions made by the theory, but also the semiotic and cognitive, and for this some input from outside linguistics will be required. The research project that natural morphology represents is thus an ambitious one. Nonetheless, natural morphology looks like a very hopeful avenue of exploration in morphological theory.

REFERENCES AND FURTHER READING

The major sources on natural morphology are Mayerthaler (1981) and Wurzel (1984a), but neither of these is particularly easy to read. An English translation of Mayerthaler is to be available soon, and this may make matters slightly easier. Dressler *et al.* (forthcoming) has been announced for several years. Otherwise only the individual papers are available. Of these, Dressler (1985) is one that illustrates the range of natural morphology, but it is extremely densely written and allusive, so that it is not easily readable.

12. Natural Morphology

The discussion of plurality in section 12.1, while based firmly on publications from the school of natural morphology, appears to leave some questions unanswered. In Turkana, a Nilotic language of North Western Kenya, a morphological distinction is made not between singulars and plurals, but between singulatives and pluratives. Objects which normally occur in isolation have a morphologically unmarked singular form, with a morphologically marked plural form. Thus the singular of the word for 'road' is *e·rot*ˋ, (where the *e* is a gender marker), and the plural is ŋi·rot·inˋ, (where the prefix marks gender, and the suffix is a plurative marker). On the other hand, objects which normally occur in groups have a morphologically unmarked plural form, and a morphologically marked singular. Thus the plural of the word for 'breast' is ŋi·sɪkɪnˋ, (where the prefix marks gender) and the singular is ɛ·sɪkɪn·aˋ, (where the prefix marks gender, and the suffix is a singulative marker). The data is taken from Dimmendaal (1983), where further details can be found. There is an intuitive sense in which this is a perfectly 'natural' system, and yet it appears to be at odds with the general presumption that plurality is always (or 'naturally') the marked category. I do not wish to imply that natural morphology cannot deal with such a phenomenon, simply that rather more elucidation is required. Mayerthaler (1981: 51ff) does deal with singulatives, which he sees as being the marked form of collectives. The point about the Turkana data is that both regular singulatives and regular pluratives are found. It is not clear from Mayerthaler's exposition whether the same is true for any of the languages he mentions.

Wurzel's discussion of Umlaut versus lack of Umlaut in German noun plurals requires a little further explanation. Hammer (1971: 7) states not only that plurals with Umlaut and a final *-e* are most frequent for masculine nouns, but also that this is the preferred way of marking the plural for masculine nouns. However, neuter nouns also prefer an Umlaut pattern, but with the suffix *-er* (as in *das Buch, die Bücher* 'book'). It is the pattern with Umlaut and suffix *-e* which is rare in feminine nouns (some 33 examples) and almost unknown for neuters (only one example: *das Floss* 'raft'). Hammer provides figures for the less common patterns and for the numbers of exceptions to the general rules, which support Wurzel's basic claims.

In regard to the iterative application of affixes as in *Ur·ur·gross·mutter, re-rewrite* discussed in section 12.3, Mayerthaler (1981: 117ff) suggests that it may be possible to formulate natural constraints on affixes which can be used in this way. His suggestion is, however, based on far too little evidence to be conclusive. He suggests that iteration of the same affix is constructionally iconic if it marks a scale showing monotonic progression. It is not clear that *meta-meta-rule* fits this category.

The data on Zulu in (11) is from Andrew Carstairs (personal communication).

13. Conclusion: Is a Synthesis Possible?

In the last Part of this book, a number of different approaches to morphology and problems in morphology have been considered. In this chapter an attempt will be made at some kind of synthesis, taking into account the points that have been raised throughout the book. To do this, a fragment of German noun morphology will be used as an example. What is done here can be contrasted with the approach taken in Chapter 10 (although it is not precisely the same set of data for which a grammar will be provided here), and in parts with the approach taken by Lieber (1981) and Zwicky (1985b). Further facts on German morphology can be gleaned from Fleischer (1975) and Hammer (1971), and from the discussion in Wurzel (1984a).

As a general notation I shall use phrase structure rules. There is a certain amount of dispute in the literature as to whether PS rules are a suitable way of writing all morphological operations (Lieber, 1981, Selkirk, 1982). It does not seem to me that the issue has been definitely settled, and until such time as it is shown convincingly that PS rules are not sufficient, they represent a conservative option: any alternative is likely to have the power of transformational rules. On the whole I am sympathetic to the general notion of phrase structure as discussed within the framework of Generalised Phrase Structure Grammar (see Gazdar *et al.*, 1985), but I have not adopted all the conventions of GPSG here. In particular, I maintain the older-fashioned (but more familiar) arrow notation for PS rules rather than the GPSG typographically more complex bracket notation. Nevertheless, I would wish these PS rules to be read as node admissibility conditions, as in GPSG. I shall comment further on some of the notions I adopt from GPSG in appropriate places.

In most cases, a Word-and-Paradigm type of statement is translatable into a PS rule quite directly. For instance, consider one of the rules used in section 10.2:

(1)	B	L	P	R
	LB	Class 9	Rule 3	$\begin{bmatrix} N \\ +dat \\ +sing \end{bmatrix}$

Class 9 was the class containing *Herz, Herzen,* and Rule 3 was the rule suffixing *-en* to the base. This can be reformulated as a PS rule in the following way:

$$(2) \quad \begin{bmatrix} N \\ +dat \\ +sing \end{bmatrix} \rightarrow \begin{bmatrix} LB \\ Class\ 9 \end{bmatrix} + en$$

In GPSG this rule would be read thus: a partial tree in which the mother node is made up of a dative singular noun and the daughter nodes are a lexical base of Class 9 and the affix *-en* is an acceptable partial tree. A tree is acceptable if all the partial trees in it are acceptable. In fact, the rule need not be as complicated as this, because of the way in which subcategorisation is handled within GPSG. In GPSG every rule is given a number, and that number serves to subcategorise the lexical categories required for the rule. So we could say that HERZ belongs to category (2), and is therefore affected by rule (2). BUCH, on the other hand, belongs to a different category, and is affected by a different rule. Mention of 'Class 9' in (2) can thus be omitted without further ado. The number of the rule (2) acts, effectively, in the same way as the 'Class 9' limitation does in the WP rule format. Instead of being marked as belonging to Class 9, *Herz* will be marked as being a member of noun type (2).

Turning now to the details of German noun morphology, we can begin with the plural inflections that were discussed in section 10.2. In that section, thirteen distinct classes of German neuter nouns were discussed. However, not all those classes are productive. In fact, only four of them are clearly productive:

(a) The class like AUTO where the plural is formed by the suffixation of *-s.*

(b) The class like MÄDCHEN where there is no overt plural marker.

(c) The class like KIND, where the plural is marked by the suffixation of *-er.*

(d) The class like BUCH, where the plural is marked by Umlaut and the suffixation of *-er.*

Two of these classes are defined phonologically, and the other two may not be distinct.

(a) The AUTO class is defined by ending in a phonologically short vowel other than /e/ (Wurzel, 1984a: 154). The class is productive for all three genders, not just neuter nouns, for instance:

(3) | Singular | Plural | Gloss |
|---|---|---|
| der Ufo | die Ufo·s | 'UFO' (masculine) |
| die Cola | die Cola·s | 'Cola' (feminine) |
| das Veto | die Veto·s | 'veto' (neuter) |

13. Conclusion: Is a Synthesis Possible?

There are a number of nouns which meet the phonological require-ments but do not have this type of plural marking (*die Firma, die Firm·en* 'firm'). Nevertheless, nouns which previously did not belong to this class tend to become members, and new phonologi-cally appropriate loan words are put into this class.

(b) Both neuter and masculine nouns which end in *-el, -en, -er* (including diminutives in *-chen, -lein*) fall into the MÄDCHEN category. There are a few nouns which fit the morphological and phonological definition of this class, but which do not make their plurals in the appropriate way. The opposing patterns are not, as far as I can tell, productive. This would be predicted. For example, only one neuter noun, KLOSTER, breaks the pattern. Such nouns will have their plural forms listed in the lexicon, not derived by general rule. As far as the neuter nouns are concerned, the produc-tivity of this class is seen most clearly with the diminutive endings.

(c) As was said in section 10.2, the KIND class and the BUCH class can be merged, if it is assumed that the Umlaut rule applies to both but has no effect on the form of the vowel in words like KIND because they are not susceptible to Umlaut.

If the proposal put forward in Chapter 8 is adopted, then the grammar need only concern itself with these productive categories. The morphological patterns of the unproductive categories will be listed in the lexicon. Just how this is to be done is not of immediate concern here, but one possibility is the use of redundancy rules as advocated by Jackendoff (1975). Such redundancy rules set up statements of formal relationships which are then referred to from lexical entries. For example a lexical redundancy rule might have the form

(4)   LB ↔ LB + *e*

This redundancy rule would be referred to in the lexical entry for a noun like BEIN 'leg' as a way of specifying the non-productive plural formation. The entire set of rules (excluding these redun-dancy rules) for deriving plurals of neuter nouns can therefore be reduced to the following:

(5) $\begin{bmatrix} N \\ +\text{nom} \\ +\text{pl} \end{bmatrix} \rightarrow \begin{bmatrix} N \\ LB \end{bmatrix} + s$

(6) $\begin{bmatrix} N \\ +\text{nom} \\ +\text{pl} \end{bmatrix} \rightarrow \begin{bmatrix} N \\ LB \end{bmatrix}$

(7)
$$\begin{bmatrix} N \\ +\text{nom} \\ +\text{pl} \end{bmatrix} \rightarrow \begin{bmatrix} N \\ \text{LB} \\ +\text{Umlaut} \end{bmatrix} + er$$

Noun class (5) will be open-ended and phonologically defined. Exceptions will be lexically listed. Rather than listing each noun such as UFO, VETO, AUTO as being a member of class (5), a preferable solution would be a redundancy rule statement according to which the class of nouns (5) is by definition the set of nouns without lexical marking which end in a phonologically short vowel which is not /e/. Such a format would account for the fact that new nouns which fit the phonological parameters appear to join this class. A similar type of logic applies to the definition of noun class (6). Class (7) is then the class of neuter nouns which has not already been covered by any other generalisation. This implies some kind of ordering between statements. Some version of the proper inclusion principle seems to be required, according to which if the set of forms subject to rule A is properly included by the set of forms subject to rule B (i.e. if the forms which can be the input to rule A are a proper subset of the forms that can provide an input to rule B), rule A must apply before rule B. Since the class of neuter nouns ending in a phonologically short non-/e/ vowel is a subset of the class of neuter nouns, rule (5) has to apply before rule (7). There is no implicit ordering relationship between (5) and (6) since neither set includes the other.

Since productive rules can never be determined by lexical marking, the noun classes defined by the rule numbers for productive rules must always be stateable in terms of some kind of redundancy rule. This rule may, of course, be extremely complex, involving several conjuncts or disjuncts. If the appropriate noun class demands lexical marking, it is evidence that the rule is not productive. This is rather different from the situation in syntax.

Without getting involved in the details of precisely what nominal categories are productive in current German, we can assume that the other rules for the nominative plural forms will look something like the following:

(8)
$$\begin{bmatrix} N \\ +\text{nom} \\ +\text{pl} \end{bmatrix} \rightarrow \begin{bmatrix} N \\ \text{LB} \end{bmatrix} + en$$

(9)
$$\begin{bmatrix} N \\ +\text{nom} \\ +\text{pl} \end{bmatrix} \rightarrow \begin{bmatrix} N \\ \text{LB} \\ +\text{Umlaut} \end{bmatrix} + e$$

204

13. Conclusion: Is a Synthesis Possible?

The rule in (8) is the main productive rule for feminine nouns, and that in (9) is the main productive rule for masculine nouns. However, not only feminine nouns use the pattern in (8) and not only masculine nouns use the pattern in (9), just as not only neuter nouns use the pattern in (7). It might therefore seem that a gain in generalisation could be achieved by allowing, for example, noun class (8) to include masculine nouns such as *der Dorn, die Dorn·en* 'thorn' and neuter nouns such as *das Bett, die Bett·en* 'bed'. If this is done it means either that there is no simple way to define the class that undergoes (8), whereas they can otherwise be defined as the class of feminine nouns, or that a list of specified masculine and neuter nouns which can undergo (8) has to be given in the grammar. The former is undesirable, in that it turns a morphologically defined class into a basically random, lexically defined class, and thus states that the rule is not really productive, which is incorrect. The latter involves stating a rule which is productive in one domain as though it were productive in another domain, which is misleading. Since this second option is also equivalent to marking the masculine and neuter nouns in this class for their own plural forms in their lexical entries, no advantage accrues from it. In general the diachronic pressures appear to be towards having the plural classes defined phonologically or morphologically (in terms of gender) (see the discussion in Wurzel, 1984a). Having only productive rules in the grammar provides some kind of answer to why this should be so. The implication, of course, is that there will never be wholesale change into a non-productive class. This contrasts with Wurzel's claim that change is towards the most common pattern. Which of these two competing claims is in fact true (if either is exclusively true) must be open to empirical verification.

The rules as they have been stated above require various phonological rescue rules. The *-e-* in the *-en* suffix in rule (8) is deleted if the base ends in a vowel or *r*, or *l* preceded by an unstressed vowel. In this sense the rules as stated are less specific than those given in section 10.2, but still I think perfectly justifiable. Similarly the use of a blatantly morphological feature [+ Umlaut] in order to trigger a phonological operation might be questioned. Since Umlaut is a morphological operation in current German, determined by morphological rather than phonological environment, this again seems to me to be justifiable. It is, however, another point which requires further consideration.

It is fairly clear in principle how the rules for deriving other case forms of nouns will work, but the details of the rules are far from clear. Consider, for example, how accusative forms are to be derived. In all the nouns that have been considered here (although this is not actually true of all nouns, in particular not those of the so-called 'weak' declension), the accusative form is identical with the nominative form. Nevertheless, the two cannot simply be equated, since masculine singular articles, for instance, are distinct in the nominative and accusative. We might, therefore, expect a rule something like the following:

$$(10) \quad \begin{bmatrix} N \\ +acc \end{bmatrix} \rightarrow \begin{bmatrix} N \\ +nom \end{bmatrix}$$

However, there are problems with a rule of this type. First of all, it is a rule of conversion. As we have seen, conversion is less natural than affixation. We would therefore expect this relationship to be shown somehow in the grammar: we would expect a conversion rule to cost more, in some sense, than an affixation rule. (The relative naturalness of conversion and affixation will depend to some extent upon language type, as is admitted by natural morphologists, but even so conversion ought to be less natural within German.) However, as it stands, rule (10) appears to cost less than an affixation rule, because it is precisely the same as an affixation rule except that it requires no operation and is, to that extent, simpler. It might be possible to solve this by a simple statement, some kind of meta-rule, that conversion rules are more costly than affixation rules. This is unsatisfactory, however, because it contains no attempt at explanation. It is simply a statement which becomes true by fiat. What, then, are the alternatives? We might have a new rule deriving accusative singulars from lexical bases, and another set of rules identical to (7), (8) and (9) except that they create accusative plural forms, not nominative plural forms. This appears wasteful, in that it fails to note what is clearly a major generalisation in German noun declensions. One way to capture this generalisation without running into problems of naturalness is to introduce a different rule type. This rule type is simply a statement of formal identity. Using it, we can reformulate (10) as follows:

$$(11) \quad \begin{bmatrix} N \\ +acc \end{bmatrix} = \begin{bmatrix} N \\ +nom \end{bmatrix}$$

The relative lack of naturalness of this rule type is then captured by the fact that it is a second rule type. The most economical system is one which contains only one rule type. In fact, there may be an advantage here. In isolating languages, most of the rules may be of this second type, with no (or very few) morphological rules of affixation. The relative naturalness of this type of language would then be captured by the fact that it operates with a single rule type

– even though that rule type is not the one which is most widely found in the languages of the world. This implies that affixation rules, natural in morphologically complex languages, are unnatural in isolating languages. This solution will be adopted here, although it also demands further consideration.

The rules specifying the other case forms can now be filled in quite quickly. The dative singular forms can be specified as follows:

(12)
$$\begin{bmatrix} \text{N} \\ +\text{dat} \\ +\text{sing} \end{bmatrix} = \begin{bmatrix} \text{N} \\ +\text{nom} \\ +\text{sing} \end{bmatrix}$$

(13)
$$\begin{bmatrix} \text{N} \\ +\text{dat} \\ +\text{sing} \end{bmatrix} \rightarrow \begin{bmatrix} \text{N} \\ +\text{nom} \\ +\text{sing} \end{bmatrix} + (e)$$

Noun class (12) is by definition the class of feminine nouns, noun class (13) is defined as the union of the classes of masculine and neuter nouns. Phonological rescue rules are then required to make sure that rule (13) does not result in an impossible sequence of vowels. Alternatively, given that a final dative *-e* is not found on a number of masculine and neuter nouns which do not end in a vowel (for example, no diminutive can take a dative *-e* – probably as a result of the phonological form of diminutives), it would be possible to define noun classes (12) and (13) on phonological grounds.

Note that rule (13) introduces another problem, since it is in effect an abbreviation of two rules, one of which is a suffixation rule, the other a statement of formal identity. Since a distinction has been drawn between these two types of rule, a formulation such as that in (13) is misleading. It might be preferable to have two distinct rules, with a free option between them. That is, there should be two alternative rules, as follows:

(14)
$$\begin{bmatrix} \text{N} \\ +\text{dat} \\ +\text{sing} \end{bmatrix} = \begin{bmatrix} \text{N} \\ +\text{nom} \\ +\text{sing} \end{bmatrix}$$

(15)
$$\begin{bmatrix} \text{N} \\ +\text{dat} \\ +\text{sing} \end{bmatrix} \rightarrow \begin{bmatrix} \text{N} \\ +\text{nom} \\ +\text{sing} \end{bmatrix} + e$$

13. Conclusion: Is a Synthesis Possible?

The rule for the dative plural will be:

(16)
$$\begin{bmatrix} N \\ +\text{dat} \\ +\text{pl} \end{bmatrix} \rightarrow \begin{bmatrix} N \\ +\text{nom} \\ +\text{pl} \end{bmatrix} + en$$

This holds in the vast majority of cases, provided that a phonological rescue rule is included to prevent it applying to forms which already end in *n*, or to delete the *-e-* if the form already ends in an *-e*. There are exceptions, however, both morphologically and semantically defined. They are included in a rule which must apply before (16):

(17)
$$\begin{bmatrix} N \\ +\text{dat} \\ +\text{pl} \end{bmatrix} = \begin{bmatrix} N \\ +\text{nom} \\ +\text{pl} \end{bmatrix}$$

Noun class (17) is the union of the sets of proper names and nouns whose plural is in *-s* (see rule (5)) (Hammer, 1971: 21).

The forms of the genitive plural can be derived by an identity operation from the nominative plural, the forms of the genitive singular are derived as follows:

(18)
$$\begin{bmatrix} N \\ +\text{gen} \\ +\text{sing} \end{bmatrix} = \begin{bmatrix} N \\ +\text{nom} \\ +\text{sing} \end{bmatrix}$$

(19)
$$\begin{bmatrix} N \\ +\text{gen} \\ +\text{sing} \end{bmatrix} \rightarrow \begin{bmatrix} N \\ +\text{dat} \\ +\text{sing} \end{bmatrix} + s$$

Here the noun class (18) is the class of feminine nouns, and the class (19) is the union of the classes of masculine and neuter nouns. A phonological rescue rule is required to insert an *-e-* between two adjacent sibilants, to avoid forms like **Krebss*, **Buschs* 'of the crab, bush' respectively.

While rules like the ones given above will account for the forms of lexemes, they say nothing about instances where particular forms occur. For example, the *-es* form of the genitive singular is used (according to Hammer, 1971: 20) with

> German (not ... foreign) mononosyllabics, or polysyllabics ending in a stressed syllable, if used as a preceding attributive genitive (the Saxon Genitive): des Tages Hitze, des Geschenkes Wert ['the heat of the day', 'the value of the gift' respectively].

Similarly, although feminine nouns cannot usually take an *-s* geni-

13. Conclusion: Is a Synthesis Possible?

tive, names and other words which may be used as vocatives do take an -s genitive when used attributively: *Annas Hut* 'Anna's hat', *Mutters Hut* 'mother's hat'. Since such rules are productive it is clear that they must be entered in the grammar somewhere. It is less clear whether they count as part of the morphology proper or whether they are syntactic rules, or precisely how, if at all, they are to be made a part of the type of rule that has been proposed here (or, for that matter, in other formal morphologies). Should there, for example, be a rule of the same form as (19) whose noun class is defined as the class of female names and the family members *Mutter* 'mother', *Tante* 'aunt'? Should this rule then only apply if called up by the syntactic component? The case of the attributive masculine and neuter -es genitives is even harder, since it involves the obligatory use of the suffix in rule (13), although that use is, in general, optional.

Turning now to derivational morphology, we can consider the case of diminutive formation. There are two diminutive suffixes in German which are clearly productive: -chen and -lein. Other diminutive endings are probably not productive in the standard language, although -el may be so in dialectal German. The two suffixes are both productive for a large number of bases in common, but there are slightly different phonological restrictions on the bases: -lein is not used if the base ends in -l or -le (unless it ends in -el: see below); -chen is not used if the base ends in -ch, -g or -ng (the spelling is frequently morphophonemic, but this could be reformulated in phonemic terms). Otherwise the two are in competition, with -chen clearly dominant. If the nominative form of the base ends in -el this is deleted before the suffixation of -lein. If the base ends in -e or -en this is deleted before either of the suffixes. Both suffixes cause Umlaut to apply to the base, unless the suffix is -chen and the base is a proper name or a word which may be used as a vocative. The various possibilities are illustrated below:

(20)	Base	Gloss	Diminutive 1	Diminutive 2
	Stadt	'town'	Städt·chen	Städt·lein
	Stall	'stable'	Ställ·chen	*
	Bach	'stream'	*	Bäch·lein
	Ring	'ring'	*	Ring·lein
	Zweig	'twig'	*	Zweig·lein
	Engel	'angel'	Engel·chen	Eng·lein
	Kiste	'chest'	Kist·chen	Kist·lein
	Haken	'hook'	Häk·chen	Häk·lein
	Karl	name	Karl·chen	*
	Frau	'woman'	Frau·chen	Fräu·lein

209

All of this can be captured in four rules, as long as the noun classes and the appropriate bases are suitably defined:

(21) $\begin{bmatrix} \text{N} \\ +\text{neut} \\ \text{LB} \end{bmatrix} \rightarrow \begin{bmatrix} \text{Base4} \\ +\text{Umlaut} \end{bmatrix} + \textit{lein}$

(22) $\begin{bmatrix} \text{N} \\ +\text{neut} \\ \text{LB} \end{bmatrix} \rightarrow \begin{bmatrix} \text{Base5} \\ +\text{Umlaut} \end{bmatrix} + \textit{lein}$

(23) $\begin{bmatrix} \text{N} \\ +\text{neut} \\ \text{LB} \end{bmatrix} \rightarrow \begin{bmatrix} \text{Base4} \\ +\text{Umlaut} \end{bmatrix} + \textit{chen}$

(24) $\begin{bmatrix} \text{N} \\ +\text{neut} \\ \text{LB} \end{bmatrix} \rightarrow [\text{Base4}] + \textit{chen}$

Base4 and Base5 (as in Chapter 10, the numbers are chosen at random and have no significance) are defined by appropriate subtraction rules: the deletion of *-e* and *-en* for Base4, the deletion of *-el* for Base5. The formulation of these rules is a matter of some concern if a PS grammar is being used, since deletions are not easily accommodated within such a grammar. It is clearly possible to write a rule of the following kind:

(25) $_{LB}[$ X e (n) $] \rightarrow$ $_{Base4}[$ X $]$

but this is really a transformational rule. In Generalised Phrase Structure Grammar, deletions are usually achieved by means of the creation of slash categories. It is not clear whether this is a possible way of deleting segmental material or not: the implications would require much greater consideration. For instance, there is an implication that tree structure continues down to a segmental level. While there is a certain amount of evidence for this from various non-linear phonologies such as metrical phonology or dependency phonology, there is no necessity for the same kind of rule format to be observed at all these levels, or for the same tree to continue down to that level of analysis. If the slash notation can be used, the definition of Base4 would be

(26)   Base4 $\rightarrow$ LB/*e*

(27)   Base4 $\rightarrow$ LB/*en*

(28)   Base4 $\rightarrow$ LB

(where '/*e*' means, informally, 'with an *e* missing'). There are obvious problems here. The -*e* or -*en* has to be final, yet this is not stated in the rule as it stands. Secondly, for the -*en* to be deleted by a single rule, the implication is that it must be dominated by a single node which does not dominate anything else. It is not clear to me whether this can be justified. Thirdly, the rules have to be ordered. The difficulties may simply be insuperable, in which case deletion rules would have to be transformational rules. If this is the case it at least helps to explain the relative unnaturalness of deletion rules.

What do we learn from this attempt at a synthesis? Each of the models discussed earlier has contributed to the treatment that has been proposed here. In the first place, much derivation is simply listed in the lexicon as suggested by the Lexicalists. Rules which are no longer productive may then become lexical redundancy rules, moving from the productive part of the grammar to the non-productive lexicon. Once there, they are available in differing degrees to different individuals, and may eventually not be used at all when words are no longer analysable. The productive rules, however, remain separate. They can be described using the general format of Word-and-Paradigm morphology, which it may be possible to re-write as some kind of phrase structure grammar, although we have seen that problems arise when this is attempted. If the wp notation is to be used, however, it would benefit from certain modifications to take account of the discoveries within natural morphology, so that rule format can reflect naturalness. In this way it ought to be possible to use the notation to make further predictions about naturalness, which can then be empirically checked on real language data.

The solution to the abstractness problem proposed in Chapter 8 has been adopted, and this has supported (and also extended) the general picture proposed by the Lexicalists without, however, saying anything about any of the details of that model.

In the question of inflection versus derivation, the type of approach presented in this chapter does not make a distinction. This can certainly be justified in terms of the discussion in Chapter 6, but further comment is required. If there is no distinction to be drawn, why is it generally upheld, felt to be valuable, and so well established? Does the distinction reflect anything in the current model? I think we can now answer these questions in a much more satisfactory way than has previously been possible. With respect to the first question, it is true that far more derivational morphology is listed in the lexicon than inflectional morphology (or, conversely, far more of the inflectional morphology is productive). We might say that, when the entire vocabulary of a language is considered, the norm for derivational morphology will be for it to be non-productive, the norm for inflectional morphology will be for it to be productive. This statement would no doubt need to be modified to cope with the case of pidgins and also with isolating languages, but seems to hold for the majority of languages with complex morphologies. It is, I would suggest, partly the perception of this norm which gives rise to the perception of the difference between inflection and derivation. The major distinction is of productivity. There is, however, another distinction which is also reflected in the type of model that has been suggested here. This was also discussed briefly at the end of Chapter 6. It relates to the number of gaps in the system. Generally speaking, it is assumed that there are fewer gaps in an inflectional paradigm than in a derivational paradigm. This can be rephrased in a rather different way. Where a lexeme uses non-productive inflectional morphology it will, in general, nevertheless have a form corresponding to every slot in the standard inflectional paradigm. There is no corresponding likelihood that every lexical base will produce a derived form for every slot in the currently productive derivational paradigm. To reword again, the potentiality of an inflectional form is more predictable on the basis of major category alone than is the potentiality of a derivational form: every verb has a third person singular present tense form and a past tense form and a past and present participle in English (with the obvious exceptions which have been discussed elsewhere and are very much a minority); not every verb has a nominalisation, an -*able* derivative, a subject nominalisation, a deverbal adjective and so on. In many cases the affixes simply do not apply to all verbs (-*able* is suffixed productively only to transitive verbs, for instance).

In the model that has been presented here, this trait is represented only indirectly: in the lexical entries for the various affixes, in the lists present in the lexicon, and so on. This seems to me to be justified, in that the major claim is that inflection and derivation work in fundamentally the same way. The difference between inflection and derivation is a by-product of historical development. This would explain why different languages draw the distinction between the two in rather different places. Bybee's notion of relevance would predict that certain features are more likely to be inflectional than others but it cannot make absolute predictions, or comparative predictions about inflections on nouns as opposed to verbs, for instance.

The major moral that I wish to draw in this chapter is that progress is being made in the study of morphology, and that much

212

13. Conclusion: Is a Synthesis Possible?

more can be made if the various schools do not remain isolated from each other. Some kind of synthesis is possible, but the synthesised result will look rather different from anything we see currently in the work being carried out on morphology.

REFERENCES AND FURTHER READING

I do not make a great deal in this chapter out of the adoption of the principles of Generalised Phrase Structure Grammar. It does seem to me, however, that several benefits might accrue from a GPSG treatment of morphology. For example, recent versions of GPSG are written in an Immediate Dominance/Linear Precedence (IDLP) format. What this means is that the linear order of elements on the right-hand side of the re-write arrow is determined by a separate set of rules from those which determine the categories to be ordered. For example, if a Verb Phrase is made up of a transitive verb and a Noun Phrase, this might be captured in an IDLP framework with an ID rule of the format

VP → NP, V

where the comma shows simply what the members on the righthand side of the rule are, and then a separate LP rule, possibly something like

[+LEXICAL] < [−LEXICAL]

(read as 'lexical nodes precede non-lexical [i.e. phrasal] nodes') defines the ordering relationships between these elements. On top of this, recent writings in GPSG suggest that the head of every construction should appear in the rule simply as 'H', and all features marking the phrase as a whole will be copied onto the head. The ID rule above should thus be re-written as

VP → NP, H

Now, the notion of head has played a large part in morphology of recent years, albeit controversially (Williams, 1981 and a number of papers criticising that, including Lieber, 1981, Selkirk, 1982, Baldi, 1983, Zwicky, 1985c). This was discussed briefly in section 9.5. More recently, Cutler et al. (1985) consider an option according to which affixes are always heads. If this is the case, any affixing rule will be of the format

X → Y, H

where X and Y are categories such as noun, adjective, verb, and where the H is the affix. The position of the H relative to its Y base will then be determined by other principles: either by linear precedence rules (for example, in Turkish any affix comes after its base, and this could easily be stated by an LP rule), or by lexical marking (affixes will carry a marking as to which side of their base they are attached). This type of approach needs to be worked out in greater detail, but seems to me to have potential.

213

APPENDIX A. Feedback Exercise for Chapter 2

As you read the following exercise, keep the page below the line you are reading covered up with a sheet of paper. Move the paper down a line at a time as you read. The answer to each question is provided on the line below the question. Do not uncover the answer until you have made your own response to the question – preferably in writing. Do not write in the book, or you will only ever be able to use it once.

If you are unable to answer a particular question, or if your response is not the same as the answer provided, read the appropriate section of the definitions, and then try to answer the question again. Do this even if you feel you 'sort of' knew the answer or if you weren't sure whether to respond with the correct answer or some other.

If you cannot make sense of the answer provided after four attempts and three re-readings of the appropriate definitions, ask your tutor for help. Similarly, if you think there is a problem that is overlooked in the answers, ask your tutor for help.

This material is designed to check and extend your understanding of material provided in Chapter 2, but it will only function properly if you are honest with yourself when you use it.

As was the case in Chapter 2, many of the example sentences are taken from Bentley & Esar (1951).

Consider (1):

(1)   An optimist is a fellow who believes that a housefly is looking for a way out.

How many orthographic words does (1) contain? (*NB*: the question is *not* how many *different* orthographic words.)

16

Now consider (2):

(2)   American motion pictures are written by the half-educated for the half-witted.

How many orthographic words does (2) contain?

11

215

Now consider (3):

(3)   There's one thing about baldness: it's neat.

How many orthographic words does (3) contain?

7

The important thing to discover from these three examples is that the definition of the orthographic word does not take meaning into account, and does not include hyphens or apostrophes as 'spaces'. We might know that *housefly, half-witted, there's* etc. contain more than one bit, but each of them is nevertheless only one orthographic word.

We discovered that (1), repeated below as (4) contains 16 orthographic words:

(4)   An optimist is a fellow who believes that a housefly is looking for a way out.

How many word-forms does (4) contain?

16

How many different word-forms does (4) contain?

13

Now look at (5):

(5)   I went to town yesterday, she has gone there this morning.

How many different word-forms are there in (5)?

11

How many different grammatical words are there in (5)?

11

How many different lexemes are there in (5)?

10

Bearing those figures in mind, consider (6) which is very similar to (5):

(6)   I walked to town yesterday, she has walked there this morning.

How many different word-forms are there in (6)?

10

How many different grammatical words are there in (6)?

11

How many different lexemes are there in (6)?

10

That is, the same word-form *walked* in (6) represents two distinct grammatical words.

Now look at (7):

(7)   Not many banks have branches on the banks of the Avon.

How many different word-forms are there in (7)?

9

How many different lexemes are there in (7)?

The answer is 10, but this may require some explanation. There are two occurrences of the word-form *banks* in (7), yet in one case it means 'financial institutions' and in the other 'slopes bordering a watercourse'. Are these the same dictionary word? The answer here is clearly 'no'. They share word-forms, but they are distinct lexemes: we could call them, as many dictionaries do, BANK¹ and BANK². So different lexemes can actually share word-forms.
Refer back to (7). How many different grammatical words are there in (7)?

10

This is a result of the facts presented in the previous discussion. In one case *banks* is 'the plural of BANK¹', in the other 'the plural of BANK²', and these are different grammatical words because they specify different lexemes, just as 'the plural of HOUSE' and 'the plural of BOOK' would be different grammatical words.
Finally in this section, consider (8):

(8)   She stoops to refill the stoops of wine, and having refilled them, wishes the wine-waiter refilled them himself.

How many different word-forms are there in (8)?

14

How many different lexemes are there in (8)?

14

How many different grammatical words are there in (8)?

16

*****

Still concentrating on the same technical terms, we now turn to a slightly different kind of exercise.
What is the word-form representing 'the plural of MOUSE'?

mice

What grammatical word does *mice* represent?

the plural of MOUSE (or a paraphrase of this)

Which lexeme is realised in *mice*?

MOUSE

How many different word-forms of the lexeme READ can you find? If you used orthography, three forms are possible: *read, reads, reading*. If you used spoken forms, there are four: /riːd/, /red/, /riːdz/, /riːdɪŋ/. /riːd/ and /red/ are distinct spoken forms, written as the same orthographic word-form *read*. No other forms are possible. Forms such as *reader* belong to a different lexeme.

Consider (9):

(9)   Whenever a man does a thoroughly stupid thing, it is always from the noblest of motives.

In (9), what grammatical word does *noblest* represent?

superlative of NOBLE

What grammatical word does *motives* represent?

plural of MOTIVE

What lexeme is realised in the word-form *does*?

DO

Why is this lexeme called DO?
There are a number of possible answers, the best of which is
    Because *do* is the citation form of that lexeme.
The reason that is true is
    Because *do* is the stem of the lexeme, and in English lexemes are named by their stems
and that is true
    By convention.
Give three other word-forms which might, under appropriate circumstances, realise the lexeme DO.

any three of *do, doing, done, did*

What do the word-forms *is*, *was* and *are* have in common?
The best answer here is 'they all realise the lexeme BE'. Other answers such as 'they are all parts of the verb "to be"', while accurate, do not use the terminology precisely. 'They are all forms of BE' is an accurate and precise alternative.
Is the following statement true: *shoot* is a form of SHOOT

Yes

Is the following statement true: *shot* is a form of SHOOT

Yes

Is the following statement true: SHOOTING is a form of *shoot*

No

Is the following statement true: SHOOTS is a form of SHOOT

No

The last few questions have dealt with notation rather than with concepts, since it is important to be able to read the kind of abbreviated statement that the notation allows if you are to understand arguments in morphology.

*****

Consider (10):

(10)   He'd be sharper than a serpent's tooth, if he wasn't as dull as ditchwater.

218

How many orthographic words are there in (10)?

> 14

How many of these word-forms contain more than one morph?

> 5

List the five.

> he'd, sharper, serpent's, wasn't, ditchwater

Divide each of these word-forms into morphs.

> he·'d, sharp·er, serpent·'s, was·n't, ditch·water

Now look at (11):

(11)   No Englishman is ever fairly beaten.

List the word-forms which contain more than one morph.

> Englishman, fairly, beaten

Divide each of these word-forms into morphs.

> English·man, fair·ly, beat·en

List the morphs from these word-forms which are roots.

> English, man, fair, beat

List the morphs from these word-forms which are affixes.

> -ly, -en

What kind of affixes are these: infixes, prefixes or suffixes?

> suffixes

What is the base to which -en was added?

Now look at (12):

> beat

(12)   My wife was too beautiful for words, but not for arguments.

There are three words here which can be analysed into more than one morph; what are they?

> beautiful, words, arguments

What kinds of affixes can be found in these words?

> suffixes

What are the roots in these words?

> beauty, word, argu(e)

The plural -s is added to *argument*. What is the technical term for *argument*?

The obvious answer is 'base'. 'Stem' is also correct, because -s is an inflectional affix. 'Base' would be true even if -ation were to be added to *argument* to give *argumentation*, while 'stem' would not be true in this case.

Now consider (13):

(13)   One should not be too severe on novels; they are the only relaxation of the intellectually unemployed.

Which words in (13) can be analysed into two or more morphs?

> novels, relaxation, intellectually, unemployed

219

List the roots from these words.

                                    novel, relax, intellect, employ
List all the suffixes from these words.

                                    -s, -ation, -ual, -ly, -ed
List all the prefixes from these words.

                                                                un-
List all the bases from these words.

        novel, relax, intellect, intellectual, employ, employed
List all the inflectional affixes from these words.

                                                            -s, -ed
Now consider the following two words which have been divided
up into morphs for you:

        person·al·iti·es   de·pol·ar·iz·ed

What are the stems for these words?

                                    personality, depolarize
Is it true that *personality* and *depolarize* are bases?

                                                                Yes
Is it true that *personality* and *depolarize* are roots?

                                                                No
What are the roots of these words?

                                            person, pol(e)
List all the derivational affixes from these words.

                            -al, -ity, de-, -ar, -iz(e)
Give four reasons for knowing that -*ed* is an inflectional affix.

        1. It produces a form of DEPOLARIZE.
        2. It doesn't change the part of speech of *depolarize*.
        3. It has a regular meaning in a lot of other words.
        4. It can be added to a wide range of verbs.

Give two reasons for knowing that -*al* is a derivational affix.
The two obvious ones are

        1. It produces a new lexeme PERSONAL from PERSON.
        2. PERSONAL is an adjective while PERSON is a noun, so it
        changes the part of speech of its base.

The following is also true, but requires justification

        3. It cannot be added to every noun to make an adjective:
        there are no words *childal, girlal, wifal, masteral, kingal.*

Note, however, that its meaning *is* fairly regular, being something
like 'an adjectival form of'.
                                *****

In older English, the word-forms *my* and *mine* were in complementary distribution as shown below:

(14) my coat   mine host
      my wife   mine husband
      my baby   mine own coat
      my goods   mine ass
      my ruff   mine undoing
      my years   mine ideas

On the basis of this data, what determines the use of the form *my*?

the following word starts with a consonant other than /h/

And what determines the use of the form *mine*?

the following word starts with /h/ or a vowel

What can we say about the conditioning of these forms?

they are phonetically conditioned (by the following sound)

Is it true that *my* and *mine* are allomorphs in this data?

Yes

What are they allomorphs of?

The expected answer here is 'a morpheme', or, if the morpheme is given a name, it is probably called {my} (although {mine} would be possible, as would something like {12345}). However, this answer oversimplifies, since when we look at the entire language, instead of just the data presented in (14), it can be argued that *my* is a portmanteau morph realising the morphemes {first person}, {singular}, {possessive}.

By the nineteenth century, the situation in (14) had changed so that for some speakers it was as shown in (15):

(15) my husband   mine host
      my hip   mine history
      my hose   mine hotel

What kind of conditioning is there now?

lexical

Can you predict whether the word *hostage* would require *my* or *mine* for speakers of the dialect shown in (15)?

The answer is 'no'. Since individual lexemes force the choice in lexical conditioning, there is no way to find a generalization.

Can you predict whether the word *hostage* would require *my* or *mine* for speakers of the dialect shown in (14)?

Yes

Which, and how can you tell?

mine because it begins with an /h/

*****

APPENDIX A. *Feedback Exercise for Chapter 2*

How many morphs are there in the word *unlikelihood*?

4

Divide it up into morphs.

un·like·li·hood

How many morphemes are realised in the word *unlikelihood*?

4

What are they?

{un}, {like}, {ly}, {hood}

Notice in particular that although the morph is -*li*- the morpheme is {ly}. As a rule we take the most widespread or basic form as the name of the morpheme, and in this case, that is -*ly*. The morphemes could have been given other names. In particular, there might be a case for renaming {un} as {negative}, but this is probably controversial, and using the form is simpler. Notice that in the written language ('although not in the spoken language) we can say that {ly} is realised by two allomorphs, -*ly* and -*li*. You might like to think about the conditioning factors for these two allomorphs.

How many morphs are there in the word *untidier*, and what are they?

3, un·tidi·er

How many morphemes are realised in the word *untidier* and what are they?

3, {un}, {tidy} and {comparative}

{er} could have been used instead of {comparative}, although a different {er} morpheme is found in words like *reader, lecturer, lover*. As a general rule, it is the grammatical morphemes which are given names different from their shapes (i.e. those which are inflectional affixes), but this is convention.

How many morphs are there in the word *tigress* and what are they?

2, tigr·ess

How many morphemes are realised in the word *tigress*, and what are they?

2, {tiger}, {ess}

Consider the following word, which has been divided into morphs:

ox·en·'s

What lexeme is realised by this word-form?

OX

What morphemes are realised in this word-form?

{ox}, {plural} and {possessive} (*or* {genitive})

Are there any portmanteau morphs?

no, each morph realises one morpheme

List two other allomorphs of {plural}.

There are a large number, including -*s* (/s/, /z/, /ɪz/), -*im*, -*ren*, -*x* (the last only in written form) and several changes of form

(possibly replacive morphs - see section 3.3) such as *-on* → *-a,*
-um → *-a, -is* → *-es.*
Consider the data in (16):

(16)	root	possessive	root	possessive
	mæn	mænz	ʃiːp	ʃiːps
	dɒg	dɒgz	gəʊt	gəʊts
	bɔɪ	bɔɪz	kʊk	kʊks
	wɔːl	wɔːlz	rælf	rælfs
	hen	henz	beθ	beθs

	root	possessive
	dez	dezɪz
	hɔːs	hɔːsɪz
	guːs	guːsɪz
	lɪz	lɪzɪz

What morphemes are realised in the word-form /mænz/?

{man}, {possessive}

How many allomorphs of the morpheme {possessive} are shown
in the data?

3

How are the allomorphs conditioned?

phonetically (by the last sound in the base)

When is the allomorph /ɪz/ used?

after /s/, /z/

In fact, it is used in other places as well, not illustrated in (16).
You can try to find the others for yourself. The pattern is actually
the same as for the 3rd person singular *-s* on verbs and for the
regular plural in English.
Now consider the data in (17):

(17)		root	possessive	plural
	(a)	pɑːθ	pɑːθs	pɑːðz
		liːf	liːfs	liːvz
		dwɔːf	dwɔːfs	dwɔːvz
	(b)	breθ	breθs	breθs
		kʌf	kʌfs	kʌfs
		riːf	riːfs	riːfs

How many morphs are there in the word-form /pɑːðz/?

2

What lexeme is realised in the word-form /pɑːðz/?

PATH

Which morphemes are realised in the word-form /pɑːðz/?

{path}, {plural}

223

How many allomorphs does {path} have?

2

What are they?

/pɑːθ/, /pɑːð/

What kind of morph is /pɑːð/?

an obligatorily bound morph

What conditions the choice of allomorph of {path}?

Whether it appears in the plural or not. It is not simply the presence of an affix, but the presence of the plural affix. Notice that this is neither lexical conditioning nor phonetic conditioning, but grammatical conditioning – it is the presence of the morpheme {plural} which triggers the choice of /pɑːð/.

In (17a) the roots have two alternating forms, but in (17b) only one form. Can we predict whether a given word, e.g. *roof* will fit into class (a) or (b)?

The answer is 'no', although the free form of the root must end in a voiceless fricative to be in class (a). The choice between class (a) and class (b) is lexically conditioned. In fact, not everyone draws the line between the two classes in the same place. For some people the plural of {roof} is /ruːfs/, for others it is /ruːvz/.

The possessive forms listed in (17) are the possessive singular. What is the possessive plural of LEAF?

leaves', /liːvz/

In the spoken form, how many morphs are there, and what are they?

2, /liːv/, /z/

What kind of morph is /liːv/?

an obligatorily bound morph

The morph /z/ is also obligatorily bound, as you would expect (it is an affix). What does this morph realise?

{plural}, {possessive}

What kind of morph does that make it?

a portmanteau morph

*****

224

APPENDIX B. Study Questions

(1) Morphology is largely concerned with analysis into morphs. This is frequently tested by problems from languages unknown to the student. Many such exercises can be found in e.g. Gleason (1955) and Nida (1949). Here a list of words of English is given. Some of these words are analysable into morphs, some are not. For each word, state what the morphs are, and what morphemes the morphs realise. In the case of portmanteau morphs, there may be more morphemes than morphs. Remember that it is important to justify your analysis. To give you some idea about how to present a morphological analysis, some examples are given below.

Examples of Analysis
The notes do not form part of the analysis, but are included to help the student. The guide below is a slightly modified version of material written by Winifred Bauer and Janet Holmes which appeared in Holmes (1984).

When you make a morphological analysis of any word W, the following steps are necessary to support your argument.

(a) A set of other words containing the relevant morphemes in W must be provided. This set must be chosen with care. Each of the morphemes in these words should, if possible, be realised by a segmentable morph; if W contains a problem of segmentation, it is useful to include at least one word which illustrates the same problem (unless W is unique). Even if W is irregular, it is the parallel with regular forms that justifies the analysis.

(b) State the morphemes in W.

(c) State how each morpheme in W is realised in morphs. You should consider *either* the written *or* the spoken form, and be consistent. In general, the spoken form is probably preferable. You should discuss your own pronunciation of the words in question if you are a native speaker of English. The pronunciations given here are widely-used ones. State whether the morphs are potentially free or obligatorily bound, and discuss allomorphs if necessary.

(d) Further discussion may be necessary to highlight particular problems.

225

EXAMPLE A: *untruthful.*

(a) i. Compare the following set: *unfair, unwise, unripe, unfruit-ful, unmindful.* These establish a pattern:

un fair
un wise
un ripe
un mindful
un fruitful

Thus

un truthful

Note

NOT *untie*, where *un-* has a reversative rather than a negative sense, and where *tie* is a verb and not an adjective like *truthful.*

NOT *unkempt*, where *kempt* is not a potentially free form.

NOT *uncle*, which is monomorphemic.

ii. Compare *truthful* with the following set: *careful, faithful, sorrowful.* These establish a pattern:

care ful
faith ful
sorrow ful

Thus

truth ful

Note

NOT *forgetful*, where *forget* is a verb, not a noun.

NOT *awful*, which is not analysable in its present meaning.

NOT *'brim'ful*, which has a different stress pattern and is different semantically.

iii. Compare *truth* with: *warmth*, the jocular *coolth*, and the somewhat irregular *depth, width.* These are probably sufficient to establish the pattern:

warm th
cool th
deep th
wide th

Thus

true th

Note: NOT *growth*, where *grow* is not an adjective, but a verb.

(b) Thus I would conclude that the morphemes in *untruthful* are {un} {true} {th} {ful}.

226

(c) i. {un} is realised by /ʌn/ (written form *un-*). Both the spoken and written forms are obligatorily bound morphs.

ii. {true} is realised by /truː/ (written form *tru-*). The spoken form is potentially free, the written form is obligatorily bound, compare the word-form /truː/ *true*.

iii. {th} is realised by /θ/ (written form -*th*). Both the spoken and written forms of the morph are obligatorily bound.

iv. {ful} is realised by /fʊl/ (written form -*ful*). Depending on your pronunciation, the spoken form may or may not be potentially free. The pronunciation given here suggests that it is. If it is potentially free, then it may be the same morpheme as is realised by the written form *full*, and the morpheme should probably be called {full}. The written form is clearly obligatorily bound.

The form is fully analysable.

(d) Two points are worth comment.

i. The variation in the written form between (*t*)*rue* and (*t*)*ru* occurs elsewhere in English: *truly, ruth* < *rue*.

ii. While there is only one regular form as a parallel for {true} + {th}, the irregular forms follow rules found elsewhere in English. For example, the /iː/ ~ /e/ alternation found in *deep/depth* is also found in pairs like *serene/serenity*.

EXAMPLE B: *children*.

(a) Consider sentences like

i. The child has come home

ii. The children have come home.

Other forms which could be substituted for *child* in (i) are *girl, cat, horse*. In (ii), forms which could be substituted for *children* include *girls, cats, horses*. In these cases we can segment

{girl} + {plural}   /gɜːl/ + /z/
{cat} + {plural}   /kæt/ + /s/
{horse} + {plural}   /hɔːs/ + /ɪz/

Note: *oxen, brethren* are not chosen as parallels because they are irregular.

(b) Since the relationship between *girl, girls* and *child, children* is the same, we can also say that *children* must be analysed as realising two morphemes

{child} + {plural}

(c) Whereas the other forms are easily analysable into morphs, *children* provides problems of analysis. There are three possible analyses:

i. /tʃɪld/ + /rən/ (written form *child·ren*).

227

ii. /tʃɪldr/ + /ən/ (written form *childr·en*).

iii. the form is unanalysable, and is a portmanteau morph.

If you choose (i), both morphs are obligatorily bound in the spoken form. In the written form, *child* is a potentially free morph. /rən/ *-ren* is an allomorph of the morpheme {plural}, and is lexically conditioned.

If you choose (ii) all the morphs are obligatorily bound in either the spoken or written forms, and /ən/ *-en* is a lexically conditioned allomorph of the morpheme {plural}.

(d) The main argument for (i) is that the morph realising {child} is very similar to the word-form *child*. The phonological alternation /aɪ/ ~ /ɪ/ illustrated in ·his pair of words is also found in other pairs of related words such as *divine/divinity, wide/width*.

The main argument for (ii) is that /ən/ also occurs in forms like *oxen*, and this analysis reduces the number of allomorphs of {plural} that have to be recognised. *Brethren*, which might appear to have /rən/ probably doesn't, since the /r/ is attributable to *brother*: /brʌðrɪnlɔ:/ contains the /r/, as does the written form *brother*. Thus *brethren* is probably best segmented as /breðr/ + /ən/ (written form *brethr·en*).

The main argument for (iii) is that there is no other plural in English which shows precisely this combination of vowel change and affix. It is probably simpler to see this as a unique change than as a series of lexically conditioned phonological change and lexically conditioned affixation process, neither of which is particularly common on its own.

EXAMPLE C: *inquire*

This example is included to illustrate how you should discuss the analysis of a more complicated word and, in particular, one where there is more than one possible morphemic analysis. There are two possible analyses of *inquire*: either it is monomorphemic or it is bimorphemic. Whichever conclusion you decide to support, it is necessary to raise all the points discussed in (a) and (d) below. In other words, deciding that *inquire* is monomorphemic does not relieve you of the necessity of discussing the arguments in favour of a bimorphemic analysis; you will need to discuss the arguments to make it clear why you find them unconvincing.

The discussion here adopts the bimorphemic analysis. This is not because it is superior to the monomorphemic analysis, but because it more obviously demands discussion of all the relevant factors.

(a) i. Compare *inquire* with *infix* (verb), *inlay, indent, inbreed, indoctrinate*. These establish a pattern:

in fix
in lay
in dent
in breed
in doctrinate

Note:

NOT *indecent* where *in-* has a negative sense, and where (*in-*)*decent* is an adjective not a verb.

NOT *incur* where *-cur* is an obligatorily bound morph, and the meaning of *in-* is not transparent: this example would not illuminate the analysis.

NOT *interest* which is undoubtedly monomorphemic.

These are sufficient to provide a basis for arguing that {in} in *inquire* is a distinct morpheme, provided that it can be shown that there is also a separate morpheme {quire}. Note that this is not necessary for *infix, inlay, indent,* and *inbreed* since their roots are potentially free forms. It would be necessary in discussing the analysis of *indoctrinate* which raises similar problems to those with *inquire*.

ii. Compare *inquire* with *acquire, require*. Although these share a formative *-quire,* it is not clear that *-quire* has the same meaning in all three words, and it is therefore not clear that it realises the same morpheme.

iii. Compare *inquire* with *query, quest, question, querist*. It can be argued that all these share a morpheme with *inquire*: there appears to be a common element of meaning associated with a partially recurrent form. If we represent that morpheme as {quer}, then *-quire* in *inquire* realises {quer}.

(b) Accepting the above arguments, I would conclude that the morphemes in *inquire* are {in} {quer}.

Problems with accepting these arguments are dealt with in (d) below. The alternative is to regard *inquire* as monomorphemic.

(c) i. If *inquire* is regarded as monomorphemic the morpheme {inquire} is realised by the morph /ɪŋkwaɪə/ (written form *inquire*). According to this solution, the form is unanalysable.

ii. If *inquire* is regarded as bimorphemic, the morpheme {in} is realised as /ɪŋ/ (written form *in-*). Both spoken and written forms are obligatorily bound morphs, unless {in} is regarded as the same morpheme as the preposition *in,* in which case the written form is a potentially free morph. The morpheme {quer} is realised by the morph /kwaɪə/ (written form *quire*). Both the spoken and written forms

229

are obligatorily bound. According to this solution, the word is fully analysable.

(d) There are a number of problems raised by the above discussion which throw doubt on the conclusion reached.

i. It is not clear that *in-* means 'in', 'into' in *inquire*. In *infix*, *inlay*, *inbreed* the meaning is quite clear, but in *indict*, *invent* a solution along these lines seems even less plausible.

ii. It is at least debatable whether the proposed morpheme {quer} does in fact have an identifiable and constant meaning in the words *query*, *quest*, *question*, *querist* and *inquire*.

iii. The morpheme {quer} postulated as underlying *query*, *quest*, *question*, *querist* and *inquire* involves phonological variation of a sort which is not common, that is: /ɪər/ ~ /e/ ~ /aɪə/ ~ /aɪr/. The written alternation of *e* with *i* is found elsewhere (for example *stink*/*stench*, *right*/*rectitude*) but even this is not regular.

Here now are some English words for you to practise with. You may also use others, but remember that some words raise extremely complex problems, while others are very simple.

anachronistic
aunties
beatnik
bedraggled
best-seller
boysenberry
bulldozer
catholic
commandant
crackerjack
degenerate
discombobulate
disinclined
entreaty
ergonomics
evacuee
habitation
highlight
his
history
inconclusive

ineffable
institutionalisation
inveterate
jeopardised
lexicalisation
lightning
linguistics
measles
monomorphemic
morphology
pious
republicanism
reserved
sociable
sorority
tablespoonful
tabloid
them
unfriendliness
Anglo-philia

(2) Are derivational affixes such as *-al*, *-ment* lexemes?

(3) Following from (2), are inflectional affixes such as *-s*, *-ing* lexemes? If your answer to (2) was negative, then you will also have a negative answer here. If your answer to (2) was positive, you will need to discuss this point.

(4) Is there a lexeme THE?

(5) How are morphs and allomorphs related?

(6) Affixes are usually defined as bound morphs. Choose one of the sets of data provided below (preferably from a language with which you have some familiarity) and decide whether this must always be the case.

(a) English
    absobloodylutely
    confronbloodytation
    guaranbloodytee
    imbloodypossible
    inbloodyfallible
    incanbloodydescent
    kangabloodyroo
    unbebloodylievable
    unibloodyversity

(b) French

sous-entendre	surchauffer	suspendre
sous-exposer	surclasser	
sous-louer	suréquiper	
sous-tendre	surestimer	
soustraire	surfaire	
sous-traiter	surmonter	

(c) German

auf·drucken	aus·drucken	be·drucken
auf·fallen	aus·fallen	be·fallen
auf·geben	aus·geben	be·geben
auf·halten	aus·halten	be·halten
auf·nehmen	aus·nehmen	be·nehmen
auf·schreiben	aus·schreiben	be·schreiben
auf·stehen	aus·stehen	be·stehen
auf·steigen	aus·steigen	be·steigen
auf·stellen	aus·stellen	be·stellen
auf·tragen	aus·tragen	be·tragen

(d) Latin

ac·curroː	re·curroː
ac·ceːdoː	re·ceːdoː
ad·duːcoː	re·duːcoː

231

```
ad·fero:    re·fero:
ad·ficio:   re·ficio:
ad·lego:    re·lego:
ad·mitto:   re·mitto:
ap·po:no:   re·po:no:
ap·porto:   re·porto:
```

(7) In each of the following pairs of words, does the word from the first column represent a morph in the word in the second column? Justify your answer carefully.

car	carriage
form	uniform
loo	Waterloo
mead	meadow
need	needle
pi	pious
private	privateer
rail	trail
roquet	croquet
wrest	wrestler

(8) In each of the following cases, do the morphs indicated represent the same morpheme or different morphemes? The arguments you use to justify your decision are more important than the conclusion you reach, so be careful to justify your position carefully. Marchand (1969) will be a useful reference for many of the cases here. More specific references to the particular affixes are not given here, though many of these cases are discussed in the literature.

(a) The prefixes *in-* (as in *inoperable*) and *un-* (as in *unnecessary*).

(b) The formative *pre-* in each of the following sets of words:

pre·cast	pre·cede
pre·clinical	pre·clude
pre·condition	pre·dict
pre·cook	pre·empt
pre·date	pre·fer
pre·destine	pre·miss
pre·disposition	pre·pare
pre-European	pre·scribe
pre·heat	pre·side
pre·judge	pre·sume
pre·molar	pre·tend
pre·occupied	pre·vent

It is possible that one or both of these lists could contain more than one morpheme {pre-}. Consult a dictionary for further examples if necessary.

(c) The suffixes *-ation*, *-ition* and *-ution* as in *perturb·ation, ador·ation; defin·ition, propos·ition; resol·ution, evol·ution.* Look in a reverse dictionary such as Lehnert (1971) for further examples.

(d) The suffixes *-ion* and *-ation* as in the following lists of words:

adapt·ation	act·ion
cit·ation	apprehens·ion
experiment·ation	assert·ion
exploit·ation	commun·ion
export·ation	descript·ion
habit·ation	dilut·ion
invit·ation	inclus·ion
justific·ation	possess·ion
palatalis·ation	product·ion
tempt·ation	protect·ion

(e) The word *most* (as in *most important*) and the formative *-est* (as in *strong·est*).

(f) The suffixes *-able* and *-ible* as in *prevent·able, sustain·able; access·ible, divis·ible.* Use a reverse dictionary such as Lehnert (1971) to find further examples.

(g) The formative *un-* in each of the following sets of words:

un·ashamed	un·bar
un·breakable	un·bend
un·conditionally	un·bosom
un·ease	un·bridle
un·economical	un·button
un·employment	un·cork
un·even	un·fetter
un·fair	un·frock
un·heated	un·horse
un·seeing	un·stitch

There may be more than one morpheme {un-} represented in either or both columns. Have all the words listed above been assigned to the correct columns?

(9) In each of the sets of data below there is a recurrent form or meaning. In each case, how many morphemes do these recurrent portions represent? If there is more than one, which words illustrate which morphemes? Most importantly, how do you know?

(a)

brandish	publish
devilish	radish
flourish	rubbish
foolish	sheepish
fortyish	smartish
greenish	waspish

	nebbish	Danish
	oldish	English
	parish	Polish
(b)	allergic	politic
	arithmetic	public
	bishopric	realistic
	catholic	rhetoric
	critic	symbolic
	heretic	traffic
	historic	vitriolic
	phonetic	vocalic
	poetic	Arabic
(c)	bikes	lasses
	boys	linguistics
	cars	men
	cherubim	mumps
	deer	oxen
	girls	planes
	houses	sheep
	kibbutzim	tableaux
	lads	women
(d)	encase	encroach
	encash	encyclopedia
	enchant	ennoble
	encircle	enslave
	enclose	ensnare
	encode	impoverish
	encourage	imprison
(e)	four	tetraplegic
	quadraphonic	
(f)	eighty	octopus
(g)	hexagon	six-sided
	sextuple	
(h)	cognate	kin
	gene	pregnant
	germ	recognise
	gonad	
(i)	arrive	rival
	derivation	river
	riparian	Riviera

(10) Is there such a thing as a bound morpheme? Justify your answer.

(11) Is *feck* in *feckless* a prefix? How can you tell?

234

(12) Is *ric* in *bishopric* a suffix? How can you tell?

(13) Is the marker of the comparative in any language known to you inflectional or derivational? Justify your answer.

(14) Do people actually create new words because of productivity, or do they only work by analogy? How can you tell the difference between the two? Does it matter to the descriptive linguist?

(15) On page 66 it was stated that 'blocking appears to be, in many instances, the derivational analogue of suppletion in inflectional systems'. Explain the comment, and discuss whether or not you would wish to agree with it, and why.

(16)
'The difference between inflection and derivation may not, in fact, have any foundation outside of the theory of grammatical structure; that is, it may be seen as corresponding to an aspect of the internal organisation of grammars, and thus as being strictly theory-internal rather than being susceptible of independent definition.' (Anderson, 1982: 587)
How does such a view of the distinction between inflection and derivation fit with the facts presented in this book? If such a view is adopted, what are the implications for 'the ordinary working linguist' (to use Fillmore's phrase)?

(17) One question that was raised in Chapter 7 was whether it is possible to distinguish between those compounds that belong to the morphology and those that belong to the syntax. Botha argues that in fact synthetic compounds are very like other morphological formations. Consider whether the division between morphological compounds and syntactic compounds could be equated with the division between synthetic and root compounds. To answer this question you will have to read Botha (1981) and Botha (1984b). You might also like to consider whether synthetic compounds could be seen as a special type of incorporation.

(18) In the first edition of *The Categories and Types of Present-Day English Word-Formation*, Marchand makes the following statement:
The prefix *in-*, however, can claim only a restricted sphere [in comparison with *un-*]: it forms learned, chiefly scientific, words and *therefore has morphemic value with those speakers only who are acquainted with Latin or French.* [Stress not in the original.]
In the second edition (Marchand, 1969: 170) the phrase 'morphemic value' is replaced by 'derivative value'. To what extent would you agree that a formative can have different morphemic value (or derivative value) for different speakers? Take care to explain your

reasons clearly, and to make reference to the definition of a morpheme, as well as to realist and instrumentalist ideas about grammar.

(19) It is sometimes claimed that the sounds in a word can add to its meaning. For example, the initial *gl-* in *gleam, glisten, glow, glare, glimmer, glint* and so on might have something to do with shining, and the initial *sl-* in *slime, slough, slip, slop, slobber, slosh, slither* and so on might have something to do with slipperiness or sliminess. Such sounds or sound combinations are termed **phonaesthemes**. Are phonaesthemes morphs realising morphemes? Justify your answer. Further examples can be found in Marchand (1969).

(20) There are some English expressions which some people write as one word, others as two or more. Using the criteria discussed in Chapter 4, see if you can show why there should be disagreement, or whether the language in fact provides a clear-cut answer to the questions. Some expressions for you to consider are *insofar as, all right, altogether, albeit, nonetheless,* but you may also be able to think of some others. You may also try the same exercise with any other language you are familiar with.

(21) In Section 5.5.1 it is stated that a common restriction on the base in a morphological process is for inflectional endings to be restricted by the declension or conjugation class of the base. Illustrate this for any four Indo-European languages. If you are not familiar with the languages, consult grammar books to find your examples.

(22) In Figure 7.1 on page 92 a network is drawn up of various morphological processes in English. One could extend the network shown there, e.g. by pointing out that acronyms and clipping have in common that they both involve shortening, and that neither involves the deletion of morphs. How does this affect the figure, and the conclusions drawn from it? Are there any other links which could be drawn? How would a language with infixation and/or reduplication affect the network shown in Figure 7.1 on page 92?

(23) In Section 11.2 it is claimed that many of the characteristics of inflection and derivation discussed in Chapter 6 can be explained by Bybee's principles of relevance and lexical generality. Test this claim. Are the characteristics discussed in Chapter 6 merely corollaries of the these principles? Can you see any other principles which might underlie those characteristics?

APPENDIX C. Definitions

ACRONYM. An acronym is a word coined from the initial letters of the words in a name, title or phrase. An example is *TESL* from *Teaching English as a Second Language.*

AFFIX. An affix is an obligatorily bound morph which does not realise (see realisation), a lexeme. Affixes thus have to make reference to some other morpheme or class of morphemes in any statement of their distribution. In the French word *recherchions* 'we were looking for' the root, which can realise the lexeme CHERCHER, is *-cherch-* and *re-, -i-* and *-ons* are affixes. The commonest types of affix are prefixes, suffixes and infixes, although circumfixes, interfixes and transfixes are also mentioned by some authorities.

AGGLUTINATIVE or AGGLUTINATING. An agglutinative language is one in which there are a number of obligatorily bound morphs, each of which realises a single morpheme. That is, there is a one-to-one correspondence between morph and morpheme in such languages. This implies that ideally there are no allomorphs in such languages. Languages usually cited as examples of agglutinative languages are Turkish and Swahili.

ALLOMORPH. An allomorph is a conditioned (see conditioning) morph. It is a conditioned realisation of a morpheme. In English the forms /t/, /d/ and /ɪd/ are phonetically conditioned allomorphs of the past tense morpheme, determined by the final sound in the stem to which they are added. In English the use of an ablaut (or vowel change) past tense for HANG but not for BANG (the past tenses are *hung* and *banged* respectively) is lexically conditioned, that is determined by the individual lexemes.

ANALYSABILITY. A word is analysable if the linguist can perceive in it some regular correlations between meaning and form, and segment the word accordingly. These correlations may or may not be perceived by the native speaker, and may or may not

237

be widely generalised or particularly productive. For example, the linguist can analyse the *-th* in *dearth*, and see it as a recurrence of the same unit that occurs in *length* and *warmth*, even though most native speakers are not aware of this, although there are not many words which use this element, and although it is no longer productive.

ANALYTIC. See **ISOLATING.**

BACKFORMATION. Backformation is the formation of words by the deletion of actual or supposed affixes in longer words. For example, the French word for 'cherry' is *cerise* which was originally borrowed into English with the final /z/. This was, however, perceived as a plural marker in English, with the result that *cherry* was created by backformation. A similar history is attached to English *pea* from an earlier *pease*.

BAHUVRIHI COMPOUND. See under **COMPOUNDING.**

BASE. A base is any item to which affixes may be added. Roots and stems are special types of base. A base is sometimes termed an **operand.**

BLEND. A blend is a new lexeme formed from parts of two or more other lexemes. There is no requirement that the blend should be made up of meaningful parts of the original lexemes, and the original lexemes are frequently unrecognisable in the blend. Examples are *stagflation* from *stagnation* and *inflation*, *smog* from *smoke* and *fog* and *tritical* from *trite* and *critical*. Blends are also called **portmanteau words.**

BLOCKING. Blocking refers to the failure of a particular lexeme to become institutionalised because of the existence of a synonymous (or, occasionally, homonymous) lexeme in general use. For example, the lexeme STEALER is not in general use because of the generally used THIEF, which has the same meaning. From the verb to SUE we do not find a derivative SUER because it would be homophonous with SEWER.

For some authorities, blocking applies only to lexemes derived from the same root, so that the example with THIEF would not be a case of blocking, but the use of TYPIST rather than TYPER would be. This is not the definition that has been adopted in this book.

Some authorities refer to blocking as **preemption.**

BOUND MORPH. See **OBLIGATORILY BOUND MORPH.**

CIRCUMFIX. A circumfix is a discontinuous affix which surrounds the base with which it occurs. In German the past participle is marked by the circumfix *ge···t* in a word like *ge·mach·t* 'made'.

CITATION FORM. See under **LEXEME.**

CLIPPING. Clipping is the process of shortening a word without changing its meaning or its part of speech, though frequently with the effect of making it stylistically less formal. Examples are *jumbo* from *jumbo jet* and *polio* from *poliomyelitis.*

CLITIC. A clitic is an obligatorily bound morph which is intermediate between an affix and a word. Clitics in English include the italicised sequences in the following examples:
He'*ll* be here in a moment.
She'*s* done it already.
The President of France'*s* beliefs.
Clitics are divided into **proclitics** which are attached before their bases, and **enclitics** which are attached after their bases.

COMPLEMENTARY DISTRIBUTION. See under **DISTRIBUTION.**

COMPOSITION. See **COMPOUNDING.**

COMPOUNDING. Compounding is the formation of new lexemes by adjoining two or more lexemes. For example, the lexeme HOUSEBOAT is a lexeme in which we can distinguish two other lexemes, HOUSE and BOAT. The lexeme HOUSEBOAT is called a 'compound lexeme', or simply a 'compound'. There are three main sub-types of compound. **Endocentric compounds** are those where the compound denotes a hyponym of the HEAD element in the compound. A houseboat is a type of boat, so HOUSEBOAT is an endocentric compound of English. The second type are called **exocentric compounds.** These do not denote a hyponym of the head element of the compound, but denote some feature of the entity which is denoted by the compound. A redskin is so called because of his red skin, but the lexeme REDSKIN does not denote a type of skin, but a type of person who has a red skin (it may, of course, also denote a potato). REDSKIN is an exocentric compound. Exocentric compounds are also called

239

possessive compounds or by the Sanskrit name **bahuvrihi compound.** The third type of compound is the **dvandva compound.** A dvandva compound denotes an entity made up of the various parts listed in the form. For example, Alsace-Lorraine is made up of the former provinces of Alsace and Lorraine. The dvandva compound ALSACE-LORRAINE lists the parts of the region which it denotes. Dvandvas are also called **copulative compounds.**

Some linguists call compounding **composition.**

CONDITIONING. A conditioning factor is one which determines which of a number of allomorphs will be found in a particular word-form. The allomorphs in question are said to be 'conditioned' by that factor. The three kinds of conditioning are phonetic, grammatical and lexical conditioning. Phonetic conditioning is when the choice of allomorph is determined by the phonetic environment in which it occurs, lexical conditioning is when the choice of allomorph is determined by the lexeme involved, grammatical conditioning is when the choice of allomorph is determined by some grammatical factor. In English the choice of /d/ or /t/ or /ɪd/ to mark the past tense is determined by the final sound in the stem: if it is /t/ or /d/, /ɪd/ is used to mark the past tense (*wanted, moulded*), if it is not /t/ but voiceless, then /t/ is used (*pushed, walked*), and if it is not /d/ but voiced, /d/ is used (*hummed, loved, sagged, played*). On the other hand, the choice between one of these forms and an ablaut (or vowel change) pattern (*swim, swam; hang, hung; shoot, shot*; etc.) is lexically determined: it is a fact about HANG that it takes an ablaut pattern, but that BANG does not. Grammatical conditioning occurs when the various allomorphs of a morpheme are determined by some grammatical (especially morphological) factor, such as gender, conjugation or declension, or the presence of a particular type of affix. For example, in Latin the ablative plural is marked by *-i:s* on first and second declension nouns, and by *-(i)bus* on other declension nouns. This distinction is grammatically conditioned.

Phonetic conditioning is called **phonological conditioning** by some authorities.

CONSTRUCTIONAL ICONICITY. This is the principle from natural morphology that a greater amount of meaning will normally be represented by a greater amount of form. This is also referred to as **diagrammaticity.**

CONVERSION. Conversion is the change in the part of speech of a form without any overt affix marking the change. The various types of *up* in the examples below can be seen to be related by conversion.

Robin climbed *up* the hill.
We'll have to *up* all the prices again.
Lee caught the *up* train at 2:30.
Things are on the *up* and up.
We all have our *ups* and downs.
I've only just got *up*.

Conversion is sometimes termed **functional shift** or **zero derivation** though some writers distinguish between these various terms.

COPULATIVE COMPOUND. See under **COMPOUNDING.**

CRANBERRY MORPH. See **UNIQUE MORPH.**

CUMULATION. Cumulation is the realisation of several morphemes in a single morph. Cumulation thus refers to the type of realisation that is found in a portmanteau morph.

DERIVATION. Derivation is one of the main branches of morphology, the other being inflection. Derivation is the process of adding affixes which (a) create new lexemes; (b) may change the part of speech of the base to which they are added; (c) may not have a regular meaning; (d) may not be fully productive and are not fully generalised. The English prefix *be-* can be found added to nouns in words like *bedew, beguile, benight, bewitch*, etc. This prefix creates new lexemes (BEDEW etc. from DEW etc.), it changes a noun into a verb, it does not have a regular meaning (in BEDEW *be-* means 'cover with', in BEGUILE 'influence by', in BENIGHT 'leave to be overtaken by' and in BEWITCH 'to affect as might a'), and it is not found added to all nouns, so that **berain, *becunning, *beday, *bewizard* etc. are not usual, or even probable, words of English.

DIAGRAMMATICITY. See **CONSTRUCTIONAL ICONICITY.**

DISCONTINUOUS MORPH. A discontinuous morph is a morph which is interrupted by some other material. The most obvious discontinuous morphs are circumfixes and transfixes. It can be argued that the perfect in English is marked by the discontinuous realisation HAVE + past participle, i.e. the italicised sequence in:

I *have* see*n* it.

DISTRIBUTION. The distribution of any unit is the sum of the contexts in which it can occur. For example, the suffix -*s* which marks the third person singular of the present tense in English can occur on the end of any non-modal verb in English (with a very few exceptions, such as *quoth*, which can easily be listed). This is thus the distribution of that element.

If two elements never occur in the same contexts, but instead divide up some set of contexts between them, they are said to be in **complementary distribution.** For example, the -*s* suffix mentioned above is pronounces /s/ after voiceless obstruents which are not sibilants, and /z/ after all other non-sibilant sounds:

Pronounced /s/	*Pronounced* /z/
ask·s	add·s
bath·s (*v*)	breathe·s
depart·s	come·s
laugh·s	call·s
stop·s	leave·s
	moo·s

These two forms are thus in complementary distribution, and are in fact allomorphs of the same morpheme.

DVANDVA COMPOUND. See under **COMPOUNDING.**

EMPTY MORPH. An empty morph is a recurrent form in a language that does not appear to be related to any element of meaning.

ENCLITIC. See under **CLITIC.**

ENDOCENTRIC COMPOUND. See under **COMPOUNDING.**

ESTABLISHED. A word is said to be established to the extent that it is in general usage in the speech community. Words which are established will generally be found listed in the major dictionaries for those languages with a lexicographic tradition. A word may be established whether it is institutionalised (see institutionalisation) or lexicalised (see lexicalisation).

EXOCENTRIC COMPOUND. See under **COMPOUNDING.**

EXPONENCE. Exponence is the term used in word-and-paradigm morphology for realisation. It is used in particular where a single morphological property is realised by a number of separate morphs, or where a number of morphological properties are realised in a single morph. The morphs are termed the **exponents** of the properties.

FEATURE PERCOLATION. Feature percolation is the term given to a variety of systems designed to ensure that a feature marked on the head of a construction is also marked on the construction as a whole.

FLECTIONAL. See **FUSIONAL.**

FORM. A form is any unit which has phonological or orthographic shape.

FORMATIVE. In this book, the term 'formative' is used to define a recurrent element of form, independent of whether it is an empty morph or whether it realises some morpheme. It is a superordinate term for morph and empty morph.

This is, however, an untraditional use, and in may works it is used as equivalent to morph, or even to morpheme.

FREE MORPH. See **POTENTIALLY FREE MORPH.**

FUNCTIONAL SHIFT. See **CONVERSION.**

FUSIONAL. An fusional language is one which contains obligatorily bound morphs but in such a way that there is no one-to-one correspondence between morph and morpheme. That is, either a morpheme may have several allomorphs, or there may be complex exponence relations holding between morph and morpheme, with a number of empty morphs and portmanteau morphs, as in the following example from Italian:

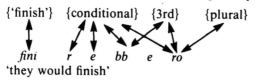

{'finish'} {conditional} {3rd} {plural}

fini *r* *e* *bb* *e* *ro*

'they would finish'

Fusional languages are also termed **flectional, inflective** and **inflectional** by different scholars.

GENERALISED. See under **PRODUCTIVE.**

GRAMMATICAL WORD. A grammatical word is the grammatical specification or description of a word-form of a lexeme as it occurs in a particular sentence. For example, the word-form *is* in the last sentence represents 'the third person singular present tense indicative of BE'. The section in quotation marks is the grammatical word. It lists the lexeme and all the inflectional (see inflection) morphemes which are realised in the word-form. Note that a single word-form may represent two different grammatical words. So in

My sheep eats grass

sheep is 'the singular of SHEEP', as can be seen by the form of the verb *eats*. (Another formulation such as 'SHEEP, singular' would be perfectly correct, as long as it covered the same information.) In

My sheep eat grass

on the other hand, *sheep* is 'the plural of SHEEP'. Conversely, the grammatical word 'the past tense of BURN' may be either of the word-forms *burnt* or *burned*:

The books burnt quickly.
The books burned quickly.

Grammatical words are called **morphosyntactic words** by some authorities.

HEAD. In a compound (see compounding) the head element is the element which
  (a) determines the gender and declension/conjugation class of the whole compound;
  (b) carries the inflectional endings which apply to the whole compound;
  (c) denotes a superordinate of the whole compound.
  In the German *Haus·frau* 'housewife', the whole compound is feminine like *Frau* and unlike *Haus*, and belongs to the same declension class as *Frau*. If housewives are discussed in the plural, the plural marker is added to *Frau* and not to *Haus*. And *Frau* 'woman' is a superordinate of *Hausfrau*. *Frau* is thus the head element.
  In English the head element is almost always the righthand element in a compound.
  In derivatives the means of determining a head is currently a matter of dispute, but many linguists believe that the notion does transfer to all morphologically complex words.

244

INCORPORATION. Incorporation is usually considered to be a special kind of compounding whereby a new verb is created by forming a compound from an existing verb and a possible argument of that verb (usually its direct object). For example, in Nahuatl, a Mexican language, there is a distinction between

ni·c·qua in nacatl
I·it·eat the flesh
'I eat the meat', 'I am eating meat'

and the version with incorporation

ni·nica·qua
I·flesh·eat
'I eat meat', 'I am carnivorous'

While English does not show incorporation of this type, the flavour of it is caught in English constructions such as *house-painting, skin-diving, gun-running*.

INFIX. An infix is an affix which is attached inside its base. In Latin *rumpo* 'I break' the *-m-* is an infix which does not occur in all verb forms: contrast *ruptus* 'broken'. The use of an infix always leads to the base being discontinuous. Infixes are usually inserted at some definite point in the base, such as after the first consonant, or before the final syllable.

INFIXATION. Infixation is the use of infixes, or the production of words using infixes.

INFLECTION. Inflection is one of the main branches of morphology, the other being derivation. Inflection is the process of adding affixes which typically (a) create word-forms of an already known lexeme, not new lexemes; (b) do not change the part of speech of the base to which they are added; (c) have a regular meaning; (d) are fully productive and extremely highly generalised. The -(*e*)*st* ending in German which marks the 2nd person singular of verbs, e.g. *machst* 'you make', *siehst* 'you see', *findest* 'you find', creates word forms of the lexemes (MACHEN, SIEHEN, FINDEN), does not change the part of speech from a verb, has a regular meaning '2nd person singular', and can be added to any verb to provide the 2nd person singular, and so is fully productive.

INFLECTIONAL. See FUSIONAL.

INFLECTIVE. See **FUSIONAL.**

INSTITUTIONALISATION. A word is said to be institutionalised if it is created by a productive morphological process and is in general use in the speech community. Institutionalisation is thus opposed to lexicalisation, although both create established words.

INTERFIX. An interfix is an affix which occurs between two bases. The *-o-* that occurs in words like *anthropology, biology, biometry, galvanometry, mythology, typology,* may be an interfix in English.

ISOLATING. An isolating language is one in which most word-forms are made up of a single morph, or, correspondingly, that only one morpheme is realised in the realisation of any lexeme. That is, there are no obligatorily bound morphs in the ideal isolating language. Chinese and Vietnamese are the examples of isolating languages usually cited.

Some sources use the term **analytic** with the same meaning.

LEVEL-ORDERING. See **STRATAL THEORY OF MORPHOLOGY.**

LEXEME. A lexeme is a dictionary word, an abstract unit of vocabulary. It is realised (see realisation) by word-forms, in such a way that the word-form represents the lexeme and any inflectional endings (see inflection) that are required. For example, *small, smaller, smallest* are all word-forms which can realise the lexeme SMALL under appropriate circumstances. While *small* only contains the lexeme SMALL, *smaller* contains the lexeme SMALL and an affix realising the morpheme {comparative}, this being an inflectional ending. Similarly, *knife, knives* are both word-forms which can realise the lexeme KNIFE. In writing, lexemes are generally distinguished by the use of capital letters, but this notation is not used by all linguists.

The **citation form** of a lexeme is that word-form belonging to the lexeme which is conventionally chosen to name the lexeme in dictionaries and the like. In English, the citation form of verbs is the stem (e.g. *love*), in Latin it is the first person singular of the present tense of the indicative (e.g. *amo*), and in French it is the infinitive (e.g. *aimer*).

LEXICALISATION. A word is lexicalised if it could no longer be produced according to productive rules. For example, the use of the suffix *-th* in words like *warmth* is no longer productive, and so all such words can be said to be lexicalised. Words may be semantically lexicalised if their meaning is no longer the sum of the meanings of their parts (e.g. the meaning of *high·ness* cannot be predicted from the meanings of *high* plus *-ness*), or phonologically lexicalised if its form cannot be predicted by productive phonological processes (e.g. if *long* were used as a base in current English, it could not become *leng*, as it does in the word *length*). Words can also be lexicalised in other ways.

MENTION. Language mention is the citation of linguistic forms in utterances. It contrasts with **language use**, which is the use of linguistic forms to produce utterances. In

The word 'the' contains three letters

There is mention of *the* where it is included in inverted commas, but use of the word *the* in the first word in the sentence.

MORPH. A morph is a constituent element of a word-form. It is the realisation of a morpheme (or sometimes of more than one, see portmanteau morph). A word-form such as /ɪn·veərɪ·əbl·z/ contains the four morphs which have been separated out by decimal points.

MORPHEME. A morpheme can be variously defined as the smallest grammatical unit of language or the smallest meaning-bearing unit of language. In fact, it has both these faces, and in most cases the morpheme represents a correlation between form and meaning at a level lower than the word. The morpheme is an abstract unit realised (see realisation) by morphs or, if by a number of conditioned items, by allomorphs. In writing, morphemes are enclosed in braces ({ }) to distinguish them from other units. For example, /t/, /d/ and /ɪd/ are phonetically conditioned (see conditioning) allomorphs of the morpheme {past tense} in English. The morph *spa* is the only morph which realises the morpheme {spa}.

Not all authorities use morpheme only in the abstract sense. For some it is also equivalent to morph. This is particularly true in American writings.

247

MORPHOLOGICAL CATEGORY. A morphological category is a superordinate of a number of morphological properties. That is, it is a general category to which a number of morphemes which are in parallel distribution can belong. For instance, the morphemes (or morphological properties) {singular} and {plural} go together to make up the morphological category of Number in most of the modern Germanic and Romance languages.

MORPHOLOGICAL PROPERTY. A morphological property is one of the set of possibilities which can realise a morphological category. For instance, the morphological category Tense, in English can be realised by either of the morphological properties present or past. Although morphological categories and properties are terms within word-and-paradigm morphology, they are nevertheless useful terms to have available in discussion. A morphological property corresponds more or less to a morpheme.

MORPHOLOGY. Morphology is the study of the forms of words (etymologically from the Greek *morphe* 'form' and *-ology* 'study': compare the German translation *Formenlehre*). In other words, it is the study of of the ways in which lexemes and word-forms are built up from smaller elements, and the changes that are made to those smaller elements in the process of building lexemes and word-forms.

MORPHOSYNTACTIC WORD. See **GRAMMATICAL WORD.**

NEO-CLASSICAL COMPOUNDING. Neo-classical compounds are words formed in the modern European languages from elements of the classical languages, in such a way that there is no native root involved. For example, the words *geo·metry*, *pluto·crat* and *theo·sophy* are neo-classical compounds in English. Neo-classical compounding is the process of forming such neo-classical compounds.

NOMINALISATION. This word has two meanings. As a countable noun it can mean the noun derived from a base which could act as either a verb or an adjective. In this sense we can say that *inducement* and *induction* are two different nominalisations from the verb *induce*. *Generality* is a nominalisation from the adjective *general*.

248

As an uncountable noun, nominalisation refers to the process of forming such nouns. In this sense we might say that the nominalisation of *induce* with the suffix -(*t*)*ion* causes a change of vowel quality.

NOTATION.

Braces: braces ({ }) enclose morphemes.
Capitals: capitals are used to mark lexemes.
Decimal point: a decimal point is used to separate morphs when this is useful for an exposition.
Italics: italics (or underlining) mark forms, that is morphs or word-forms. They are also used in this book to mark words.

OBLIGATORILY BOUND MORPH.
An obligatorily bound morph is a morph which cannot stand on its own as a word-form. An obligatorily bound morph can only form a word-form in combination with some other morph or morphs. In *absolutely*, *-ly* is an obligatorily bound morph, since it must be attached to some other morph (in this case *absolute*) to make a word-form. Most sources call obligatorily bound morphs just **bound morphs**. Note that obligatorily bound morphs, like potentially free morphs are usually identified in terms of their spoken form.

OPERAND. See BASE.

ORTHOGRAPHIC WORD.
An orthographic word is a unit which, in print, is bounded by spaces on both sides. For example the sentence

My sheepdog isn't afraid of being rammed.
1   2   3   4   5   6   7

contains seven orthographic words as indicated. An orthographic word is a word-form in the written language.

PARADIGM.
A set of forms corresponding to some subset (defined in terms of a particular morphological category) of the grammatical words from a single lexeme is termed a paradigm. Paradigms are frequently presented in tabular form, like this paradigm from Latin:

amo:	ama:mus
ama:s	ama:tis
amat	amant

249

A paradigmatic relationship is the relationship held by substitutable items within a paradigm. The relationship between *-o:* and *-a:s* in the paradigm above is a paradigmatic relationship.

PHONOLOGICAL WORD. The phonological word is an equivalent for the spoken language to the orthographic word for the written language. While the orthographic word is a word-form defined in terms of orthographic criteria, the phonological word is a word-form defined in terms of phonological criteria such as stress, vowel harmony and the like.

POLYSYNTHETIC. A polysynthetic language is a language with a particularly high concentration of obligatorily bound morphs which bear a high semantic load. For example, in Labrador Inuttut, as well as there being obligatorily bound morphs meaning 'passive', 'intransitive', 'perfect', 'causative' and marking case relations, there are obligatorily bound morphs with meanings such as 'want', 'easy', 'often', 'be able', 'ask' and the like. The languages most often cited as examples of polysynthetic languages are the Eskimo languages.

PORTMANTEAU MORPH. A portmanteau morph is a morph which realises (see realisation) more than one morpheme. The morph *-a* on the end of the word-form *bella* in the Italian phrase *la mia bella cugina* 'my beautiful (female) cousin' realises both {feminine} (contrast *il mio bello cugino* 'my handsome (male) cousin') and {singular} (contrast *le mie belle cugine* 'my beautiful (female) cousins'), and is thus a portmanteau morph.

PORTMANTEAU WORD. See **BLEND**.

POSSESSIVE COMPOUND. See under **COMPOUNDING**.

POTENTIALLY FREE MORPH. A potentially free morph is a morph which can stand on its own as a word-form. In *absolutely*, *absolute* is a potentially free morph, since *absolute* is a possible word-form. Most sources call potentially free morphs just **free morphs**. Note that potentially free morphs, like obligatorily bound morphs are usually identified in terms of their spoken form.

POTENTIATION. One morphological process potentiates another if it creates a base suitable for that other process to apply to.

For example, the affixation of -*ise* to an adjective such as *general* potentiates -*ing* suffixation, since *generaling* is not a possible word of English, but *generalising* is.

PREEMPTION. See **BLOCKING.**

PREFIX. A prefix is an affix which is attached before its base. In *untroubled* there is just one prefix, *un-*.

PREFIXATION. Prefixation is the use of prefixes, or the production of words using prefixes.

PRIMARY COMPOUND. See under **SYNTHETIC COMPOUND.**

PROCLITIC. See under **CLITIC.**

PRODUCTIVE. A process is said to be productive to the extent that it can be used in the creation of new forms in a language. In morphology, a process can be said to be **generalised** to the extent that its results can be seen in known words. Most authorities use the term 'productive' for both these meanings. For example, the 3rd person singular present tense -*s* on the end of forms like *loves, wanders, types* is productive: it can be added to any new verb to make the third person singular of the present tense. It is not completely generalised, however, since there are a very few verbs (modals such as *can, may, must, will* etc., and *beware*) which do not have a 3rd person singular -*s* form.
   An item may show **individual productivity** if a single person uses it productively, but this productivity is not shared in the community at large.

PROTOTYPE. The prototype of a category has all the features that are typically associated with that category across languages. Actual examples of the category in various languages will differ from the prototype in that they may not display all the properties which are typical of the prototype, and they will also display other properties which are not typical of the prototype. The prototype is thus a cross-linguistic ideal.

REALISATION. In the sense used here, 'realise' means 'to make real'. Realisation (as an uncountable noun) is then the act of making real or (as a countable noun) an object which makes something else real. Abstract entities (whose technical name often ends in *-eme* in linguistics) are realised by entities which have a form (which you can see, write down, tape-record, hear etc. etc.). So word-forms realise lexemes and any relevant inflectional affixes, morphs or allomorphs realise morphemes. Morphemes and lexemes are units of analysis constructed by the linguist to make the analysis possible; word-forms and morphs are the raw material on which the linguist has to operate to provide an analysis.

REDUPLICATION. Reduplication has two meanings. The first is the formation of new affixes by repeating some part of the base (possibly the whole base). The second is the formation of new words using affixes created in this manner.

With the first meaning, we can say that the prefix showing future in the following Tagalog examples is created by reduplication of the first consonant and vowel of the base:

su·sulat	'will write'
ba·basa	'will read'
ʔa·ʔaral	'will teach'
ʔi·ʔibig	'will love'

In the second meaning, we can say that forms like *susulat* are created by reduplication.

REPLACIVE MORPH. A replacive morph is the replacement of a phoneme or sequence of phonemes in one word-form with a different phoneme or sequence of phonemes to make a related word-form. For example, the vowel changes in the examples below could be analysed as replacive morphs:

s*i*ng	s*a*ng	s*u*ng	s*o*ng
sh*oo*t	sh*o*t		
c*o*me	c*a*me		

The replacive morph in the last example is /ʌ/ → /eɪ/ (orthographically *o* → *a*). For such replacement of (strings of) phonemes to be analysable as replacive morphs, it should ideally be shown that there is a parallel affixed form elsewhere in the language.

It should be noted that any analysis which includes replacive morphs is controversial, and there is always an alternative way of viewing the data.

ROOT. A root is that part of a word-form which remains when all inflectional (see inflection) and derivational (see derivation) affixes have been removed. It is the basic part of a lexeme which is always realised, and it cannot be further analysed into smaller morphs. In the English word *wordiness* the root is *word.* In the Latin word *ama:bunt* 'they will love' the root is *am-.* Notice that in this latter case the root is an obligatorily bound morph. In a word such as *typewriter* there are two roots, *type* and *write* even though there is only one lexeme.

ROOT COMPOUND. See under **SYNTHETIC COMPOUND.**

SEMI-PRODUCTIVITY. A process is said to be semi-productive if it is not fully productive in the sense that it does not apply to all possible bases defined solely in terms of the part of speech to which they belong. For example, suffixation of -*age* to a verb to produce a noun is semi-productive because although it can be added to *carry, marry* and *wreck* to give *carriage, marriage* and *wreckage* respectively, it is not added to *bear, espouse* and *smash* to give **bearage, *espousage* and **smashage.* Semi-productivity is sometimes seen as a defining feature of derivational as opposed to inflectional morphology (see derivation and inflection).

It should be noted that the validity of the notion of semi-productivity is strongly questioned in this book.

SIMULFIX. See **SUPERFIX.**

STEM. A stem is a base to which inflectional (see inflection) affixes can be added. In *stupidities* the stem is *stupidity* although the root is *stupid.*

Some scholars use the term 'stem' with a different meaning, so care should be taken when the term is met in the literature.

STRATAL THEORY OF MORPHOLOGY. The stratal theory of morphology is a theory whereby different classes of affixes are added to bases in such a way that all the affixes from one class or stratum have to be added before affixes from the next class or stratum can be added. This is also sometimes referred to as **level-ordering,** since each stratum or level is ordered with respect to all others.

SUBJECT NOMINALISATION. A subject nominalisation is a nominalisation which denotes the entity which would be the subject of the verb which has been nominalised. For example, a *beater* is a machine which beats. The beater is what does the

253

beating, so is the subject of the verb *beat* from which *beater* is derived. *Beater* is a subject nominalisation.

SUBTRACTIVE MORPH. A subtractive morph is a morph which is removed by some morphological process. Consider the following sets of active an passive forms from Maori:

active	passive	gloss
huri	huri·hia	'turn'
inu	inu·mia	'drink'
karanga	karanga·tia	'call'
mau	mau·ria	'seize'
noho	noho·ia	'sit'
paa	paa·ngia	'touch'
tomo	tomo·kia	'enter'

The passive in such cases is not predictable from the active, because the presence or absence of an initial consonant in the morph realising {passive}, and the nature of the consonant is not predictable. It is thus frequently proposed as a more economical description for the fact that the base form for deriving all the forms listed above should contain a final consonant, which should be subtracted to provide the active form.

It should be noted that analyses which depend on subtractive morphs are frequently controversial, and that it appears that speakers of Maori memorise a number of lexically conditioned (see under conditioning) passive allomorphs, rather than using a subtractive morph.

SUFFIX. A suffix is an affix which is attached after its base. In *prematurely* there is just one suffix, *-ly*.

SUFFIXATION. Suffixation is the use of suffixes, or the production of words using suffixes.

SUPERFIX. The term 'superfix' refers to suprasegmental internal modification of a base, i.e. change of tone or stress in a base, when this has the same effect as adding an affix. The stress difference between pairs such as

'abstract	abs'tract
'absent	ab'sent
'frequent	fre'quent

can be seen as a superfix. Superfixes have also been termed **suprafixes** and **simulfixes**.

SUPPLETION. When two forms in a paradigm are not related to each other regularly but have idiosyncratic forms for a particular lexeme we speak of suppletion, and the forms concerned as being suppletive forms. For example, if we compare the verbs GO and WALK in English, we can see that GO has a suppletive past tense form:

go   walk
goes   walks
going   walking
went   walked

SUPRAFIX. See **SUPERFIX.**

SYNCRETISM. Syncretism is the neutralisation of two forms in a paradigm, so that two different grammatical words are realised by homonymous word-forms. For example, in Latin there is consistent syncretism between the Dative and Ablative plural, so that *reːgibus* could be either the Dative or the Ablative plural of REX 'king'.

SYNTHETIC. A synthetic language is one which is not analytic. Agglutinative, fusional and polysynthetic languages are all synthetic.

SYNTHETIC COMPOUND. A synthetic compound is a compound whose head element (in English the right-hand element) contains a verbal base, and where the modifying element in the compound is an element which could occur in a sentence as an argument of that verb. For example, if we compare the synthetic compound *book launching* with the sentence *Somebody launched the book,* we see that the same verbal element {launch} is present in both, and that the direct object of the verb is used as the modifying element in the compound. Other synthetic compounds are *street cleaner, language description, time sharing* and so on.

Synthetic compounds are also termed **verbal compounds** or **verbal-nexus compounds.** They are contrasted with **root compounds** (also called **primary compounds)** which do not have such a structure. Root compounds include *text-book, computer graphics, town hall* and the like.

TRANSFIX. Transfixes are discontinuous morphs which are interspersed throughout the bases with which they occur. They are

255

mostly found in the Semitic languages. For example, the following data from Egyptian Arabic illustrates a transfix of the form 'CaaCiC (where 'C' indicates a consonant of the root) which produces subject nominalisations.

'katab	'write'	'kaatib	'clerk'
'rikib	'ride'	'raakib	'rider'
'sikin	'inhabit'	'saakin	'inhabitant'
'naʃar	'publish'	'naaʃir	'publisher'

UNIQUE MORPH. A unique morph is one which only occurs in a single collocation in a language. In English, *-ric* in *bishop·ric* is a unique morph because there are no other words which have the same suffix. Unique morphs are sometimes called **cranberry morphs** because the first element in *cranberry* is supposed to be a unique morph.

USE. See under **MENTION.**

VERBAL COMPOUND or VERBAL-NEXUS COMPOUND. See **SYNTHETIC COMPOUND.**

WORD. Word is a superordinate term for grammatical word, lexeme and word-form. That is, it is a term which can be used without specifying which of the more specific kinds of 'word' one means.

Note that this is not the way in which all linguists use the term. For some it means word-form, for others lexeme, and for others grammatical word. Only the context can make clear which is meant.

WORD-AND-PARADIGM. Word-and-paradigm is an approach to morphology which gives theoretical centrality to the notion of the paradigm, and which derives the word-forms representing lexemes by a complex series of ordered rules which do not assume that the word-form will be easily analysable into morphs, or that each morph will realise a single morpheme.

WORD-FORM. A word-form is a form which can stand in isolation and which represents the particular shape (orthographic or phonological) in which a lexeme occurs. Thus *am, are, be, been, being, is, was, were* are all different word-forms which, in the appropriate circumstances, can realise (see realisation) the lexeme BE. There is a single word-form *help* which can be

a verb or a noun, and which can serve various functions as a
verb (imperative, infinitive, etc). Word-forms in the spoken
language can be transcribed. Word-forms in the written
language can be termed orthographic words. In print, word-
forms are distinguished by italics (underlining in typescript or
manuscript).

ZERO DERIVATION. See **CONVERSION.**

ZERO MORPH. A zero morph is analysed where there is no overt
marker of a particular morpheme, even though one would be
expected on the basis of parallel examples in the language.
For example, in Latin there is no overt marker of nominative
singular on the lexeme PUER 'boy', even though there is one
on a parallel lexeme DOMINUS 'lord'.

nominative	puer	domin·us
accusative	puer·um	domin·um
genitive	puer·i:	domin·i:
dative	puer·o:	domin·o:

The nominative singular of PUER might thus be analysed as
puer·∅, with the zero morph holding the place usually taken
by overt affixes.

It should be noted that analyses with zero morphs are always
controversial, and that alternative analyses are always possible.
Even if zero morphs are permitted in an analysis, care should
be taken to avoid their proliferation.

References

Allen, M. (1978). *Morphological Investigations*. PhD thesis, University of Connecticut.

Anderson, J. (1980). 'Towards dependency morphology: the structure of the Basque verb'. In J. Anderson & C.J. Ewen (eds), *Studies in Dependency Phonology*, Ludwigsburg, 227-71.

Anderson, S.R. (1977). 'On the formal description of inflection', *Papers from the Thirteenth Regional Meeting of the Chicago Linguistic Society*, 15-44.

Anderson, S.R. (1982). 'Where's morphology?' *Linguistic Inquiry* 13, 571-612.

Anderson, S.R. (1985a). 'Typological distinctions in word formation'. In T. Shopen (ed), *Language Typology and Syntactic Description III*, Cambridge: Cambridge University Press, 3-56.

Anderson, S.R. (1985b). 'Inflectional morphology'. In T. Shopen (ed), *Language Typology and Syntactic Description III*, Cambridge: Cambridge University Press, 150-201.

Anshen, F. & Aronoff, M. (1981). 'Morphological productivity and phonological transparency', *Canadian Journal of Linguistics* 26, 63-72.

Aronoff, M. (1976). *Word Formation in Generative Grammar*. Cambridge, Mass.: MIT Press.

Aronoff, M. (1980). 'The relevance of productivity in a synchronic description of word-formation'. In J. Fisiak (ed), *Historical Morphology*, The Hague: Mouton, 71-82.

Aronoff, M. (1983). 'A decade of morphology and word formation', *Annual Review of Anthropology* 12, 355-75.

Asher, R.E. (1982). *Tamil*. Amsterdam: North Holland.

Ashton, E.O. (1944). *Swahili Grammar*. London: Longman.

Austin, P. (1981). *A Grammar of Diyari, South Australia.* Cambridge: Cambridge University Press.

Baldi, P. (1983). 'On some recent claims in morphological theory', *General Linguistics* 23, 171-90.

Barnhart, C.L., Steinmetz, S. & Barnhart, R.K. (1973). *A Dictionary of New English.* London: Longman.

Barnhart, C.L., Steinmetz, S. & Barnhart, R.K. (1980). *The Second Barnhart Dictionary of New English.* New York: Harper & Row.

Bauer, L. (1978a). *The Grammar of Nominal Compounding with special reference to Danish, English and French.* Odense: Odense University Press.

Bauer, L. (1978b). 'On lexicalization', *Archivum Linguisticum* 9, 3-14.
259

References

Bauer, L. (1980). 'In the beginning was the word', *Te Reo* 23, 73-80.

Bauer, L. (1983). *English Word-formation*. Cambridge: Cambridge University Press.

Bauer, W. (1981a). 'Hae.re vs ha.e.re: a note', *Te Reo* 24, 31-6.

Bauer, W. (1981b). *Aspects of the Grammar of Maori*. PhD thesis, University of Edinburgh.

Bauer, W. (1982). 'Relativization in Maori', *Studies in Language* 6, 305-42.

Bazell, C.E. (1966). 'Linguistic typology'. In P. Strevens (ed), *Five Inaugural Lectures*, London: Oxford University Press, 27-49.

Beard, R. (1982). 'The plural as a lexical derivation', *Glossa* 16, 133-48.

Bentley, N. & Esar, E. (eds) (1951). *The Treasury of Humorous Quotations*. London: Dent.

Bergenholtz, H. & Mugdan J. (1979). *Einführung in die Morphologie*. Stuttgart etc.: Kohlhammer.

Blake, F.R. (1925). *A Grammar of the Tagalog Language*. New Haven: American Oriental Society.

Bloomfield, L. (1935). *Language*. London: Allen & Unwin.

Booij, G. (1977). *Dutch Morphology. A study of word formation in generative grammar*. Dordrecht: Foris.

Botha, R.P. (1981). 'A base rule theory of Afrikaans synthetic compounding'. In M. Moortgat, H. v.d. Hulst & T. Hoekstra (eds), *The Scope of Lexical Rules*, Dordrecht: Foris, 1-77.

Botha, R.P. (1984a). *A Galilean Analysis of Afrikaans Reduplication. Stellenbosch Papers in Linguistics* 13.

Botha, R.P. (1984b). *Morphological Mechanisms*. Oxford etc: Pergamon.

Brandt, S. (1984). 'Does "cranberry" contain a cranberry morpheme?' *Nordic Linguistic Bulletin* 8/3, 6-7.

Brown, E.K. & Miller, J.E. (1980). *Syntax: a linguistic introduction to sentence structure*. London: Hutchinson.

Brown, G. (1977). *Listening to Spoken English*. London: Longman.

Bybee, J.L. (1985). *Morphology: a study of the relation between meaning and form*. Amsterdam: Benjamins.

Carroll, J.M. (1979). 'Complex compounds: phrasal embedding in lexical structures', *Linguistics* 17, 863-77.

Carstairs, A. (1983). 'Paradigm economy', *Journal of Linguistics* 19, 115-25.

Carstairs, A. (1984a). 'Outlines of a constraint on syncretism', *Folia Linguistica* 18, 73-85.

Carstairs, A. (1984b). *Constraints on Allomorphy in Inflexion*. Indiana University Linguistics Club. A revised version is now more readily available under the title *Allomorphy in Inflexion*, London: Croom Helm, 1987.

Carstairs, A. (1984c). 'Paradigm economy in the Latin third declension', *Transactions of the Philological Society* 117-37.

Chomsky, N. (1970). 'Remarks on nominalization'. In R. Jacobs & P. Rosenbaum (eds), *Readings in English Transformational Grammar*, Waltham, Mass.: Ginn, 184-221.

260

References

Chomsky, N. & Halle, M. (1968). *The Sound Pattern of English.* New York: Harper & Row.
Clark, E.V. & Clark, H.H. (1979). 'When nouns surface as verbs', *Language* 55, 767-811.
Comrie, B. (1981). *Language Universals and Linguistic Typology.* Oxford: Blackwell.
Crystal, D. (1980). *A First Dictionary of Linguistics and Phonetics.* London: Andre Deutsch.
Cutler, A., Hawkins, J. & Gilligan, G. (1985). 'The suffixing preference: a processing explanation', *Linguistics* 23, 723-58.
Dardjowidjojo, S. (1979). 'Acronymic patterns in Indonesian', *Pacific Linguistics* Series C, 45, 143-60.
Derbyshire, D.C. (1979). *Hixkaryana.* Amsterdam: North Holland.
Derwing, B.L. (1973). *Transformational Grammar as a Theory of Language Acquisition.* Cambridge: Cambridge University Press.
Derwing, B.L. (1976). 'Morpheme recognition and the learning of rules for derivational morphology', *Canadian Journal of Linguistics* 21, 38-66.
Derwing, B.L. & Baker, W.J. (1979). 'Recent research on the acquisition of English morphology'. In P. Fletcher & M. Garman (eds), *Language Acquisition,* Cambridge: Cambridge University Press, 209-23.
Dik, S.C. (1980). *Studies in Functional Grammar.* London, etc.: Academic Press.
Dimmendaal, G.J. (1983). *The Turkana Language.* Dordrecht: Foris.
Dressler, W. (1977). 'Wortbildung bei Sprachverfall'. In H.E. Brekle & D. Kastovsky (eds), *Perspektiven der Wortbildungsforschung,* Bonn: Bouvier, 62-69.
Dressler, W. (1981). 'General principles of poetic license in word formation'. In W. Weydt (ed), *Logos Semantikos in Honorem E. Coseriu II,* Berlin: de Gruyter, 423-31.
Dressler, W. (1982). 'Zur semiotischen Begründung einer natürlichen Wortbildungslehre', *Klagenfurter Beiträge zur Sprachwissenschaft* 8, 72-87.
Dressler, W. (1985). 'On the predictiveness of natural morphology', *Journal of Linguistics* 21, 321-37.
Dressler, W. (1986). 'Explanation in natural morphology, illustrated with comparative and agent-noun formation', *Linguistics* 24, 519-48.
Dressler, W., Mayerthaler, W., Panagl, O. & Wurzel, W. (forthcoming). *Leitmotifs in Natural Morphology.* Amsterdam: Benjamins.
Einarsson, S. (1945). *Icelandic.* Baltimore: John Hopkins Press.
England, N.C. (1983). *A Grammar of Mam, a Mayan Language.* Austin: University of Texas Press.
Fleischer, W. (1975). *Wortbildung der deutschen Gegenwartssprache.* Tübingen: Niemeyer.
Fortescue, M. (1984). *West Greenlandic.* London: Croom Helm.
Fudge, E. (1984). *English Word-Stress.* London: George Allen & Unwin.

References

Gazdar, G., Klein, E., Pullum, G. & Sag, I. (1985). *Generalized Phrase Structure Grammar.* Oxford: Blackwell.

Gleason, H.A. (1955). *Workbook in Descriptive Linguistics.* New York, etc.: Holt, Rinehart and Winston.

Greenberg, J.H. (1954). 'A quantitative approach to the morphological typology of language'. In R.F. Spencer (ed), *Method and Perspective in Anthropology,* Minneapolis: University of Minnesota Press, 192-220.

Greenberg, J.H. (1963). 'Some universals of grammar with particular reference to the order of meaningful elements'. In J.H. Greenberg (ed), *Universals of Language,* Cambridge, Mass.: MIT Press, 58-90.

Haiman, J. (1985). *Natural Syntax.* Cambridge: Cambridge University Press.

Halle, M. (1973). 'Prolegomena to a theory of word formation', *Linguistic Inquiry* 4, 3-16.

Hammer, A.E. (1971). *German Grammar and Usage.* London: Edward Arnold.

Hockett, C. (1947). 'Problems of morphemic analysis', *Language* 23, 321-43. Reprinted in M. Joos (ed), *Readings in Linguistics I,* Chicago: University of Chicago Press, 1957, 229-42.

Hockett, C.F. (1954). 'Two models of grammatical description', *Word* 10, 210-31. Reprinted in M. Joos (ed), *Readings in Linguistics I,* Chicago: University of Chicago Press, 1957, 386-99.

Holmes, J. (1984). *Introduction to Language Study: a workbook.* Revised edition. Wellington: Victoria University.

Householder, F.W. (1966). 'Phonological theory: a brief comment', *Journal of Linguistics* 2, 99-100.

Jackendoff, R. (1975). 'Morphological and semantic regularities in the lexicon', *Language* 51, 639-71.

Jakobson, R. (1960). 'The gender pattern of Russian'. In R. Jakobson, *Selected Writings II,* The Hague: Mouton, 1971, 184-6.

Jespersen, O. (1909). *A Modern English Grammar on historical principles. Part I: sounds and spellings.* London: George Allen and Unwin and Copenhagen: Munksgaard.

Jones, D. (1977). *English Pronouncing Dictionary.* London: Dent. 14th edition revised by A.C. Gimson.

Karlsson, F. (1983). *Finnish Grammar.* Porvoo, etc.: Werner Söderström Osakeyhitiö.

Karlsson, F. & Koskenniemi, K. (1985). 'A process model of morphology and lexicon', *Folia Linguistica* 19, 207-31.

Kennedy, B.H. (1962). *The Revised Latin Primer.* Revised by J. Mountford. London: Longman.

Kilani-Schoch, M. & Dressler, W.U. (1984). 'Natural morphology and Classical vs. Tunisian Arabic', *Wiener Linguistische Gazette* 33-34, 51-68.

Kroeber, A.L. (1954). 'Critical summary and commentary'. In R.F. Spencer (ed), *Method and Perspective in Anthropology,* Minneapolis: University of Minnesota Press, 273-99.

References

Kwee, J.B. (1965). *Indonesian*. London: The English Universities Press.

Lapointe, S.G. (1981). 'A lexical analysis of the English auxiliary system'. In T. Hoekstra, H. v. d. Hulst & M. Moortgat (eds), *Lexical Grammar*, Dordrecht: Foris, 215-54.

Lass, R. (1984). *Phonology: an introduction to basic concepts*. Cambridge: Cambridge University Press.

Lawler, J.M. (1977). '*A* agrees with *B* in Achenese: a problem for Relational Grammar'. In P. Cole & J.M. Sadock (eds), *Grammatical Relations* (Syntax and Semantics 8), New York etc: Academic Press, 219-48.

Lees, R.B. (1960). *The Grammar of English Nominalizations*. Bloomington: Indiana University Press and The Hague: Mouton.

Lehnert, M. (1971). *Reverse Dictionary of Present-Day English*. Leipzig: VEB.

Levi, J.N. (1978). *The Syntax and Semantics of Complex Nominals*. New York, etc.: Academic Press.

Lewis, G.L. (1967). *Turkish Grammar*. Oxford: Oxford University Press.

Lieber, R. (1981). *On the Organization of the Lexicon*. Indiana University Linguistics Club.

Lightner, T.M. (1975). 'The role of derivational morphology in generative grammar', *Language* 51, 617-38.

Lightner, T.M. (1981). 'New explorations in derivational morphology'. In D. Goyvaerts (ed), *Phonology in the 1980's*, Ghent: Story-Scientia, 93-9.

Lightner, T.M. (1983). *Introduction to English Derivational Morphology*. Amsterdam and Philadelphia: John Benjamins.

Lukas, J. (1937). *A Study of the Kanuri Language*. Oxford: Oxford University Press. Reprinted by Dawsons, 1967.

Lyons, J. (1968). *Introduction to Theoretical Linguistics*. Cambridge: Cambridge University Press.

Lyons, J. (1977). *Semantics*. Cambridge: Cambridge University Press.

Marchand, H. (1964). 'A set of criteria for the establishing of derivational relationship between words unmarked by derivational morphemes', *Indogermanische Forschungen* 69, 10-19.

Marchand, H. (1969). *The Categories and Types of Present-Day English Word-Formation*. München: C.H. Beck. Second edition.

Marle, J. van (1985). *On the Paradigmatic Dimension of Morphological Creativity*. Dordrecht: Foris.

Matthews, P.H. (1970). 'Recent developments in morphology'. In J. Lyons (ed), *New Horizons in Linguistics*, Harmondsworth: Pelican, 96-114.

Matthews, P.H. (1972). *Inflectional Morphology: a theoretical study based on aspects of Latin verb conjugation*. Cambridge: Cambridge University Press.

Matthews, P.H. (1974). *Morphology: an introduction to the theory of word-structure*. Cambridge: Cambridge University Press.

Mayerthaler, W. (1980). 'Ikonismus in der Morphologie', *Zeitschrift für Semiotik* 2, 19-37.

263

References

Mayerthaler, W. (1981). *Morphologische Natürlichkeit*. Wiesbaden: Athenaion.

McMillan, J.B. (1980). 'Infixing and interposing in English', *American Speech* 55, 163-183.

Mitchell, T.F. (1956). *An Introduction to Egyptian Colloquial Arabic.* London: Oxford University Press.

Mitchell, T.F. (1962). *Colloquial Arabic.* London: The English Universities Press.

Mugdan, J. (1986). 'Was ist eigentlich ein Morphem?' *Zeitschrift für Phonetik, Sprachwissenschaft und Kommunikationsforschung* 39, 29-43.

Nida, E. (1949). *Morphology: the descriptive analysis of words.* Ann Arbor: University of Michigan Press.

Ohlander, S. (1976). *Phonology, Meaning, Morphology.* Göteborg: Acta Universitatis Gothoburgensis.

Orr, J. (1962). *Three Studies on Homonymics.* Edinburgh: Edinburgh University Press.

Plank, F. (1981). *Morphologische (Ir-)Regularitäten.* Tübingen: Gunter Narr.

Plank, F. (1984). 'Romance disagreements: phonology interfering with syntax', *Journal of Linguistics* 20, 329-49.

Quirk, R., Greenbaum, S., Leech, G. & Svartvik, J. (1972). *A Grammar of Contemporary English.* London: Longman.

Radford, A. (1981). *Transformational Syntax.* Cambridge: Cambridge University Press.

Robins, R.H. (1959). 'In defence of WP', *Transactions of the Philological Society* 116-44.

Robins, R.H. (1964). *General Linguistics: an introductory survey.* London: Longmans. Revised edition, 1967.

Rowlands, E.C. (1969). *Yoruba.* London: Hodder & Stoughton.

Samuels, M.L. (1972). *Linguistic Evolution.* Cambridge: Cambridge University Press.

Sapir, E. (1911). 'The problem of noun incorporation in American languages', *American Anthropologist* 13, 250-82.

Sapir, E. (1921). *Language.* London: Harvest.

Sasse, H.-J. (1984). 'The pragmatics of noun incorporation in Eastern Cushitic languages'. In F. Plank (ed), *Objects*, London etc.: Academic Press, 243-68.

Scalise, S. (1984). *Generative Morphology.* Dordrecht: Foris.

Selkirk, E.O. (1982). *The Syntax of Words.* Cambridge, Mass.: MIT Press.

Siegel, D. (1974). *Topics in English Morphology.* PhD thesis, MIT. Published in 1979. New York: Garland.

Smith, L.R. (1982a). 'Labrador Inuttut (Eskimo) and the theory of morphology', *Studies in Language* 6, 221-44.

Smith, L.R. (1982b). 'An analysis of affixal verbal derivation and complementation in Labrador Inuttut', *Linguistic Analysis* 10, 161-89.

References

Stein, G. (1970). 'Zur Typologie der Suffixentstehung', *Indogermanische Forschungen* 75, 131-63.

Stein, G. (1977). 'The place of word-formation in linguistic description'. In H.E. Brekle & D. Kastovsky (eds), *Perspektiven der Wortbildungsforschung*, Bonn: Bouvier, 219-35.

Suomi, K. (1985). 'On detecting words and word boundaries in Finnish: a survey of potential word boundary signals', *Nordic Journal of Linguistics* 8, 211-31.

Taylor, A.J. (1970). 'Reduplication in Motu', *Pacific Linguistics* Series C, 13, 1235-43.

Thiel, G. (1973). 'Die semantische Beziehungen in den Substantivkomposita der deutschen Gegenwartssprache', *Muttersprache* 83, 377-404.

Thomas, D.D. (1971). *Chrau Grammar*. Honolulu: University of Hawaii Press.

Thompson, L.C. (1965). *A Vietnamese Grammar*. Seattle: University of Washington Press.

Tiersma, P.M. (1985). *Frisian Reference Grammar*. Dordrecht: Foris.

Townsend, C.E. (1975). *Russian Word-formation*. Columbus, Ohio: Slavica.

Trudgill, P. (1974). *Sociolinguistics: an introduction*. Harmondsworth: Penguin.

Vennemann, T. (1974). 'Words and syllables in natural generative grammar'. In A. Bruck, R.A. Fox & M.W. LaGaly (eds), *Papers from the Parasession on Natural Phonology*, Chicago: Chicago Linguistic Society, 346-74.

Waugh, L.R. (1976). *Roman Jakobson's Science of Language*. Lisse: Peter de Ridder.

Wheeler, C.J. & Schumsky, D.A. (1980). 'The morpheme boundaries of some English derivational suffixes', *Glossa* 14, 3-34.

Williams, E. (1981). 'On the notions "Lexically Related" and "Head of a Word"', *Linguistic Inquiry* 12, 245-74.

Williams, S.J. (1980). *A Welsh Grammar*. Cardiff: University of Wales Press.

Williams, T. (1965). 'On the "-ness" peril', *American Speech* 40, 279-86.

Wurzel, W.U. (1980). 'Some remarks on the relations between naturalness and typology', *Travaux du cercle linguistique de Copenhague* 20, 103-13.

Wurzel, W.U. (1984a). *Flexionsmorphologie und Natürlichkeit*. Berlin: Akademie-Verlag.

Wurzel, W.U. (1984b). 'On morphological naturalness', *Nordic Journal of Linguistics* 7, 165-83. = Summary in Wurzel (1984a).

Wurzel, W.U. (1985). 'Morphologische Natürlichkeit und morphologischer Wandel: zur Vorhersagbarkeit von Sprachveränderungen'. In J. Fisiak (ed), *Papers from the 6th International Conference on Historical Linguistics*, Amsterdam: Benjamins and Poznan: Adam Mickiewicz University Press, 587-99.

References

Zwicky, A.M. (1978). 'On markedness in morphology', *Die Sprache* 24, 129-43.

Zwicky, A.M. (1985a). 'Clitics and particles', *Language* 61, 283-305.

Zwicky, A.M. (1985b). 'How to describe inflection', *Proceedings of the Eleventh Annual Meeting of the Berkeley Linguistics Society*, 372-86.

Zwicky, A.M. (1985c). 'Heads', *Journal of Linguistics* 21, 1-29.

Zwicky, A.M. & Pullum, G.K. (1983). 'Cliticization vs. inflection: English *n't*', *Language* 59, 502-13.

Index

ablaut, 27
abstractness, 15, 116-8, 120-2
Achenese, 22
acronym, 39-40, 91-3, 237
Adjacency Condition, 141
affix and affixation, 11-12, 19-25, 41,
    47, 86, 99-100, 110-5, 122, 170,
    177, 206, 207, 213, 237
    ordering, 20, 22, 52, 132-5, 146-8,
    173-7
Afrikaans, 25, 26, 196
agglutinative or agglutinating, 166-73,
    180, 190-1, 237
agreement, 84, 177
Allen, M., 129, 134-5, 148, 149
allomorph, 13-6, 18, 80, 82, 112, 114,
    122, 149, 172, 237
alternation, 93
    See also allomorph, phonology
analogy, 64
analysability, 61, 122, 211, 237
analytic. See isolating
Anderson, S. R., 74, 84-5, 153-4, 162-3
aphasia. See language disorders
Arabic, 25, 197, 256
Aronoff, M., 66-8, 129, 130, 142, 195-6
assimilation, 93, 97

backformation, 32-3, 90-3, 134, 238
bahuvrihi. See compound and
    compounding, exocentric
base, 12, 112, 115-20, 122, 156-60,
    219-20, 238
Basque, 19
Bauer, L., 120-2
blend, 39, 91-3, 238
blocking, 66, 69, 238
Bloomfield, L., 5, 48-9
boundary, 132-5
Bybee, J., 173-9, 185

Carstairs, A., 179-84
category
    morphological, 74, 162, 248

267

syntactic, 12, 69, 75-7, 84-5, 103,
    111, 176
Chinese, 4, 84, 154, 167, 246
Chomsky, N., 5, 125, 126-7, 128, 187
Chrau, 23, 97
circumfix, 22-3, 197, 239, 241
citation form, 192, 218
clipping, 33, 40, 67, 90-3, 239
clitic, 99-100, 131, 239
commutation, 10, 49, 82
composition. See compound and
    compounding.
compound and compounding, 25, 33-7,
    41, 42, 95, 131, 149, 239-40
    dvandva, 36, 146, 240
    endocentric, 35, 135, 239
    exocentric, 35, 137, 139, 239
    heads in, 139, 244
    in stratal ordering, 134, 146-7
    meaning in, 35-6, 143
    morphological form, 23, 34-5
    root, 36, 101, 255
    similarities with word-formation, 40,
    89-93, 101, 112, 154
    synthetic, 36, 101, 255
    syntactic aspects, 47, 49, 91, 100-4
    See also neo-classical compound
concreteness. See abstractness
conditioning, 114-5, 221-4, 240
    grammatical, 14, 95, 224
    lexical, 14, 18, 95, 100, 114, 221
    phonetic, 14, 114, 149, 221
consonant mutation, 26, 95
constituency, 49, 53, 143-6, 171
constraints, 140-1, 195-6
conversion, 32, 77, 82, 90-3, 111, 134,
    157, 206, 241
copulative compound. See compound
    and compounding, dvandva
cranberry morph. See unique morph
cumulation. See portmanteau morph
Czech, 46, 51

Danish, 27, 34, 35, 42, 51

Index

Index

271

Index